INSIDERS' GUIDE® TO

GETTYSBURG

HELP US KEEP THIS GUIDE UP TO DATE

Every effort has been made by the author and editors to make this guide as accurate and useful as possible. However, many things can change after a guide is published—phone numbers change, facilities come under new management, etc.

We would love to hear from you concerning your experiences with this guide and how you feel it could be improved and be kept up to date. While we may not be able to respond to all comments and suggestions, we'll take them to heart and we'll also make certain to share them with the author. Please send your comments and suggestions to the following address:

The Globe Pequot Press
Reader Response/Editorial Department
P. O. Box 480
Guilford, CT 06437

Or you may e-mail us at:

editorial@GlobePequot.com

Thanks for your input, and happy travels!

INSIDERS' GUIDE® SERIES

INSIDERS' GUIDE® TO
GETTYSBURG

KATE HERTZOG

INSIDERS' GUIDE®

GUILFORD, CONNECTICUT
AN IMPRINT OF THE GLOBE PEQUOT PRESS

The prices and rates in this guidebook were confirmed
at press time. We recommend, however, that you call
establishments before traveling to obtain current information.

To buy books in quantity for corporate use
or incentives, call **(800) 962–0973**
or e-mail **premiums@GlobePequot.com.**

INSIDERS' GUIDE®

Text design by LeAnna Weller Smith
Maps by XNR Productions, Inc. © Morris Book
Publishing, LLC

ISBN 978-0-7627-3786-4

Manufactured in the United States of America
First Edition/Second Printing

To loved ones who no longer walk this earth. I carry you with me every day . . . in my heart.

And to my husband, Tim, who's been there through it all—thanks for walking the path of life with me.

CONTENTS

CONTENTS

Directory of Maps

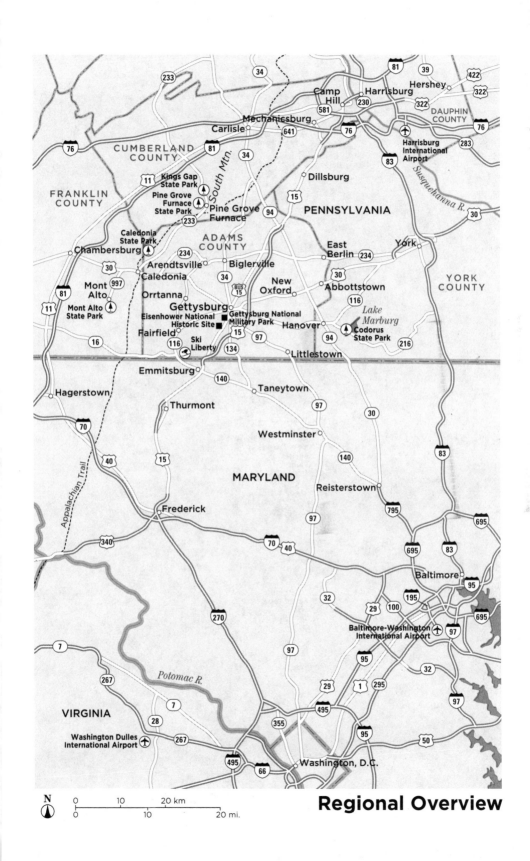

Regional Overview

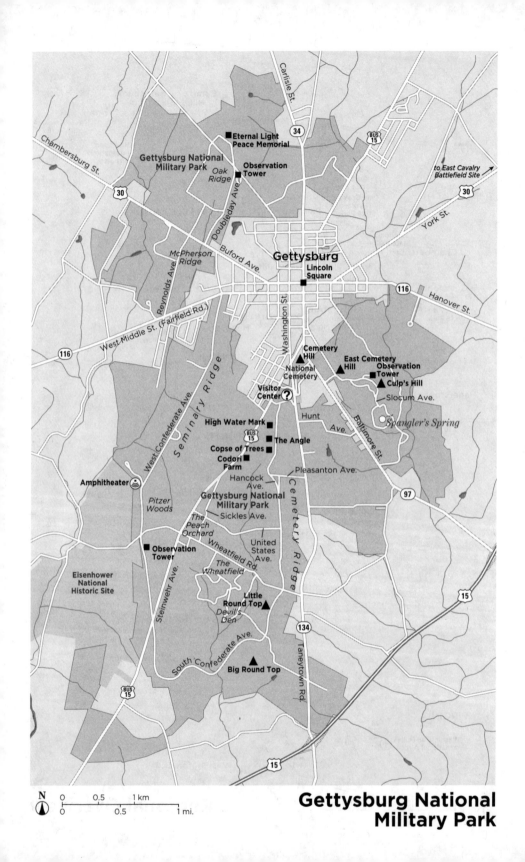

Gettysburg National
Military Park

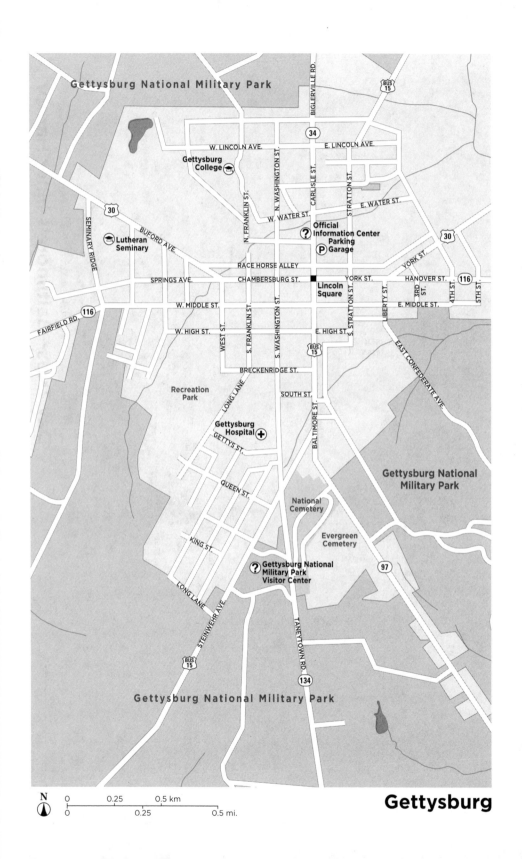

Gettysburg

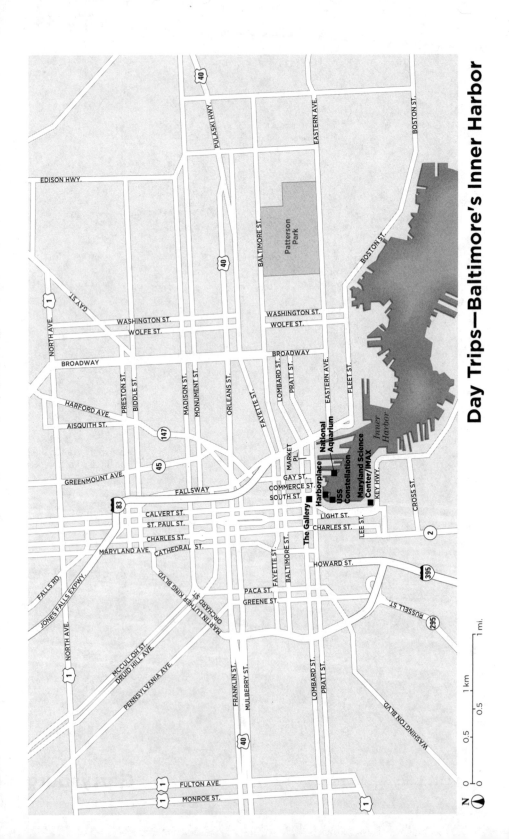

Day Trips—Baltimore's Inner Harbor

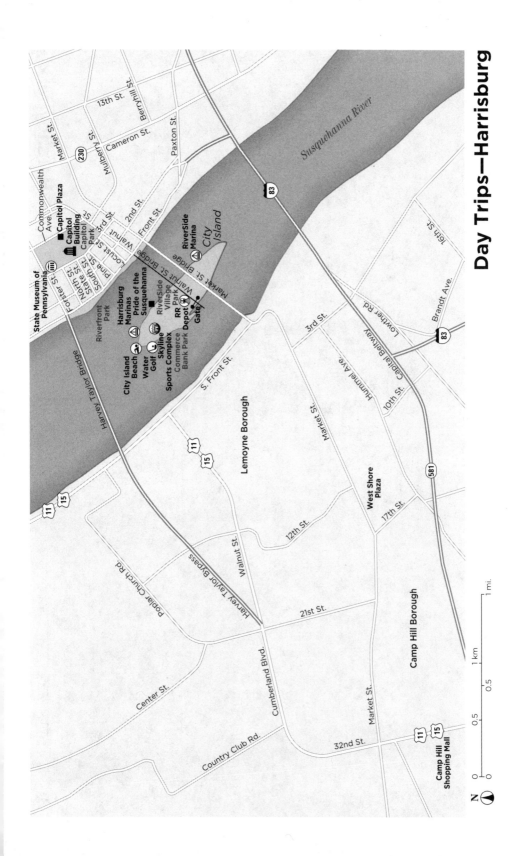

Day Trips—Harrisburg

Susquehanna River

State Museum of Pennsylvania

Commonwealth Ave.
Market St.
Cameron St.
Mulberry St.
13th St.
Berryhill St.
Paxton St.

(230)

Capitol Plaza
Capitol Building
Capitol Park

Forster St.
North St.
State St.
South St.
Pine St.
Locust St.
2nd St.
3rd St.
Walnut St.
Front St.

Riverfront Park

Harrisburg Marinas
Pride of the Susquehanna
City Island Beach
Water Golf
Skyline Sports Complex
Commerce Bank Park
RiverSide Village
RR Depot
Gate

RiverSide Marina

Harvey Taylor Bridge

Walnut St. Bridge
Market St. Bridge

City Island

83

16th St.
Brandt Ave.
Lowther Rd.
3rd St.
Hummel Ave.
10th St.
Capital Beltway

83

581

S. Front St.

11
15

Lemoyne Borough

Market St.
12th St.
17th St.

West Shore Plaza

Harvey Taylor Bypass
Walnut St.
Poplar Church Rd.
21st St.
Cumberland Blvd.
Center St.
Country Club Rd.
32nd St.
Market St.

Camp Hill Borough

11
15

Camp Hill Shopping Mall

N

0   0.5   1 km
0   0.5   1 mi.

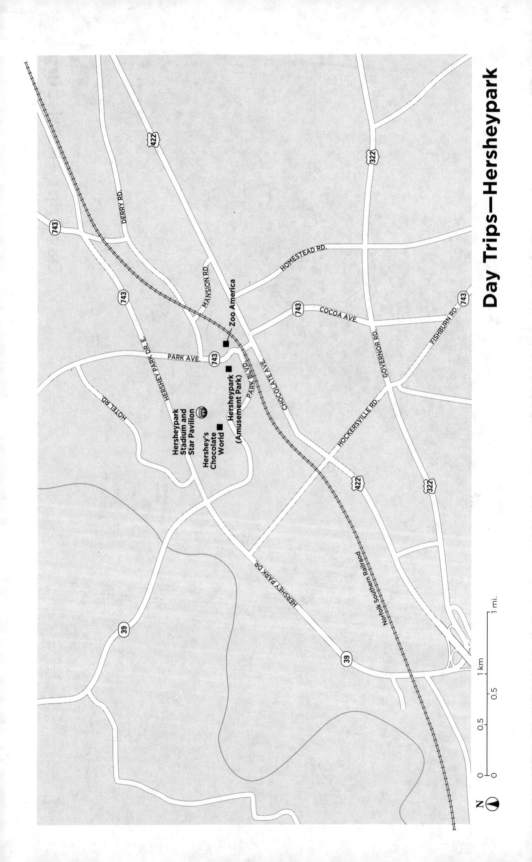

Day Trips—Hersheypark

PREFACE

When I first considered writing *Insiders' Guide to Gettysburg*, I had already edited about 20 books in the Insiders' series, so I figured I had a firm grasp of what was entailed in creating an interesting guide. Having lived in Mechanicsburg, a mere half an hour from Gettysburg, for more than 30 years, I felt I had a good feel for the Gettysburg area. My, were my eyes opened when I began the research for this book. Gettysburg is a world unto itself, a world that encompasses so much more than visiting the battlefield that surrounds the town.

Gettysburg is essentially a small town with a huge history. Most first-time visitors are here to see where the famous battle of the Civil War took place in July 1863. Some travel great distances and others drive in for the day. Many visitors come back time and again, and some become permanent residents in order to be closer to the history that emanates from the area. But there are also those who live in the area who visit the battlefield once, or maybe never at all. For them, Gettysburg is a rural oasis, with bluegrass festivals, apple festivals, fairs, and recreational opportunities to enjoy throughout the year. And yet the diverse visitors, this rural atmosphere, and all of its history mesh together very well.

As I researched this guide, I was heartened by the sincere interest the residents of Gettysburg take in their town. Gettysburg has grown into a huge tourist attraction without losing its hometown feeling. Everyone I interviewed for this book was enthusiastic and excited about not only Gettysburg's past but also Gettysburg's future. And to be sure, Gettysburg is in a state of evolution. There's work being done all around town—new ways being developed to see the battlefields, new hotels being built, new events being promoted.

I'm thrilled to have had the opportunity to discover all that Gettysburg has to offer—on the battlefield and off. Besides the military history that permeates the area, you'll also be able to enjoy first-rate theater performances and cultural events, wonderful dining experiences, free concerts, and fun pubs, just to name a few of the ways you can spend your time while visiting the area. I hope this guide shows you what I found—a fun, vibrant town that has something for everyone.

Many people contributed to the creation of this book, and I'd like to take this opportunity to say thank you. Many Gettysburg residents took time to converse and tell some great stories, and I'm grateful to each and every one, especially Andrew Manley, Chuck Caldwell, Brian Kennell, Nancy Rice, Ronn Palm, and Tim and Debbie Sheads. My thanks also go out to my husband, Tim, and my former college roommate and good friend Becky Snyder DiRosa, who both gave invaluable feedback on my work in progress. And this guide would not be in your hands today without the dedicated staff of Globe Pequot Press; thanks to everyone who had a part in its formation. Special thanks go to acquisitions editor Stephanie Hester and to senior editor Mimi Egan, who always took a personal interest and who made it seem like fun rather than work.

HOW TO USE THIS BOOK

Gettysburg, Pennsylvania, appears in every book that covers the Civil War, and the events that occurred here in July 1863 are known to all who study history. Entire books have been written on the Battle of Gettysburg, and many past and present (and no doubt future) scholars have devoted entire lifetimes to studying the military strategies employed by the opposing forces engaged at the town of Gettysburg. This guide will not recount the battle, nor will it provide new insights on the conflicts involved in this battle, or the Civil War in general. Instead, it will give you a good idea of what you can expect to find in the town of Gettysburg today. Of course, the battlefield is a major attraction, and you'll find lots of information on battlefield tours and sites in the Gettysburg National Military Park chapter. But you'll also get a thorough exploration of all the other great ways to spend your time here at Gettysburg.

After practical tips on getting here and a beefy history of the town, there are listings of the best places to eat and stay, followed by what's available in the way of shopping, sightseeing, and cultural events. Be warned—there's a lot to pick from. The Attractions chapter alone is divided into general, ghostly, and historical attractions! You'll also discover what recreational activities are available and some ideas on ways to spend your evenings. A separate chapter highlights area events and sites that are especially appealing to kids. Trips to the area's five state parks are included, as are day trips to the Inner Harbor at Baltimore, Maryland, Pennsylvania's capital city of Harrisburg, and the amusement-park rides of Hersheypark. Throughout the book you'll also find lots of Insiders' Tips (indicated by 🄸) which are helpful hints or bits of trivia

about the area. There are also "Close-Up" boxes, which focus in-depth on places, events, or persons of special interest.

Most of the sites people come here to see are within a few miles of Lincoln Square, which, just as it was during the Battle of Gettysburg, is the center of town. For that reason, Lincoln Square will serve as the geographic center in chapters that contain a lot of information. The chapter introduction will tell you if information is arranged in a format other than alphabetically. Smaller chapters have their entries arranged alphabetically while larger ones may be arranged in a number of different ways. For instance, entries in the Hotels, Motels, and Resorts chapter are listed by direction from the square while entries in the Shopping chapter are listed by category, then by direction from the square. If you're at Culp's Hill and perusing the book to see where to eat lunch, you'll find the restaurant entries broken down by direction from the square and then listed in alphabetical order.

A town name (and state if in Maryland) is provided in the entry only if the address is not in Gettysburg. Most readers will find plenty to do right within the town limits, and that is the overall scope of *Insiders' Guide to Gettysburg*. However, no book on Gettysburg would be complete without mentioning some places outside of town, such as the Fairfield Inn, a bed-and-breakfast only 8 miles from Lincoln Square that houses one of the oldest taverns still operating in America (see the Bed-and-Breakfasts and Guesthouses chapter). And some places are such fun they're worth a short drive, which is certainly the case with Mr. Ed's Elephant Museum in Orrtanna (see the Attractions chapter).

Gettysburg hosts almost two million

visitors each year, so some advance planning is in order. Use this guide to become familiar with what the town and the battlefield have to offer. The reenactment of the Battle of Gettysburg is July 1 through July 3, and this is when the town is busiest. But Gettysburg is a year-round destination, with many businesses using special offers during the winter months to draw visitors to town. You'll find First Friday sales each month at area merchants, many bed-and-breakfasts offer specially priced romantic getaways, and new events seem to pop up every year.

Since it is difficult to absorb all the history and fun of Gettysburg in one trip, use this guide to narrow your choices and plan what to see on your return trip. Once

you've experienced Gettysburg's small-town charm and monumental history, you'll definitely want to come back for more.

Perhaps you've considered relocating to Gettysburg, so you can enjoy all it and the surrounding region have to offer at your leisure. If so, this book can help you get to know Gettysburg quickly and intimately. Use it to find out about local events held throughout the year, to check out the nightlife scene, and to discover the recreational opportunities in Gettysburg's backyard. If you decide to join the many others who have relocated to Gettysburg, the Relocation chapter will provide contact information to get your planning under way.

AREA OVERVIEW

ettysburg is the county seat of Adams County, which consists of 21 townships and 13 boroughs. (See Adams County Vital Statistics later in this chapter.) The southern part of the county abuts the Mason-Dixon Line, and the borough of Gettysburg sits at the crossroads of two national highways—U.S. Route 30 and U.S. Route 15. The Gettysburg National Military Park, which commemorates the famous Civil War battle that was fought here in July 1863, surrounds the town on the south, west, and north sides.

This is a small town that fate took hold of and never let go. Generals Meade and Lee didn't plan a battle at Gettysburg, and President Lincoln was only asked to say a few words when he dedicated the cemetery that had been created to honor those who died fighting here. But the significance of those actions lives on, with almost two million people coming to Gettysburg annually to connect with the area's past.

Surrounded by other rural communities, Gettysburg retains its small-town ambience despite the influx of tourists every year. The *Gettysburg Times* newspaper regularly prints pictures of locals on their birthdays. Rich in cultural heritage, Gettysburg is home to Gettysburg College and the Lutheran Theological Seminary, both established in the early part of the 19th century. The college is in the northern part of town while the seminary is at the town's western edge.

Lincoln Square is the center of town, and most directions in this guide start from this spot. The Gettysburg National Military Park Visitor Center, where you should begin your tour of the battlefield, is to the south of the square. South of the square is also where you'll find the greatest concentration of restaurants, shopping, and sightseeing opportunities.

Visitors also come to see attractions other than the battlefield. The Eisenhower National Historic Site draws many who wish to see the farm where the 34th president resided with his wife, Mamie. Some come to seek out ghosts, others come to enjoy the rural landscape and nearby skiing, and still others come to attend the area festivals. And those of us lucky enough to live here don't have to travel far at all to take part in all the history and fun the Gettysburg area has to offer. Perhaps

Emergency Sirens

Adams County's emergency-alert system uses sirens to alert fire and rescue personnel as well as the general public to emergencies. Four types of sirens are used; each siren is three minutes long but the siren modes differ. A standard wavering siren means fire personnel are to report to their stations, while an extra-long wavering siren means rescue personnel should also report to their fire stations. A long and steady siren tells the public to tune to their radio (1320 AM) for essential emergency information, and a short wavering siren indicates that the public should go to the nearest shelter or take the best cover immediately available.

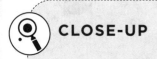

CLOSE-UP

Gambling at Gettysburg?

Chance Enterprises, represented by area businessman David LeVan (owner of Battlefield Harley Davidson/Buell; see the Shopping chapter), announced plans in April 2005 to bid to develop a gambling resort near the intersection of US 15 and US 30 east of the borough of Gettysburg. Governor Ed Rendell introduced the idea of slots in Pennsylvania as part of his campaign for governor in 2003, promoting the idea as a way to aid education and curb rising property taxes in the state. A slots law was passed in July 2004 that guarantees Philadelphia will get two stand-alone casinos, Pittsburgh will get one stand-alone casino, and two other stand-alone casinos will go elsewhere in the state. There also will be seven racetrack/casinos and two resort hotel casinos. Licenses for the casinos will be awarded by the Pennsylvania Gaming Control Board.

The resort proposed by Mr. LeVan and his group of investors would have a hotel, several restaurants, a spa, and a gambling parlor initially containing about 3,000 slot machines. If Mr. LeVan is awarded the bid, the resort would be up and running in 2008. More information about the proposed resort can be found at www.cross roadsgaming.com.

Many area residents oppose the casino, and they've organized a grassroots effort named No Casino Gettysburg to ensure the resort never becomes a reality. So far, No Casino Gettysburg has

circulated petitions, hosted nationally known anti-casino speakers, held candlelight vigils, polled visitors and residents, and sponsored a Stop the Slots bike ride to garner attention to their cause. Plans are under way to have reenactors march on the state capital of Harrisburg to deliver their anti-casino message to legislators. The group also attends every public meeting of the Pennsylvania Gaming Control Board and lobbies local and national legislators and politicians on the cause.

The awarding of sites for slots in Pennsylvania is expected to be a laborious process, and no one knows whether No Casino Gettysburg will be successful in keeping gambling from Gettysburg. But it is inspiring to see a grassroots effort taking shape and taking off. No Casino Gettysburg started with a few citizens in April 2005, and in three months the group had garnered enough national attention to generate 145,000 hits to the message board on their Web site.

If you'd like to help stop gambling from becoming part of the the Gettysburg experience, contact No Casino Gettysburg, P.O. Box 3173, Gettysburg, PA 17325; (717) 334-6333; www.nocasino gettysburg.com. No Casino Gettysburg accepts donations and sells T-shirts, totes, and bumper stickers to raise money. Petitions can be signed online, at many area businesses, and at various downtown locations on Saturdays.

Numbers to Keep Handy

Fire, Police, Ambulance: 911

Gettysburg Police (non-emergency): (717) 334-1168

Pennsylvania State Police: (717) 334-8111

Gettysburg Hospital: (717) 334-2121

Gettysburg National Military Park: (717) 334-1124, ext. 431

Eisenhower National Historic Site: (717) 338-9114

Gettysburg-Adams County Area Chamber of Commerce: (717) 334-8151

Gettysburg Convention and Visitors Bureau: (717) 334-6274

Time of Day: (717) 334-0505, ext. 1000

Weather/Temperature: (717) 334-0505, ext. 1131

that's why you meet people who have traveled to Gettysburg year after year without fail. And maybe it's why you won't be in town long before you meet someone who decided to set up a permanent home in the area.

Of course, all the people enjoying themselves at Gettysburg can make for quite a crowded little town. The tourist season now extends from April through December, and during the summer the attractions, restaurants, and streets are packed. But the nice part about Gettysburg is that it's still a small town not only in size but also in heart. So don't be in a terrific hurry to see and do everything there is available. Stop and talk to the people who live here, who manage and work at the attractions, shops, and restaurants in town. Many are genuinely immersed in the history that surrounds them, and the stories they have to tell are really something to hear. Some have ancestors who lived here during the battle, and many know every detail of the history of the house in which they reside.

Although the residents of Gettysburg relish their history, don't be fooled into thinking they're stuck in the past. Community leaders and business people are constantly trying to strike a balance between retaining the rich history of the past while finding new ways for the town to thrive. Sometimes residents disagree on the best way to move forward, but everyone agrees that Gettysburg is looking to the future as well as the past.

Adams County Vital Statistics

Area: 526 square miles

Average Winter Low Temperature: 19 degrees Fahrenheit

Average Summer High Temperature: 86 degrees Fahrenheit

Average Snowfall: 32.2 inches

Average Rainfall: 40.99 inches

County Population: 91,292 (2000 Census)

Gettysburg Population: 7,490

"Pillow" Tax: 3 percent; this is a tax on lodging that is in addition to the 6 percent state sales tax.

Major Nongovernmental Area Employers: Knouse Foods Cooperative; Lincoln Intermediate Unit #12; Gettysburg College; Gettysburg Hospital

GETTING HERE, GETTING AROUND

GETTING HERE

Most visitors to Gettysburg arrive by car, probably because no forms of mass transit stop here. The train gets you only as close as Harrisburg, Pennsylvania, or Baltimore, Maryland. (For Amtrak information, call 800-872-7245 or visit www.amtrak.com.) The nearest bus stop is in Hagerstown, Maryland, and it's a secondary stop without amenities.

If you do decide to travel by train, neither of the stations has rental-car kiosks. At Harrisburg you can make arrangements for Enterprise (717-238-7541, 800-736-8222) to drop off a car for you. The station in Baltimore has a phone on which you can call Hertz, or you can take a shuttle to Baltimore-Washington Airport and pick from the many rental-car companies located there. Those traveling from a distance will probably end up flying into one of the area's international airports and renting a car from there.

There is one other option—and it's a good one. If you make arrangements in advance, **Gettysburg Tours** (778 Baltimore Street; 717-334-6296) will pick you up at the Baltimore-Washington, Dulles, or Harrisburg airports or at the train stations.

If you're doing the driving, you will want to eventually use one of two major highways to get to Gettysburg. U.S. Route 30 is the major east-west road, and U.S. Route 15 is the major north-south route. US 30 takes you directly to the heart of downtown at Lincoln Square, and US 15 has six Gettysburg exits. (Consult "Which Exit Do I Take from U.S. Route 15?" in this chapter to see which exit will best serve you.)

Airports

Baltimore-Washington
International Airport (BWI)
Baltimore, Maryland
(410) 859-7111, (800) 435-9294
www.bwiairport.com
BWI is a large airport with 4 concourses, 69 jet gates, and 12 commuter gates that are serviced by 27 commercial airlines. Some of the better-known airlines that fly here are Aer Lingus, American Airlines, British Airways, Continental, Delta Airlines, Icelandair, Midwest Airlines, Northwest Airlines, SouthWest Airlines, United Airlines, and US Airways. (See the Airline Information box for airline phone numbers and Web sites.)

There are numerous amenities at the airport, including restaurants, food concessions, gift shops, an outdoor walking/jogging trail, and an observation gallery that offers a virtual tour of airport operations and the chance to listen to real-time communications between the tower, ground control, and aircraft. High-speed wireless Internet access is available at all the food courts and at the US Airways Club.

In 2003 a new rental-car facility opened, and there is a free shuttle service to transport passengers between the facility and the airport. The ride takes approximately 10 minutes. The following companies currently run rental-car kiosks.

Alamo: (410) 859-8092, (800) 832-7933; www.alamo.com

Avis: (410) 859-1680, (800) 331-1212; www.avis.com

Budget: (410) 859-0850, (800) 527-0700; https://rent.drivebudget.com

Airline Information

Aer Lingus: (800) 474-7424;
www.aerlingus.com
Air Canada: (888) 247-2262;
www.aircanada.com
Air France: (800) 321-4538;
www.airfrance.com
Alitalia: (800) 223-5730;
www.alitaliausa.com
American Airlines: (800) 433-7300;
www.aa.com
American Eagle: (800) 433-7300;
www.aa.com
British Airways: (800) 247-9297;
www.ba.com
Continental: (800) 525-0280;
www.continental.com
Delta Airlines: (800) 221-1212;
www.delta.com
Icelandair: (800) 223-5500;
www.icelandair.com

KLM Royal Dutch Airlines: (800)
225-2525; www.nwa.com
Lufthansa: (800) 645-3880;
www.lufthansa.com
Midwest Airlines: (800) 452-2022;
www.midwestairlines.com
Northwest Airlines: (800) 225-2525;
www.nwa.com
SAS: (800) 221-2350; www.sas.com
SouthWest Airlines: (800) 435-9792;
www.southwest.com
TransMeridian: (866) 435-9862;
www.tmair.com
United Airlines: (800) 241-6522;
www.ual.com
US Airways: (800) 428-4322;
www.usairways.com

Dollar: (800) 800-4000;
www.dollar.com
Enterprise Rent-A-Car: (800)
736-8222; www.enterprise.com
Hertz: (410) 850-7400, (800) 654-3131;
www.hertz.com
National Car Rental: (410) 859-8860,
(800) 227-7368; www.nationalcar.com
Thrifty Car Rental: (410) 850-7139,
(800) 367-2277; www.thrifty.com
To travel to Gettysburg after picking
up your rental car, take Interstate 195 to
Interstate 95 North. Travel I-95 for only a
couple of miles and turn left onto Interstate 695 and follow I-695 to Interstate
795. At the Reisterstown exit, take Maryland Route 140 North to Westminster,
Maryland, where you will pick up Pennsylvania Route 97 North, which will take you
directly into Gettysburg.

**Washington Dulles
International Airport (IAD)
Dulles, Virginia
(703) 572-2700
www.mwaa.com**
There are four concourses at this gigantic
airport, which has more than 30 major airlines serving it. Most travelers arrive at
either Concourse A or B, which have 67
gates between them. Just about every
major airline flies into here, including Air
Canada, Air France, Alitalia, American Airlines, British Airways, Continental, Delta,
KLM, Lufthansa, Northwest Airlines, SAS,
United Airlines, and US Airways. (See the
Airline Information box for airline phone
numbers and Web sites.)
Dulles has all the amenities you would
expect, with myriad shopping and eating
options to please everyone in your party.

Wireless high-speed Internet access is available throughout the airport.

For rental cars, information screens and courtesy telephones are located in the main terminal's lower level at the Ground Transportation Centers. Those renting cars are transported to the agencies by shuttle bus. To catch a bus, go down any ramp from the Baggage Claim Level and proceed outside to the second curbside. The following companies currently operate out of Dulles.

Alamo: (800) 832-7933; www.alamo.com

Avis: (800) 331-1212; www.avis.com

Budget: (800) 527-0700; https://rent.drivebudget.com

Dollar: (800) 800-4000; www.dollar.com

Enterprise Rent-A-Car: (800) 736-8222; www.enterprise.com

Hertz: (800) 654-3131; www.hertz.com

National Car Rental: (800) 227-7368; www.nationalcar.com

President Eisenhower selected the site for Washington Dulles International Airport in 1958, and he attended the dedication ceremony that was held in November 1962. The airport was named for John Foster Dulles, who served as Ike's secretary of state from 1953 to 1959.

Thrifty Car Rental: (800) 367-2277; www.thrifty.com

To drive to Gettysburg from the airport, take Virginia Route 267 (Dulles Expressway) west to Leesburg, where you pick up US 15 North. (Consult the Which Exit Do I Take from U.S. Route 15? box to determine which exit you want to take to enter Gettysburg.)

Which Exit Do I Take from U.S. Route 15?

There are six Gettysburg exits off US 15, and many travelers just take the first one they come to. This can result in a lot of frustration, especially if you take an exit that leads you to the southern part of town and you have to fight tons of traffic to arrive at your hotel at the north end of town. So be a smart traveler—get off at the exit that takes you closest to your destination. The exits are listed in the order you come to them while traveling to Gettysburg from the north.

Routes 394 (Hunterstown) and U.S. Business Route 15—This exit takes you directly to Gettysburg College, located in the northern end of town.

York Street (US 30)—This east-west road takes you to Lincoln Square.

Hanover Street (Route 116)—This east-west road merges with US 30 and takes you to Lincoln Square. US 30 can get awfully busy, so this is sometimes a more relaxing alternative.

Baltimore Street (Route 97)—This exit brings you into the southern end of town and to Baltimore Street. This is also the exit for the Gettysburg Village Factory Stores.

Taneytown Road (Route 134)—This is the best exit to take if you're going straight to the battlefield.

Steinwehr Avenue (US Business 15/Emmitsburg Road)—This exit takes you into the southern end of town and to Steinwehr Avenue. This is also the exit for Boyds Bear Country. (See the Attractions chapter.)

U.S. Route 30 was the first cross-country road built in the United States. Completed in 1913, it stretches from New York City to San Francisco. A large mural on the exterior wall of the Dollar General store facing Springs Avenue, just off US 30, is one of 11 Pennsylvania murals that commemorate the history of the road.

Harrisburg International Airport (HIA)
Middletown
(717) 948-3900, (888) 235-9442
www.flyhia.com

Although not as large as the other more well-known airports in the area, Harrisburg International Airport unveiled a new state-of-the-art terminal and multimodal transportation facility in 2004. The Y-shaped terminal has 12 departure gates, and the first floor of the transportation facility, which is connected to the terminal via a climate-controlled sky bridge, houses the rental car ready/return lot.

Seven airlines service HIA: Air Canada, American Eagle, Continental, Delta, Northwest, TransMeridian, and US Airways. (See the sidebar for airline phone numbers and Web sites.) Airport amenities include food concessions, a restaurant that serves drinks and classic American fare, and a gift shop. The entire terminal is wired for free wireless Internet access, and there's an observation deck on the third floor for watching planes arrive and depart.

The traffic circle of Lincoln Square isn't as confusing as it may seem at first. Just remember that drivers in the circle have the right-of-way. If the thought of navigating around the circle sets your teeth on edge, avoid it by taking Washington Street for north-south travels and Middle Street for your east-west trips.

The following companies provide rental cars for HIA travelers, and their kiosks can be found on the first floor of the transportation facility.

Avis: (717) 948-3720, (800) 331-1212; www.avis.com

Budget: (717) 944-4019, (800) 527-0700; https://rent.drivebudget.com

Enterprise: (717) 795-0900, (800) 736-8222; www.enterprise.com

Hertz: (717) 944-4081, (800) 654-3131; www.hertz.com

National Car Rental: (717) 948-3710, (800) 227-7368; www.nationalcar.com

Thrifty Car Rental: (717) 944-9024, (800) 367-2277; www.thrifty.com

When you leave the airport in your rental car, follow the signs to the Pennsylvania Turnpike (Interstate 76) and head west toward Pittsburgh. From the turnpike, exit onto US 15 South, and travel about 25 miles to the Gettysburg exits.

GETTING AROUND

Downtown Gettysburg is pretty easy to navigate. Lincoln Square is the center of town, and the town's four main streets emanate from the square. These streets are named for the towns you reach when you travel them. North of the square is Carlisle Street, south is Baltimore Street, east is York Street, and west is Chambersburg Street. Confusion begins to seep in only once you leave the downtown area, where all the roads change names and all eventually split into different roads.

Carlisle Street heads north and splits into US Business 15 and Route 34. US Business 15 heads northeast and back to US 15, and Route 34 heads north to Biglerville and Carlisle. Baltimore Street travels south to a light at a Y intersection. If you go straight (left) at the light, Baltimore Street becomes Baltimore Pike (Route 97), which leads to US 15. If you turn right at the light, you're now on Steinwehr Avenue and will come to another light. At this light, Steinwehr Avenue continues straight and leads to US 15. If you turn left you'll be on Taney-town Road (Route 134), which also takes you to US 15.

York Street heads east and splits into US 30 (York Road) and Route 116 (Hanover Road). Both roads eventually lead to US 15. Chambersburg Street travels west and is called Buford Avenue for a bit before again being called Chambersburg Road. Route 116 can also be taken westward, but you must go south of the square and pick up Middle Street, which becomes Route 116 and is called Fairfield Road as it heads west.

Most visitors choose to walk to the major attractions, which are mostly along the major routes I've described. Battlefield tour buses pick up at most of the hotels, and they also take you to other major attractions. There's also a trolley that oper-ates from mid-April to mid-October. A map of the trolley route is available at the Gettysburg Tour Center (778 Baltimore Street; 717-334-6296). The trolley stops at the square, at the southern end of Balti-more Street, along Steinwehr Avenue, and at the visitor center.

The closer you are to Lincoln Square, the more you pay to park. Meters around the square cost 75 cents per hour with a limit of two hours. Around the borough costs range from 20 to 60 cents an hour, and parking limits vary. Meters outside the borough cost 20 cents per hour with a parking limit of 12 hours.

There's free parking at the Gettysburg National Park Visitor Center, but most parking downtown consists of metered street parking, small lots on side streets that also have meters, and a parking garage on Race Horse Alley, which runs behind the Gettysburg Hotel. To reach the garage, take York Street from the square and make a left onto Stratton Street. Make another left onto Race Horse Alley and the garage is on your right. Parking in the garage is 50 cents per hour with no hourly limit.

HISTORY 🏛

NATIVE AMERICAN HISTORY

The area of Gettysburg was originally the land of the Susquehannock Indians, who occupied the area along the Susquehanna River and its branches from southern New York State to the north end of Chesapeake Bay. It's believed Susquehannock was an Algonquin name meaning "people of the muddy river." The tribe probably had a population of 5,000 to 7,000 members in 1600, but not a great deal of information about them exists because Europeans rarely visited their inland villages during early exploration. In 1608 Capt. John Smith was the first European to meet the Susquehannock, and he described them as giants. They must have been very tall because the Swedes who met the Susquehannock 30 years later also commented on their height.

Besides being farmers, hunters, and fishermen, the Susquehannock were fierce warriors who were feared by many of the tribes around them. They were enemies of the Iroquois and trading partners with the Erie and Huron tribes of Ontario. The French were the next Europeans to make contact with the tribe, and in battle the Susquehannock sided with the French and the Huron against the Iroquois. Despite this, the Susquehannock were able to maintain trading relationships with all the European nations that were then exploring the area. This allowed them to obtain armaments from their European trading partners, which helped them maintain a strong position during the Beaver Wars, a time of intertribal warfare from 1630 to 1700 to determine which tribes would dominate the lucrative European fur trade.

But all this warfare, combined with epidemics brought on by contact with the settlers, began to take its toll. In the 1650s the Susquehannock ceded their lands in the lower Susquehanna valley to the English, and in 1676 the last 300 Susquehannock surrendered to the Iroquois. In 1706 the Iroquois allowed them to set up a village in the Susquehanna Valley, where they became known to Pennsylvania colonists as the Conestoga, from the name of their last village in Pennsylvania. Quaker missionaries arrived, some tribe members left, and the Conestoga village was converted to a Christian community. By the end of the French and Indian War in 1763, there were only 20 of the Susquehannock left, and they were a peaceful community. Unfortunately, tensions between colonists and Indians were very high at this time, and the last Susquehannock were massacred in Lancaster County by a mob of colonists named the Paxton Boys. Although the tribe was no longer, Susquehannock descendants are found among the Iroquois, Delaware, and Tuscarora people.

WHITE SETTLEMENT

In 1736 the land west of the Susquehanna River was purchased from the Indians as part of Chester County, one of the original three counties of Pennsylvania. Chester County was eventually divided, and out of that division, Lancaster County came into being; subsequently, Lancaster County itself was divided, and York County came into being. In 1800 York County was divided, and Adams County was established. Eventually, Gettysburg was named as the county seat of Adams County.

The first white settlers came to the area we know as Gettysburg in 1734. They began the Marsh Creek Settlement, which was developed from 1736 to 1760 by pioneers of German, Scotch, and Irish descent. In the 1760s, Samuel Gettys purchased from John Penn (grandson of William Penn) a land grant of more than 300 acres that surrounded a crossroads where the Philadelphia-Pittsburg (east-west) and Baltimore-Shippensburg (north-south) roads met. Realizing the potential of the crossroads during this time of settlement expansion, Gettys built a tavern there in 1772, where he sold supplies and refreshments and a bed for the night to settlers who were moving to the west and to the north from Maryland. Continental troops were mustered at the Gettys' Inn and Tavern during the Revolutionary War.

Samuel Gettys died in 1783, and some of his land was auctioned off to satisfy his debts. His son James bought 116 acres of the land, which included the tavern, in 1785, and by 1790 he had laid out a town of 210 lots, which was named Gettystown in his honor. Because of its location at a crossroads, the town grew steadily and, as Gettysburg, it was named the county seat of the newly formed Adams County in 1800. The first session of the new county's court was held in the Gettys' Tavern in 1802, the first courthouse was erected in the square in 1804, and Gettysburg was incorporated as a borough in 1806.

The first half of the 19th century brought the establishment of Gettysburg as an agricultural transportation corridor and the founding of two educational facilities within the town, the Gettysburg Lutheran Theological Seminary in 1826 and Pennsylvania College, now called Gettysburg College, in 1832. The years between 1830 and 1860 saw the town develop the industry of carriage and wagon making, and in 1858 the Gettysburg Railroad was extended into town, connecting Gettysburg with other markets. By 1860 Gettysburg had 2,400 residents and 10 roads leading into town. It was said at the time that all roads led to Gettysburg, a fact that propelled the town to its fate in July 1863.

THE BATTLE OF GETTYSBURG

General Robert E. Lee's Confederate army of 75,000 men and Gen. George G.

Meade's Union army of 97,000 men met by accident at Gettysburg in July 1863 when a Confederate brigade sent to Gettysburg for supplies observed a forward column of the Union cavalry. This chance encounter led to the Battle of Gettysburg, what many believe to be the turning point of the Civil War. The battle went on for three days, culminating in Pickett's Charge, where Maj. Gen. George E. Pickett ordered a massed infantry of some 12,000 Confederate troops across an open field and toward the Union center on Cemetery

---

Casualty counts include not only soldiers killed but also those wounded, captured, or missing at the end of a battle. At Gettysburg about 7,100 of the 51,000 total casualties were actually killed in the three days of the battle.

Ridge. Pickett's men reached the Union line, but they failed to break it. Confederate casualties from the charge totaled 6,800 in 50 minutes, and the Battle of Gettysburg was at an end. The casualty count was 51,000, making Gettysburg the bloodiest battle in American history. More men fought and more men died than in any other battle on North American soil. Although the Civil War continued for almost two years after Gettysburg, the Confederacy never recovered from its losses there, and General Lee never attempted another offensive operation of such proportions.

The Battle of Gettysburg raged in the town itself, and many citizens had their houses overtaken by soldiers from both sides of the conflict. Although the three days of the battle were hard on the townsfolk, only one citizen, Jennie Wade, was killed during the action. The harder part came after the warfare, when the citizens' homes were turned into hospitals, and the townspeople had to deal with the ugly aftermath of war.

 CLOSE-UP

Lincoln's Gettysburg Address

Gettysburg is lucky to have its very own Abraham Lincoln living right in town. His name is James Getty, and his resemblance to Lincoln is uncanny. Mr. Getty has been portraying Abraham Lincoln since 1978, and he puts on a show every summer at the Gettysburg Battle Theatre (see the listing on Mr. Lincoln Returns to Gettysburg in the Attractions chapter for details). He also plays Lincoln at town events, such as Remembrance Day, which commemorates when Lincoln traveled to town to say a few words during the dedication of the National Cemetery on November 19, 1863. Those few words have lived on in history, and most of us learn the words to the address as schoolchildren. For those whose memories may not reach back that far, here is Abraham Lincoln's famous speech.

"Four score and seven years ago our fathers brought forth, upon this continent, a new nation, conceived in Liberty, and dedicated to the proposition that all men are created equal.

"Now we are engaged in a great civil war, testing whether that nation, or any nation so conceived, and so dedicated, can long endure. We are met here on a great battlefield of that war. We have come to dedicate a portion of it as a final resting place for those who here gave their lives that that nation might live. It is altogether fitting and proper that we should do this.

"But in a larger sense we can not dedicate—we can not consecrate—we can not hallow this ground. The brave men, living and dead, who struggled, here, have consecrated it far above our poor power to

LINCOLN'S GETTYSBURG ADDRESS

The National Cemetery at Gettysburg is the first cemetery that was dedicated exclusively to the burial of soldiers. A few days after the battle, then-governor A. G. Curtin appointed David Wills, a prominent attorney, to establish a cemetery for the Union soldiers who had died in the fighting. Wills invited President Abraham Lincoln to make a speech at the dedication, which was held November 19, 1863. Lincoln traveled by train from Washington, D.C., the night before the dedication and stayed in David Wills' house on Lincoln Square. The morning of the ceremony, he traveled from Lincoln Square south on Baltimore Street to Evergreen Cemetery, earning the route its name—The Historic Pathway. Although Lincoln's speech was only two minutes in length, it is probably one of the most quoted speeches in American history. (See the Close-up for the memorable words of Lincoln's Gettysburg Address.)

To create the National Cemetery, 17 acres were purchased on Cemetery Hill at the apex of what had been the triangular battle line of the Union Army. Exhumation of the bodies began on October 27, 1863, and this work wasn't completed until

add or detract. The world will little note, nor long remember, what we say here, but can never forget what they did here. It is for us, the living, rather to be dedicated here to the unfinished work which they have, thus far, so nobly carried on. It is rather for us to be here dedicated to the great task remaining before us— that from these honored dead we take increased devotion to that cause for which they here gave the last full measure of devotion—that we here highly resolve that these dead shall not have died in vain; that this nation shall have a new birth of freedom; and that this government of the people, by the people, for the people, shall not perish from the earth."

—President Abraham Lincoln

Gettysburg resident James Getty portrays President Lincoln at town events and throughout the country as well as in the show he performs at Gettysburg Battle Theatre. LEWISBURG, PA STUDIO

March 18, 1864. Lots in the cemetery were given to each state with dead on the field. Graves were arranged in a semicircular plan with the land allotted to each state converging on a central point. A space of two feet wide was allotted for each body, and the bodies were laid with their heads toward the center. The headstones are uniform in size and contain the name, regiment, and company, if obtainable, of each soldier. Because the cemetery is part of the battlefield, it contains monuments that were erected in honor of Union regiments that fought on the soil. Union cannons that were part of the fighting are also found in the cemetery.

The cemetery was completed in 1872, and by the battle's 25th anniversary in 1888, many traveled to Gettysburg to view the battlefields and the cemetery. A massive reunion of the Blue and Gray was held in Gettysburg on the 50th anniversary in 1913. The townspeople of Gettysburg have played willing hosts to visitors and have taken great care to preserve the town's history.

DWIGHT D. EISENHOWER

During WWI, then-captain Eisenhower fell in love with the area around Gettysburg

Volunteers were plentiful at the beginning of the Civil War, but volunteer numbers eventually dropped off. This led both sides to begin drafting men, with the South beginning its conscription in 1862 and the North following suit in 1863.

when he was the commanding officer at Camp Colt in 1918. Camp Colt was a tank-training camp that at one time housed 8,000 soldiers. During training, weapons were mounted on flatbed trucks that sped around camp as trainees took aim at Little Round Top, the famous hill that figured so prominently in the Battle of Gettysburg.

Eisenhower loved the rural area, and in the 1950s he purchased a farm just west of where the Confederates were positioned on Seminary Ridge. The home served as a weekend retreat for the president, and it was here that he hosted many world leaders, including Nikita Khrushchev, Winston Churchill, and Charles De Gaulle. After the presidency, Eisenhower and his wife, Mamie, retired here.

Today the home has been preserved and is open to the public as part of the Eisenhower National Historic Site.

GETTYSBURG TODAY

The town of Gettysburg takes its role in history very seriously, and preserving that history is very important to its residents.

But the town is not just a preserved showplace. It's a thriving tourist town that also hosts diverse interests—rural countryside to play in, festivals to attend, and art and culture to absorb. The town currently has so many improvement projects going on that it's hard to keep track of them all. The Lincoln Train Station off Carlisle Street is being restored and will serve as a welcoming center for tourists. The Wills House on Lincoln Square, where Lincoln stayed before giving his famous address, is being renovated. A new complex called Gateway Gettysburg is in the works, which will have hotels, conference centers, restaurants, shops, and an eight-screen movie complex. The historic Majestic Theater on Carlisle Street reopened in 2005 as a performing-arts venue. In fact, there are so many diverse improvements going on that it's estimated to be 10 years before they're all completed.

And it's not just the town that's renovating. The Gettysburg National Military Park has planned a $95 million project that will include a new visitor center, an artifact museum, and a cyclorama gallery in one building that will be about half a mile south of the existing center.

But even as Gettysburg plans its future, it remains deeply connected to its rich history. That was recently proven when work on the renovation of the Lincoln Train Station unearthed three railroad ties within the original rail bed that carried President Lincoln's train to Gettysburg in 1863. The future of Gettysburg lies in its reverence of the past.

HOTELS, MOTELS, AND RESORTS

Gettysburg offers a wide range of accommodations with so many choices that I've included a separate chapter on bed-and-breakfasts and guesthouses and one on campgrounds and RV parks. This chapter will focus on the hotels and motels in the area, from which there are many to choose. I've also included two resorts, one with skiing and one with golfing, which are located next to each other about 10 miles west of town.

Competition to attract business compels most area hotels and motels to offer a wide range of services as standard fare. Although motels don't have as many amenities as hotels, many people prefer the ease of parking right at their front door. Expect most motels in the area to offer phones and cable or satellite TV in the rooms, free coffee and free newspapers, and microwaves and refrigerators available for a fee. Most hotels include these motel amenities as well as offering in-room hair dryers, irons and ironing boards, coffeemakers, a pool, free local calls, and pickups for battlefield tours. Almost all offer smoking rooms; I'll tell you if an establishment offers only smoking or smoke-free rooms. All the businesses in this chapter accept credit cards and, if you're eligible, make sure to ask about AAA or AARP discounts when making reservations. The hotels listed here are wheelchair accessible, but although most of the motels have ground-level rooms, the rooms are not really equipped for wheelchair access. You should assume that pets are not welcome unless specifically mentioned.

Since there are a good number of hotels and motels available in Gettysburg, I've first broken them down by geographic location from Lincoln Square and then listed them alphabetically. I realize that many travelers decide what sites they want to be close to and then pick a hotel or motel based on its location in relation to those sites. Although there is nothing wrong with this method, remember that walking in Gettysburg can be an experience in itself, and the trolley is also available to zip you around town.

PRICE CODE

Prices quoted are for one night's lodging in a basic room with one or two people in the room during the season, which is April through December. State and local taxes are not included. Pennsylvania has a 6 percent sales tax, and Adams County has an additional 3 percent "pillow tax."

$	Less than $70
$$	$71 to $99
$$$	$100 to $135
$$$$	$136 and higher

LINCOLN SQUARE

**Best Western
Historic Gettysburg Hotel** $$$$
**1 Lincoln Square
(717) 337-2000, (866) EST-1797, (800) 528-1234 (reservations)
www.hotelgettysburg.com**
Established in 1797, this is the premier hotel in town. When you enter the lobby, the rich woods and deep-pile carpets give you a good feel for the hotel's quiet elegance. Sitting on the square, its six floors contain 96 guest rooms and 26 suites that are outfitted with Civil War–period furnishings, and the hotel staff dressing in period costume completes your transfor-

mation to the days of the past. The name of the hotel's restaurant—Centuries on the Square—says it all. Here you can enjoy casual fine dining daily (see the Restaurants chapter). There's also a historic English pub on-site—McClellan's Tavern, which has a turn-of-the-century mahogany Van Tromp Bar imported from Brick Lane in England. The Gettysburg Hotel is featured on the Historic Gettysburg Walking Tour (see the Attractions chapter), and it's also listed on the National Register of Historic Places and on the Historic Hotels of America for the National Trust for Historic Preservation.

All the amenities you would expect to find are here. In addition, there's room service from 7:00 A.M. to 9:00 P.M., babysitting and dry-cleaning services and in-room movies are available, and local calls are free if they're less than 30 minutes long. You'll also have free high-speed Internet access, free transportation to the battlefield bus tour, complimentary afternoon tea, and turndown service. Two-room family units are available, children younger than age 17 stay free in the room with a paying adult, and fireplaces and Jacuzzi baths grace the hotel's suites.

NORTH OF LINCOLN SQUARE

Blue Sky Motel $
2585 Biglerville Road
(717) 677-7736, (800) 745-8194
www.blueskymotel.com
This motel has 17 rooms to choose from, ranging from a room with a double bed and a shower stall to suites with two double beds, a sleeper sofa, and a living room. In between, you'll find family rooms outfitted with a fridge and efficiencies outfitted with kitchens. The Blue Sky is nothing more than it appears to be—a small motel that offers clean, affordable lodging. It's not fancy, but it is run by friendly people who want your stay in Gettysburg to be a happy experience. You won't have a paper delivered or have a free continental break-

fast here, but there is a wake-up service and a late-check-in service, local calls and morning coffee are free, and battlefield tours pick up at the motel. Located a little less than 5 miles north of the square and practically next to the National Apple Harvest Festival held in Arendtsville (see the Annual Events and Festivals chapter), Blue Sky Motel, which was built in 1950, had its rooms completely gutted and renovated in 2000. You'll find rooms with modern heating and air-conditioning and random-width hardwood panels that have caused more than one guest to say it felt like he was staying in a cabin. Technically, you won't find any nonsmoking rooms here. If you request it at the time of your reservation, the staff will do an intense cleaning of your room, including wiping down the walls and cleaning the carpets. In the summertime, you'll find a playground, a picnic area where you can barbecue, and a pool. Since the motel sits on four acres, there's also plenty of room for horseshoes, croquet, badminton, and volleyball. With notice, the motel will also pick up discount tickets to Hersheypark (see the Day Trips chapter) for you.

SOUTH OF LINCOLN SQUARE

America's Best Inn $$$
301 Steinwehr Avenue
(717) 334-1188, (800) 237-8466
(reservations)
www.gettysburgbestinn.com
Owned by Choice Hotels, America's Best Inn certainly has one of the best locations in town. It sits between the American Civil War Museum and the Lincoln Train Museum on Steinwehr Avenue, right across from the Gettysburg National Military Park (GNMP) Visitor Center. This two-story hotel was built in the 1960s and offers 77 rooms, which are routinely renovated on a rotating basis. Most of the rooms have double beds, but some are equipped with king-size beds. If you want a smoking room, call early; all but two

rooms are nonsmoking. And call early if you want one of the eight "evergreen" rooms, which feature air and water filters, or the one room that comes equipped with a small efficiency kitchen. A free deluxe continental breakfast is available to guests, and you can get free coffee in the office 24/7. When you're done touring, you can relax by the outdoor pool or enjoy high-speed Internet access in your room. Children younger than age 18 stay for free with a parent, and pets are allowed for a fee of $10 per pet per night.

Budget Host—Three Crowns Motor Lodge $-$$
205 Steinwehr Avenue
(717) 334-3168, (800) 729-6564
(reservations)
www.onlinehotels.com

The Budget Host and the Colton Motel (see subsequent listing) have been owned by the same people since 1996. This franchise motel, which is painted red, white, and blue, has 29 rooms with either one king-size bed or two double beds. It also has a fabulous location—you're only about a block from the GNMP Visitor Center and 6 blocks south of Lincoln Square. Built during the 1940s and 1950s, the motel rooms have undergone constant upkeep, and they receive a renovation every year. Besides comfortable rooms, you'll also have access to the outdoor pool, data ports, and free local calls, and children younger than age 18 stay free with a paying guest. The Budget Host began offering a free continental breakfast for guests in 2005, and a copy of the *Gettysburg Times* newspaper is available in the lobby. If you want, feel free to bring your four-legged friend; pets are allowed. If you have Internet access, be sure to check out the motel's Web site—it has a great slideshow of the motel.

Colton Motel $$
232 Steinwehr Avenue
(717) 334-5514, (800) 262-0317
(reservations)
www.onlinehotels.com

The Colton has the dubious distinction of being the last independently owned motel in the borough of Gettysburg. But there's nothing dubious about the distinction of sleeping on hallowed ground on Cemetery Ridge, with the National Cemetery as the motel's backdrop. This is where soldiers from the Ohio 73rd Company D Infantry unit held the Union line at the burr of the fishhook before it started to bend around Culp's Hill. The exterior of the Colton, which was built in 1953, is painted blue and gray, and the rooms have been kept up well. In fact, they're currently being updated to make each one a little different. Sitting only 100 yards north of the visitor center at GNMP, the motel has the benefit of an ideal location to walk to restaurants and attractions. If you love to talk history, be sure to chat with the manager, who lives on the property. He's a treasure trove of Civil War history, one of many former visitors to Gettysburg who decided to make the town his home. (See the Close-up within this chapter.)

The Colton has 25 rooms, including family rooms, and all rooms but the family suite are on the ground level. The second-story family suite has three bedrooms with four double beds, and there's also a family room available that has three queen-size beds. The motel has an outdoor pool and Internet access is available. You can also make free local calls, and the office has complimentary coffee and a copy of the *Gettysburg Times* and the *Hanover Evening Sun* newspapers available. There's a great slideshow of the hotel's rooms on the Internet if you want to check it out.

Country Inn & Suites by Carlson $$$
1857 Gettysburg Village Drive
(717) 337-9518, (800) 456-4000
(reservations)
www.countryinns.com/gettysburgpa

Just about anyone from Gettysburg can tell you where this hotel is—it sits across from the Gettysburg Village Factory Stores (see the Shopping chapter). Located only 2.9 miles from Lincoln Square, Country Inn & Suites is also close

CLOSE-UP

Drawn to Gettysburg

You'll meet many residents of Gettysburg who will tell you they were drawn here. Some have traveled to the battlefield since their youth and eventually felt the need to relocate to the area. Andrew Manley, manager at the Colton Inn, is one such person. His first visit to the battlefield was in 1968 as an eight-year-old on vacation with his family. Manley returned often and walked the battlefield many times, feeling compelled to visit the area but never really knowing why. On a battlefield visit in the late 1990s, he stumbled across the grave of one Timothy Manly (as the spelling appeared on the headstone), and he wondered . . . could this be a family relative? He decided to do some research, which eventually turned into a lot of research, and he discovered that Timothy Manley (the headstone has the spelling wrong) was, indeed, a relative—a great-great-cousin.

Timothy Manley was a private in the 63rd Irish Brigade who was mortally wounded in the battle for the Rose Wheatfield on July 2, 1863. He was taken to the Camp Letterman Field Hospital (a marker for the hospital is near the Giant grocery store on York Road), where he died of his wounds in early September. His body was buried on the hospital grounds but was later exhumed and interred in the National Cemetery just days before Lincoln arrived in November to say a few words in honor of the fallen Union soldiers. Lincoln well might have gazed upon Timothy's grave as he delivered what would be his most famous speech—the Gettysburg Address.

After living in many parts of the country, Andrew Manley decided after 9/11 that he wanted to live in Gettysburg. He picked up and moved from Las Vegas to Gettysburg with only the promise of a job interview, which never materialized once he hit town. But Manley felt he was destined to stay here; in fact, he says, he felt the spirit of Timothy Manley calling him to Gettysburg. After a lot of hardship, Manley was offered a job at the Colton Motel as its manager, which he readily accepted. As he often did, Andrew Manley visited the battlefield and placed a flag upon his great-cousin's grave. Only when he was back in the office of the Colton did he realize he could easily view the flag he had placed there. The great pull he had felt all his life was finally real-

to Boyds Bear Country (see the Attractions chapter) and the battlefield. The three-story hotel was built in May 2001 and has 83 rooms, 35 of them standard rooms with two queen-size beds and the rest suites. There are five types of two-room suites to pick from, all with refrigerator, microwave, and wet bar, and some are equipped with two-person Jacuzzis. An indoor pool and fitness center round out your exercise options, and rooms have data ports and high-speed Internet access. Or perhaps you'd rather relax with a good book—feel free to borrow one from the hotel's lending library and return it on your next visit to a Country Inn &

ized, and he was at peace, knowing he had found where his home was meant to be. Manley feels that his great-cousin is also finally at peace and that his spirit was able to move on to its eternal resting place.

"Old soldiers never die, they just stand sentry" is Manley's take on the line from an army ballad that Gen. Douglas MacArthur made famous. He believes his great-cousin was standing sentry, waiting for him to come to Gettysburg. Andrew Manley meets many visitors to Gettysburg who are drawn here but cannot exactly say why. His advice to them is to follow their feelings—perhaps they have a sentry waiting for them as well.

The National Cemetery sits behind the Colton Motel, and you're sleeping on hallowed ground when you stay at this motel. KATE HERTZOG

Suites. A donation is made to a literacy organization for every book returned. Having complimentary beverages and cookies available 24/7 is one of many ways this chain hotel makes you feel at home. They also feed you a deluxe complimentary continental breakfast and welcome guests younger than age 18 traveling with a parent for free. Hungry travelers will find restaurants in the food court in the nearby outlet mall and a TGI Fridays restaurant beside the hotel. Although the hotel accepts AAA discounts, they stopped accepting AARP in February 2005.

Cozy Country Inn $-$$
103 Frederick Road, Thurmont, MD
(301) 271-4301
www.cozyvillage.com

History buffs won't mind the 18-mile drive south from Gettysburg on U.S. Route 15 that's required to reach the Cozy, which is on the list of America's Historic Inns. To them, staying in one of the inn's 21 historic, quaint, and unique rooms and cottages that are decorated in the style of presidents and dignitaries who have visited Camp David and/or the Cozy Country Inn will be worth the drive. In April 2005 the Camp David Museum opened, and now you can view pictures, many never before seen by the public, of past presidents visiting Camp David. The also-famous Cozy Restaurant, which seats 150 and is the oldest restaurant in Maryland still operated by descendants of its founding family, offers both lavish buffets and an a la carte menu. The Cozy has a lounge where you can get a tall, cool drink. Or, if you prefer, order from room service, which is offered from 11:00 A.M. to 9:30 P.M. Your free continental breakfast, which is served in the lobby during the week, is served in the restaurant on the weekend. The inn and restaurant are part of Historic Cozy Village, which offers some unique shops for you to browse.

Econo Lodge $$$
945 Baltimore Pike
(717) 334-6715, (800) 334-6192
www.gettysburgeconolodge.com

The Econo Lodge is owned by Choice Hotels, as are many hotels in town. You'll find the lodge 1.5 miles from Lincoln Square, across from the Battlefield Military Museum (see the Attractions chapter) and beside the Pike Restaurant (see the Restaurants chapter). Its location puts it within walking distance of the battlefield and the National Cemetery and only 1 block from the Gettysburg Tour Center. This two-story motel has 42 rooms, with a queen-size bed in some rooms and two double beds in others. There's also a room that has three beds in order to accommodate families. Families will also enjoy the free continental breakfast that's offered in season and the outdoor pool.

Eisenhower Inn & Conference Center $$$
2634 Emmitsburg Road
(717) 334-8121, (800) 776-8349
(reservations)
www.eisenhower.com

With 307 rooms available, this is one of the largest hotels in the area. Located only 4.5 miles south of Gettysburg on U.S. Business Route 15, the Eisenhower Inn is next door to and associated with the All-star Events Complex (see the Attractions and Kidstuff chapters), which has tons of recreational choices for you and the kids, such as go-karts, minigolf, fishing, and tennis, just to name a few. The Eisenhower actually consists of two connected buildings. The Eisenhower I is the original facility, and the Eisenhower II is the addition. All rooms in the Eisenhower II are non-smoking, and about half the rooms in the Eisenhower I are also nonsmoking. The standard rooms offer double beds, and there are some rooms with one king-size bed. Queen leisure rooms are all located in the Eisenhower II and include two queen-size beds and a sleeper sofa; executive rooms are also equipped with microwave and minifridge, as are the presidential suites, which also have a living room and bedroom. More than 100 rooms come with a microwave and minifridge for your convenience.

In addition to the expected amenities, such as in-room coffeemakers, hair dryers, and irons and ironing boards, you'll also enjoy an indoor/outdoor pool with a Jacuzzi, a guest laundry, dry saunas, an exercise room, and Internet access. The pool area, with its open sky dome and cabana seating area, is an especially inviting place for relaxation. When hunger hits, choose from the on-site deli, called the Marketplace, or Richard's Restaurant and Lounge, which has a French Country motif and seats 120. Or enjoy the luxury of calling room service, which operates from morning to early afternoon and in the evening.

Gettysburg Travelodge   **$$$**
613 Baltimore Street
(717) 334-9281, (800) 578-7878
(reservations)
www.travelodge.com
Located opposite the Gettysburg Tour
Center (see the GNMP chapter), this chain
hotel has 47 rooms that are equipped
with double, queen-size, or king-size
beds. The hotel actually consists of two
buildings—one that was constructed in
May 2000 and a second, recently reno-
vated building that used to be the Her-
itage Motor Lodge. Suites with a king-size
bed, a queen-size pullout bed, a micro-
wave, a refrigerator, and a whirlpool tub
are available, as is Sleepy Bear Den, a
suite geared toward folks traveling with
kids. Although the hotel does charge for
local calls, a dial-up Internet connection is
available, and children younger than age
18 stay free with an adult. A select num-
ber of rooms have balconies, and you can
park directly in front of some of the
ground-floor rooms. Parking is free. Walk-
ing to major attractions is a breeze from
here; you're only 7 blocks south of Lincoln
Square and 3 blocks from the GNMP Visi-
tor Center. To round out your travel stay,
you'll receive a free continental breakfast
and daily newspaper. And feel free to
bring your pet—they're welcome at the
Travelodge.

Holiday Inn Battlefield   **$$$**
516 Baltimore Street
(717) 334-6211, (800) HOLIDAY
www.ichotels.com
This Holiday Inn was completely remodeled in 2003. Most of its 111 rooms have
two double beds, but there are a few
rooms that have king-size beds, microwaves, refrigerators, and whirlpools in
the bathroom. The Brigades Food Wine
& Spirits Restaurant & Lounge (see the
Restaurants chapter) is located in the
hotel, which is adjacent to the Gettysburg Tour Center. You'll also find a fitness center, outdoor pool, and guest
laundry, and pets are welcome in most

rooms. Although this hotel is very conveniently located, some guests note that
it can be quite noisy and that you can
hear your neighbor easily, so if you're a
light sleeper, you might want to make a
different lodging choice.

Quality Inn Gettysburg
Motor Lodge   **$$$-$$$$**
380 Steinwehr Avenue
(717) 334-1103, (800) 228-5151
(reservations)
www.gettysburgqualityinn.com
All of the 109 rooms in this two-story
motel are nonsmoking, and most have
either one king-size bed or two double
beds. There are some rooms with three
double beds, and eight spa rooms have a
whirlpool in the bathroom. One efficiency
suite with a kitchen is also available. All
rooms are renovated on a rotating basis.
Owned by Choice Hotels, the Quality Inn
offers high-speed Internet access and
allows children younger than age 18 to
stay free with a parent. In the morning,
enjoy a free expanded continental break-
fast in the Victorian breakfast cottage,
which dates from the 1880s, and then
walk to the battlefield and attractions
nearby. Depending upon the season, you
can relax in the outdoor or indoor
(heated) pool, or perhaps in the whirlpool
in the pool area. There's also a fitness
room with a sauna, and a putting green is
available in summer. Be sure to check out
the inn's unique underground cocktail
lounge, which is called the Reliance Mine
Saloon (see the Nightlife chapter). The
Quality Inn Gettysburg received the
Reader's Choice Award by the *Gettysburg
Companion* magazine in December 2004.

EAST OF LINCOLN SQUARE

Comfort Inn   **$$$**
871 York Road
(717) 337-2400, (800) 4CHOICE
www.choicehotels.com
This 80-room hotel located 1 mile east of

Lincoln Square was built in 1990, and its indoor heated pool was just redone in 2003. There's a Jacuzzi in the pool area, and Jacuzzi suites, which come with a minifridge, are also available. As with other Choice Hotels, children younger than age 18 stay free in a parent's room, and rooms have high-speed Internet access. Most rooms have queen-size beds, but some are outfitted with king-size beds. Although only two stories, the hotel is equipped with an elevator, and it's adjacent to the Gettysburg Family Fun Center (see the Kidstuff chapter). The hotel offers a free continental breakfast and 24-hour free coffee and tea, and there's also a Perkins Family Restaurant adjacent for more substantial fare. Pets are allowed at $10 per night, per pet.

Don't attempt to walk to the downtown area from hotels east of the square, with the exception of the Super 8. York Road (U.S. Route 30) is a busy highway, and walking along it is not a safe practice.

Days Inn Gettysburg $$$
865 York Road
(717) 334-0030, (800) DAYS INN (reservations)
www.daysinngettysburg.com

Located a mile east of Lincoln Square on York Road, the Days Inn has 112 rooms with king- and queen-size beds. You can choose a room with two queen-size beds; a Work Zone Room, with a king-size bed, comfy recliner, and two-line data-port phone; an Executive Room, with its sofa sitting area; or a Jacuzzi Room, outfitted with a king-size bed, sofa, and Jacuzzi for two. To round out your stay, there's a heated outdoor pool open from May through September, a fitness center that's open 6:00 A.M. to 11:00 P.M. daily, a complimentary deluxe continental breakfast, complimentary hot beverages 24 hours per day, and guest laundry facilities. If you

choose a room that doesn't have a refrigerator or microwave, they are available for rent. The Perkins Family Restaurant is adjacent to the hotel. This Days Inn has won numerous Days Inn awards, including the Chairman's Award for Quality every year since 1993.

Hampton Inn $$$$
1280 York Road
(717) 338-9121, (800) HAMPTON (reservations)
www.hamptoninngettysburg.com

This chain hotel was built in 1996, and since 2000 it's already had its rooms and lobby renovated—this place is kept up to date. And it keeps up on its technology, also. The Hampton Inn has high-speed wireless Internet throughout the hotel. You can cruise the Web in your room and while enjoying the free continental breakfast that's included in your stay! And although there's no room service available, the Ruby Tuesday restaurant next door delivers.

With 79 rooms within four stories, the Hampton has two elevators for guests' convenience. Most rooms have two double beds, but there are also two-bedroom family rooms that sleep six, and King suites, which are outfitted with a fireplace, Jacuzzi, kitchenette, and sofa bed, are available. Active guests have access to an indoor pool, a spa, and a fitness room, and 75 percent of the rooms are nonsmoking. A free continental breakfast that has some hot entrees is served, and guests younger than age 18 stay for free with a paying guest. As with all Hampton Inns, your satisfaction is 100 percent guaranteed—if not, your money is returned.

Hilton Garden Inn $$$$
1061 York Road
(717) 334-2040
www.hiltongardeninn.com

The 88 guest rooms in this chain hotel that opened in July 2004 come with either two queen-size beds or one king-size bed, and all rooms have microwaves as well as refrigerators. If you like to stay connected with the world while you travel, you'll have access to private voice mail, complimentary high-speed Internet, and data ports. When hunger strikes, you can order food from the Ruby Tuesday next door, which delivers. Or you can find food as well as sundries at the 24-hour Pavilion Pantry. The Hilton Garden Inn does have a breakfast-only restaurant, which is open to the public. You can work off any unwanted calories by using the cardio equipment in the fitness center or doing laps in the indoor pool. There's also a Jacuzzi available for relaxing at the end of a long day of sightseeing.

Holiday Inn Express $$$
869 York Road
(717) 337-1400, (800) HOLIDAY
www.hiexpress.com/gettysburgpa
Renovated in January 2003, the two-story Holiday Inn Express has 51 rooms and 2 suites. Double beds outfit 46 of the rooms, and the remaining 5 rooms have king-size beds. One of the suites has a king-size bed and a queen-size pullout couch while the other has two queen-size beds in separate rooms and a full kitchen. Thirty-eight of the rooms and the two suites are non-smoking. If you don't like climbing steps, book a first-floor room—there's no elevator. There is a large indoor pool and a whirlpool. As at all Holiday Inn Express locations, you can partake in the complimentary deluxe continental Express Start™ Breakfast, and there is 24-hour coffee service also. Phones are equipped with voice mail, data ports are available, and there's high-speed Internet access. Small pets are allowed, but in smoking rooms only.

Homestead Motor Lodge $
1650 York Road
(717) 334-3866
This small 10-room motel 2.5 miles east of Lincoln Square offers travelers nice, no-frills (and no pool) accommodations. The Homestead is family owned and operated. Four of its rooms have a queen-size bed, and the other six have two double beds.

If you're interested in the Days Inn's Jacuzzi rooms, book early—there are only three.

Five of the rooms have a microwave and refrigerator, and all your local calls are free. The rooms are a decent size and decorated nicely. Although this is a strip motel on the outskirts of town, the price is right and the place is quiet and clean.

Super 8 Motel—Gettysburg $$$
606 York Street
(717) 334-4274, (800) 800-8000
www.super8.com
This Super 8 opened in spring 2000, and its 52 guest rooms are large enough to accommodate two queen-size beds. King deluxe suites, complete with whirlpool tub, sofa bed, microwave, and refrigerator, are also available. Located 1 mile east of Lincoln Square, this three-story motel has a large lobby, interior corridors, and an elevator. You'll be treated to a free continental breakfast, and the motel also has an indoor pool and a spa. Although there are data ports in the rooms, the lobby is the only place where free wireless high-speed Internet access is available.

WEST OF LINCOLN SQUARE

Carroll Valley Resort $$$
121 Sanders Road, Fairfield
(717) 642-8211, (888) 330-4206
(800) 548-8504 (reservations)
www.carrollvalley.com
This is the Gettysburg area's golf resort, although many people also stay here when swooshing down the slopes of Ski Liberty, which is but steps away. The stone mountain lodge you'll drive up to is where you register, and the actual accommodations are located in the two-story building just behind the lodge. The resort's restaurants, fitness and billiards rooms, and banquet and conference facilities are also within the

lodge. For your accommodation choices, you can pick between a room with a view of the Catoctin Mountains south of Gettysburg or a view of the golf course. The resort has 58 rooms, of which 46 are standard rooms equipped with two double beds. The other 12 rooms are parlor rooms. Eight of the parlor rooms have two double beds and a Jacuzzi tub, and four of them have a king-size bed, a sofa, and a Jacuzzi tub. You can enjoy fireside dining at The Inn at Carroll Valley, and casual dining for breakfast or lunch is available downstairs in The Tavern on the Green restaurant. For golfers, the resort has a driving range and two 18-hole Ault & Clark championship golf courses (see the Golf chapter). You'll have a choice of lots of different golf packages, with lodging, breakfast, and dining included in packages.

Liberty Mountain Resort and Conference Center $$$
78 Country Club Trail, Carroll Valley
(717) 642-8282
www.libertymountainresort.com

Liberty Mountain Resort is nestled at the bottom of the 16 ski slopes of Ski Liberty (see the Recreation chapter). It's open year-round right beside the Carroll Valley Resort (see the previous listing). The Liberty Mountain Hotel sits on a hill above the ski lodge, which also contains McKee's Tavern. Wireless Internet is available throughout the hotel and the ski lodge. If you book a mountainside room, you'll have a balcony to relax on and take in the views. All 41 rooms are individually decorated with a country motif and include cable, voice mail, and computer ports. The luxury suite has a bedroom with a king-size bed and a balcony, a separate living room that also has a balcony, a fully

equipped kitchenette, a bathroom with a two-person whirlpool tub and an oversize shower with glass block walls, and a stackable washer/dryer. Ski and Stay packages are available in winter, and in summer guests enjoy the outdoor swimming pool or a round of golf at the Carroll Valley Resort.

Quality Inn Larson's at General Lee's Headquarters $$$
401 Buford Avenue
(717) 334-3141
www.gettysburgusa.com, www.the gettysburgaddress.com

With many of its rooms overlooking the battlefield at historic Seminary Ridge, this Quality Inn is adjacent to the small stone house that was owned by Thaddeus Stevens and that served as the headquarters of Gen. Robert E. Lee during the Battle of Gettysburg. In fact, General Lee's Headquarters Museum (see the Attractions chapter) is on-site and free to guests of the inn. The Lutheran Theological Seminary (see the Education chapter) is adjacent to the inn. The inn is also a pickup site on the Battlefield Tour, and the jumping-off point for the Ghosts of Gettysburg Candlelight Walking Tours of Seminary Ridge (see the Attractions chapter).

Owned by Choice Hotels, the inn has 41 rooms and 7 suites. The rooms come in a variety of bed choices, and each suite is unique. One suite might have a Jacuzzi while another will have a fireplace. Four of the suites are in Civil War–era buildings, and they have full-size kitchens. All the rooms are ground level while two of the suites are two stories. In addition to free coffee in the lobby, you also receive a free continental breakfast. The fitness center and outdoor pool lure active sports-oriented guests, while the hotel's gift shop satisfies guests who prefer to exercise their credit cards. You can also pamper yourself by using the inn's valet laundry service. And you won't go hungry (or thirsty) while staying here—the Appalachian Brewing Co. brewpub (see the Restaurants chapter) is located beside the inn.

Gen. George Patton and President Dwight D. Eisenhower are two famous military leaders who have stayed at the Quality Inn Larson's at General Lee's Headquarters.

BED-AND-BREAKFASTS
AND GUESTHOUSES

Bed-and-breakfasts and country inns abound in the Gettysburg area. At last count, there were almost 40 within 20 to 25 miles of Gettysburg. For the purposes of this book, an establishment will be considered a country inn if it offers breakfast to nonguests as well as guests. The accommodations included here are either within or very close to Gettysburg proper. They include in-town homes and homes surrounded by acres in the country. At the end of the chapter, three guesthouses that are available for rent are also included. These are not bed-and-breakfasts; you rent the entire house and you take care of your own meals.

Many of the bed-and-breakfasts included here were built in the 1700s, and some retain parts of the original homes, such as wide plank flooring. Some of the homes have bullet holes and bloodstained floors to attest to the role they played during the Battle of Gettysburg. Others are Victorian charmers, with period antiques gracing the rooms. Still others are rural nirvanas, with lots of open space and outdoor activities to keep you busy. Each bed-and-breakfast has unique qualities, with history and location playing only one part. Some innkeepers run small, intimate abodes, with guests receiving lots of individual attention, while others are bigger establishments, with group activities offered.

Once you've narrowed your choices, you might want to employ the services of one of the bed-and-breakfast associations available to you. These organizations allow you to find out about vacancies, special offers, and the nuances of their member inns. See the Gettysburg Bed-and-Breakfast Associations box within this chapter for contact information.

Web sites are given for all the bed-and-breakfasts; if possible, take the time to visit these sites. Most have views of the rooms available to guests as well as pictures of the house and common rooms. This allows you to get a good idea of where you're going to feel the most comfortable during your stay.

This chapter is arranged geographically, with the inns categorized by their direction from Lincoln Square. You can count on all the bed-and-breakfasts to have a two-night minimum stay during the season (April through December) and to impose an additional charge for more than two people in a room. Most offer customized packages and special-event deals, as well as off-season savings, so be sure to ask!

Unless otherwise noted, assume that smoking and pets are not allowed. Also assume that an accommodation isn't wheelchair accessible unless that fact is specifically noted. If credit cards aren't accepted, that will be mentioned in the establishment's entry. (Be aware that some inns require a personal check rather than a credit card to hold your reservation.) For those readers who sneeze when they see a dog or cat, I'll let you know if a home has a resident pet.

The degree to which a bed-and-breakfast welcomes children varies widely. Some have set age limits, and just about all request that children be "well-behaved." Since this term is subjective, it's probably best to talk directly to the innkeeper as to whether you and your child will find the accommodations suitable.

Here's one bit of advice you need to remember: Check on cancellation policies before you book. These vary considerably, depending on your time and length of stay.

Gettysburg Bed-and-Breakfast Associations

Bed and Breakfasts INNside Gettysburg
www.bbonline.com/pa/innsidegettys
burg

This site consists of seven bed-and-breakfasts with a physical Gettysburg address that organized to promote their businesses during the off-season and midweek times. The inns cooperate to provide winter weekend packages for guests. The following inns belong to this association: the Baladerry Inn, the Battle-field Bed & Breakfast Inn, the Brafferton Inn, The Brickhouse Inn, The Doubleday Inn, the Gaslight Inn, and the James Gettys Hotel.

Country Bed & Breakfasts of Gettysburg
www.gettysburgbnbs.com

Five owner-owned and -operated country inns banded together to promote their attentive and personalized service by forming this association. The participating inns are the Baladerry Inn, the Brierfield II, the Gettysburg Pond View Farm, the Red Bud Inn, and the Slocum House Inn.

Inns of the Gettysburg Area
(717) 624-1300, (800) 587-2216
www.bbonline.com/pa/gettysburg

This bed-and-breakfast association consists of 20 historic inns in and around Gettysburg. When you call, an innkeeper will be able to tell you which members have available lodging. Participating inns that are included in this chapter are A Quiet Knight Bed & Breakfast, A Sentimental Journey Bed & Breakfast, the Baladerry Inn, the Battlefield Bed & Breakfast Inn, the Brafferton Inn, The Brickhouse Inn, the Brierfield II, the Cashtown Inn, The Doubleday Inn, the Farnsworth House Inn, the Gaslight Inn, the Gettysburg Pond View Farm, the Gettystown Inn, the Herr Tavern & Publick House, the Keystone Inn Bed & Breakfast, the Lightner Farmhouse, and the Slocum House Inn.

Prices quoted are for one night's lodging with one or two people in the room during the season, which is April through December. State and local taxes are not included. Pennsylvania has a 6 percent sales tax, and Adams County has an additional 3 percent "pillow tax."

PRICE CODE

$	Less than $95
$$	$96 to $120
$$$	$121 to $160
$$$$	$161 and higher

NORTH OF LINCOLN SQUARE

Brierfield II Country Guest Cottages $
1060 Belmont Road
(717) 334-8725
www.gettysburgcottages.com

Owner and innkeeper Nancy Rice opened the first Brierfield Bed and Breakfast in town in 1988, but she closed it in 1998 and opened the Brierfield II out in the country so she could give greater attention to fewer guests. The Brierfield II consists of two country guest cottages that sit at the end of a gravel path that winds from the main house along a beautiful pastoral setting. Each cottage comes equipped with a private bath, guest-controlled heat and air-conditioning, a kitchen, and a TV. The Pool House features a private porch for taking in all the beauty around you. A queen-size cherry canopy bed graces the Salt Box Cottage, and the Pool House Cottage has a king-size bed that can be converted to twin beds. A phone for guests' use is located in the main brick ranch house.

The one-story cottages are surrounded by 16 acres in the country, 4 of which are wooded, making them especially perfect for couples wanting to enjoy the bed-and-breakfast experience while still having privacy. But Nancy also caters to business and government workers, who enjoy corporate and government per diem rates while relaxing in the peaceful surroundings. Nancy loves being able to cater to her guests, and she certainly does this at breakfast time. Guests are asked not only what they'd like for breakfast but also when they'd like it served. Breakfast is laid out in the sunroom at the back of the main house, where picture windows allow you to start your day off right with a beautiful view of nature. Nancy loves the bed-and-breakfast business, and it shows. Ninety percent of her business comes from repeat guests or referrals from past guests.

Cornerstone Farm
Bed and Breakfast $$$–$$$$
305 Crooked Creek Road
(717) 334-8205, (888) 334-8205
www.cornerstonefarmbandb.com

The Cornerstone Farm was built in the 1890s and is surrounded by more than 100 acres of private farmland where you'll find quarter horses, cattle, and lots of wildlife. Birders will delight in the large variety of Eastern species and warblers found in the area. You can arrange a guided horseback ride among the Texas longhorn cattle on the farm, which is near the site of the first shot of the Battle of Gettysburg and adjacent to what was a Confederate Civil War hospital. Or if you prefer, you can ride in the large outdoor

ring. The Cornerstone can also arrange an escorted horseback tour of the battlefield. Cross-country skiing is available on the grounds in winter.

Quiet patios and private dining tables make the Cornerstone an oasis for relaxation. The living room features French doors that open to the patio and the swimming pool and cabana, which are surrounded by gardens. Each of the five guest rooms comes with a cozy fireplace and private bath, and there's central air-conditioning throughout the house. The Sunrise, Lincoln, and Log Cabin Rooms have king-size beds, with the Log Cabin's being a four-poster bed. The Charleston Room has a black cherry queen-size canopy bed, while the Blue Room is outfitted with twin beds. One room, the Sunrise Room, is wheelchair accessible, and the Lincoln Room, with its private balcony that looks out across miles of country land, is requested the most often. To complete your perfect stay, gourmet breakfasts of fresh fruits, home-baked breads and pies, a hot entree, and a side dish are served daily. Your scrumptious breakfast is served in a large dining room that has floor-to-ceiling windows, and tables are outfitted with fine linen, flowers, and candlelight.

The Cornerstone welcomes children age 10 and older. There are strict regulations on smokers, with specific designated outdoor smoking areas.

The Doubleday Inn $$
104 Doubleday Avenue
(717) 334-9119
www.doubledayinn.com

Splendid views of Gettysburg and the battlefield await you at The Doubleday Inn. Nestled on Oak Ridge and adjoined by the battlefield on three sides, the Peace Light Memorial, Confederate artillery on Oak Hill, and the Railroad Cut are all within walking distance. The inn is named for Gen. Abner Doubleday, who assumed command of the 1st corps at what is now the site of the inn upon the death of General Reynolds. General Doubleday held off Confederate forces that greatly outnum-

General Doubleday, for whom the Doubleday Inn is named, was a captain stationed at Fort Sumter when Confederate troops attacked the fort and the Civil War began. Captain Doubleday gave the command for the first Union shot to be fired in response. It was thought for a long time that Doubleday also invented the game of baseball, but this isn't true. He did, however, refine the sport by organizing the game and modifying some of the basic rules.

bered his own for seven hours, allowing the Union forces to regroup that evening and enabling them to place themselves in a strategically advantageous position for the second day of the battle.

Today the centrally air-conditioned Doubleday Inn offers nine guest rooms decorated in English country fashion with Civil War accents, and each room has a private bath. Eight of the rooms are for double occupancy, and one is for single occupancy. Two large patios offer a panoramic view of 8 to 10 miles, and there are also great views from the second-floor deck, named "The Porch on Oak Ridge." Within the house, you'll find some artwork by Dale Gallon, a premier Civil War artist whose studio is in Gettysburg. Ruth Anne and Charles Wilcox, your delightful hosts, treat their guests to afternoon tea or refreshments and a full candlelight country breakfast daily. On selected nights, they also host a battlefield historian who leads a discussion on the Battle of Gettysburg. Ruth Anne and Charles welcome well-behaved children age eight and older, and there are designated outside smoking areas.

The Doubleday has been featured in *Washingtonian Magazine, New York Magazine,* and *Potomac Magazine,* as well as being included in the books *Secrets of Entertaining from America's Best Innkeepers* (Globe Pequot Press) and *Teatime at the Inn* (Rutledge Hill Press).

Slocum House Inn $
200 Blue Berry Road, Gardners
(717) 528-7390
www.slocumhouseinn.com
Sitting on 25 acres just north of Gettysburg and named for Union general Warner Slocum, this restored circa-1759 home enfolds you in country experiences. Here you can walk along country lanes, wander through the gardens, relax by the pond, and swim in the outdoor pool, all just minutes from the heart of Gettysburg. Originally built as a settler's log cabin, the home has been expanded with stone additions but still maintains its original character. Owner and innkeeper Carol Shafer has decorated the inn in Williamsburg style with period antiques and reproductions throughout. While relaxing in comfy seating and enjoying the common room's fireplace, guests are invited to partake of satellite TV, VCR tapes, the well-stocked bookshelves, and complimentary beverages.

Slocum House Inn has three guest rooms, and a fourth room can be combined with one of the guest rooms to create a two-room suite. General Slocum and his division generals provide the rooms' names. The Greene Room is in the guest cottage and provides plenty of privacy. This romantic room is outfitted with a queen-size canopy bed, gas log fireplace, private bath, cherry wood furniture, and colonial wall stencils. Also located in the guest cottage is the Geary Room. Here you'll find a four-poster queen-size bed, private bath, a Queen Anne wing chair perfect for reading beside the gas log fireplace, and colonial decorating. The Williams Room is upstairs in the section of the main house that was built in the 1750s. It boasts wide pine floors and low ceilings, and it has a private bath, a queen-size bed with a handmade quilt, and stenciled walls. This is the guest room that can be combined with the Slocum Room, also upstairs in the main house and also with a queen-size bed, to form a two-bedroom suite with a shared bath.

Carol serves a full breakfast in the dining room, and she fills you up with coffee, juice, fruit, fresh baked goods, and gourmet dishes that are prepared fresh daily.

The Slocum House Inn does not accept credit cards, so you will have to use cash or a personal check to pay for all this country living. Children age 14 and older are welcome at the inn.

SOUTH OF LINCOLN SQUARE

A Quiet Knight Bed & Breakfast   **$$**
267 Baltimore Street
(717) 337-3886, (877) 828-8828
www.gettysburg.com/gcvb/aqknight.htm
If you enjoy admiring beautiful antiques, you'll love A Quiet Knight. Innkeepers Bill and Linda Knight bought this two-story brick Civil War–era home in 1999, totally renovated the inside, and decorated it with 19th- and 20th-century antiques acquired from local Gettysburg estates. The house was beside the street that was the dividing line between the troops during the Gettysburg battle, and a Rebel sharpshooter was shot in the attic.

Three guest rooms are available on the second floor, each with cable TV and private bath. There's central air-conditioning downstairs and window units in each guest room, allowing guests to control the temperature in their quarters. The Lincoln Room, which retains its original mantel above a nonworking fireplace, has a queen-size bed and overlooks Baltimore Street, where Lincoln traveled on his way to Evergreen Cemetery to deliver his address. A white-iron, queen-size bed graces the Lee Room, and the Women of Gettysburg Suite is named for the women civilians of Gettysburg who served during the battle; it has a sitting room, a study area, and a full-size bed.

Bill is the resident chef, and his legendary breakfasts are served at 8:30 in the dining room. Cloth tablecloths, linen napkins, and fine china set the stage for Bill's delicious fare, which might include fruit smoothies, baked pears, baked apples, homemade pancakes with homemade syrup, or some of his other mouthwatering offerings. Bill and Linda tried serving afternoon snacks, but they found that most guests are out exploring during the day. So instead, they have a complimentary room that has a fridge where guests can store any refreshments and goodies they bring home. And you don't have to worry about parking at this intown inn—off-street parking is available for guests. Many guests never move the car once they check in. They walk to their destinations and enjoy the convenience of staying at an inn centrally located within the historic district.

A Sentimental Journey
Bed & Breakfast   **$**
433 Baltimore Street
(717) 337-0779 (10:00 A.M. to 5:00 P.M.),
(717) 642-5188 (5:00 to 10:00 P.M.),
(888) 337-0779
www.aceshighgallery.com
Owners and innkeepers Barbara and Steve Shultz were raised in Gettysburg, and at one time Steve was the chef at the historic Farnsworth House (see the listing within this chapter). A Sentimental Journey, their latest venture, houses the b&b as well as their first business, the art/picture framing studio and gallery of aviation art the couple began in 1992. (See The Arts chapter for more on Aces High Gallery.)

Built in 1928 of burgundy bricks, this three-story home has five romantic guest rooms, each decorated in an early 1900s time period. One room has a turn-of-the-19th-century motif, complete with an iron queen-size bed and claw-foot tub, and another is decorated in WWI memorabilia, including a turn-of-the-20th century phone and a doughboy uniform. A third room is decked out in art deco style, and two rooms honor the WWII era, one depicting the home front and one honoring the men who fought in the CBI (China, Burma, India) theater. All the rooms have cable TV and air-conditioning, and all except the CBI room have queen-size beds and private baths. The CBI room has a full-size bed and is half price when rented in conjunction with the art deco room (the rooms also share a bath). A continental breakfast is laid out in the 1950s kitchen for you to enjoy, and off-street parking is available to guests. If you and your sweetheart want to journey back to the romantic days of yesteryear, let A Sentimental Journey's 1940s porch glider transport you to a gentler, slower time. Located in the historic district, this bed-and-breakfast is close to all the Gettysburg attractions, and off-street parking is available.

Baladerry Inn at Gettysburg $$$
40 Hospital Road
(717) 337-1342
www.baladerryinn.com

The Baladerry Inn consists of three homes that are surrounded by four acres at the edge of the battlefield near Little Round Top. At the end of a winding driveway, you'll spy the Carriage House on the right and the Main House and the brick Federal-style 1812 House on the left. Looking at the homes against their backdrop of huge trees, you know you're about to experience country graciousness at its best. These homes give new meaning to the word *spacious*. Staying at the Baladerry also allows you to experience a bit of history—the 1812 House served as an Army of the Potomac field hospital during the Battle of Gettysburg. Today guests gather around the massive brick fireplace in the 1812 House's two-story great room, which is also where breakfast is served. For guests who enjoy the great outdoors, the sprawling grounds offer a brick terrace off the 1812 House that serves as a gathering spot and a garden gazebo for more private rendezvous. There is also a tennis court, so be sure to pack your racket.

Accommodations are spread out among the houses—two rooms are in the Main House, two rooms are in the 1812 House, and four rooms and a suite are in the Carriage House. All are named for flowers. The two-room Cottage Rose Suite is outfitted with a sunroom with a full-size sofa bed, a large bedroom with king-size bed, a private patio, a fireplace, and a private entrance adjacent to the tennis court. All the rooms but one have queen-size beds, and the Primrose Room, in the 1812 House, has twin beds that can be converted to a king-size bed. The Primrose Room's private bath is across the hall; the rest of the rooms have a private bath within the room. All the accommodations have in-room phones and air-conditioning. In the Carriage House, the Rose and Daisy Rooms have private patios while the Marigold and Shamrock Rooms have a fireplace and sitting area. The Windflower Room, in the 1812 House, has a whirlpool tub. While the Garden and Tulip Rooms in the Main House may not have a patio or fireplace, they do enjoy the luxury of being close to the common areas.

A full country breakfast is served in the two-story great room. You might feast on sausage and stuffed French toast with apricot sauce or crepes Suzinn with bacon garnish or one of the many other delicious choices. The inn wants you to have the perfect vacation, and they'll arrange for deliveries of flowers, chocolates, and wine. They'll also work with you to create your ideal personalized evening. Children age 12 and older are welcome.

Battlefield Bed & Breakfast Inn $$$$
2264 Emmitsburg Road
(717) 334-8804, (888) 766-3897
www.gettysburgbattlefield.com

History abounds at the Battlefield Bed & Breakfast Inn, an 1809 stone farmhouse that sits on 30 acres of the South Cavalry Battlefield. The eight guest rooms within the inn are named for and decorated with Civil War art related to the units that fought on the property during the Battle of Gettysburg. Four are standard rooms with queen-size beds, and the other four are either specialty rooms with fireplaces and more than one bed or are suites. All of the rooms have a private bath and air-conditioning. Your stay also includes a full two-course breakfast served by staff costumed in Civil War attire. Along with orange juice, coffee, and tea, the first course might be poached pears and raisin rum muffins or apple cobbler with whipped cream, followed by a second-course selection of heart-shaped pancakes with bacon, fried egg, and farm potatoes or raspberry cream crepes with ham and farm potatoes. (If you haven't guessed, the Battlefield is famous for their farm potatoes.) Breakfast is served at 9:00 A.M. in the great room overlooking the pond. Or, if you prefer, you can arrange to have a private breakfast in the Lincoln Room. If you like to get an earlier start on your day, just let innkeeper Florence Tarbox know when you check in, and breakfast will be fixed at a time chosen by you.

The inn conducts Civil War history presentations with hands-on demonstrations at 8:00 A.M. in the gathering room. The programs change daily, allowing guests to attend a different program each day of their stay. A Wednesday afternoon program that focuses on Civil War weapons, including teaching the participants how to fire a musket, began in 2004. The history programs are available to inn guests only and are free, but you're to make your reservation when you check in. Ghost stories, theme weekends, and special packages are also offered by the inn. If you're planning on riding your own horse on the battlefield, you can board your horse here. Three box stalls equipped with hay racks and water buckets are supplied, and you provide the feed.

The Brickhouse Inn Bed & Breakfast $$$
452 Baltimore Street
(717) 338-9337, (800) 864-3464
www.brickhouseinn.com

A stay at the Brickhouse Inn transports you back to the Victorian era. Located in the heart of the historic district, the imposing 1898 three-story brick Victorian home and adjacent circa–1830 residence are decorated with innkeepers Craig and Marion Schmitz's family heirlooms and selected antiques reminiscent of the turn of the 20th century. Although the feel is Victo-

rian, complete with some original wood floors and chestnut woodwork, the amenities are modern, and off-street parking directly behind the inn allows you to forget about driving while you walk to area sites.

Each of the 10 guest rooms, which are named for states represented in the Battle of Gettysburg, comes with a private bath, individually controlled air-conditioning and ceiling fans, and a telephone. Cable TV can be arranged upon request. The beds are covered with cozy comforters and are queen-size except for the Virginia Room, which has a full-size bed. Located on the third floor in the rear of the house, this slightly smaller room decorated in summer colors and white lacy curtains is Marion's favorite. The most popular room of returning guests is the Delaware Room, a two-room suite with a gas stove in the original fireplace, 1868 pine floors, an original claw-foot tub, and a private first-floor entrance. The other rooms have their own charms. There are bay windows in the Maryland, South Carolina, Tennessee, and New York Rooms, a private porch in the North Carolina Suite, and claw-foot tubs in the New England and North Carolina Suites and the Georgia Room. The Ohio Room has an Amish feel and is decorated with a matching antique oak dresser and washstand.

Breakfast is served out on the garden patio during warmer weather, and it always includes the inn's signature dish, Marion's Pennsylvania Dutch Shoo Fly pie, made from a secret family recipe. You'll also be served a hot entree, fruit, juice, coffee, and bread or muffins. Later in the day, guests are invited to gather on the wraparound porch for afternoon lemonade and homemade cookies. All in all, the Brickhouse Inn promises genteel accommodations with all the conveniences of the modern world and the added attraction of an in-town location.

Farnsworth House Inn $$$
401 Baltimore Street
(717) 334-8838
www.farnsworthhouseinn.com

The Farnsworth House is considered one

of the most haunted inns in America. The tradition of ghost telling in Gettysburg began here, and you can partake in the inn's candlelight ghost walks and visit the Civil War Mourning Theatre downstairs. (See the Attractions chapter for more on these and other places in Gettysburg where you can hear eerie stories and possibly see a ghost or two.) If you want to take every opportunity to try to contact the otherworld, why not stay in one of the inn's haunted guest rooms —5 of the 11 guest rooms are supposedly haunted, and spirits have been known to walk the halls. It's not surprising that Civil War spirits roam the house—the house was in the midst of some heavy fighting during the Battle of Gettysburg. (For more on the house's history and role in the battle, see the Close-up in this chapter.)

Located in the historic district, this Victorian beauty on the Register of Historic Places is decorated throughout with 19th-century antiques. Each of the guest rooms is air-conditioned and has a private bath, and many of the baths have claw-foot-tub/shower combinations. Two of the rooms, both with four-poster queen-size beds, are rented only to adults. The Lincoln Room has a mirrored two-person Jacuzzi, and the Belle Boyd Room, named for a notorious Confederate spy, has a large oil painting of a reclining nude and a two-person Jacuzzi with a stained-glass window. The significance of some of the guest-room names may elude you unless you know the home's history. The McFarland Room, the only room with twin beds rather than a queen-size bed, is named for John McFarland, who built the house. The Catherine Sweney Room, which has stained-glass windows, is named for one of the Sweney family members who lived in the house during the Battle of Gettysburg, and the Sara Black Room, with its queen-size canopy bed, is named for a previous owner. Featuring unique Bradbury/Bradbury ceiling and hallway panels and a cherry four-poster bed, the Shultz Room is named for the current owners. The remaining rooms are named for historic figures,

and their names are familiar to everyone. Longstreet and Chamberlain are the two newest rooms, and you'll also find the Custer, Jennie Wade, and Eisenhower Rooms. (By the way, the Eisenhower Room is named for Mamie, not Ike, and it has a beautiful working brick fireplace.)

Open to the public, the Farnsworth House serves breakfast to guests in the authentically restored dining rooms, which are accented by oil paintings of Generals Lee and Meade. The main dining room features candlelight and period-dressed waitstaff, and here you will find Civil War–era fare served for lunch and dinner, such as game pie, peanut soup, sweet potato pudding, and the like. If the weather is nice, you may want to dine in the patio garden beside the spring-fed stream. For more casual fare, the Killer Angel Tavern fits the bill. Also on the grounds are the Farnsworth House Military Impressions bookshop (see the Shopping chapter) and the Gettysburg Quartermaster (see the GNMP chapter), both great places for Civil War buffs to spend some time.

Gaslight Inn $$$–$$$$
33 East Middle Street
(717) 337-9100, (800) 914-5698
www.thegaslightinn.com

This in-town 1872 three-story Italianate-style yellow brick house exudes elegance, with its windows veiled in lace and a wrought-iron gate that opens to a brick path that takes you past a beautiful gaslight to the old-fashioned covered front porch. As you enter the house, where you might be greeted by the resident Labrador retriever, there are two parlors separated by pocket doors and a dining room decked out with a chandelier and oriental carpet.

The Daisy Room, which is customized to accommodate disabled guests, is on the first floor and opens onto a large brick patio that's beside a pond. There are eight more guest rooms on the second and third floors. The second floor also has the sitting room, with a television, video library, full bookshelves, and an entrance to the cov-

The Farnsworth House

The Farnsworth House is the central part of a complex that sprawls along Baltimore Street and contains a tavern, a bookshop, and a sutlery in addition to the bed-and-breakfast and its outside dining area. The oldest part of the house was built in 1810, followed by the brick structure in 1833, and the original walls, flooring, and rafters remain intact. The Sweney family lived in the Farnsworth House during the Battle of Gettysburg, and they sheltered Confederate sharpshooters. One hundred bullet holes can be seen in the south side of the house, where it was ravaged by Union soldiers. It's believed one of the Confederate sharpshooters in the house accidentally shot Jennie Wade, the only civilian to perish in the three days of fighting. (See the Attractions chapter for information on the tour of the Jennie Wade House.) Bullet holes are also visible in the door that's in the back room of the dining area on the home's first floor. In the early 1900s the house was opened as a lodging home by the George E. Black family. The Loring H. Shultz family purchased the home in 1972 and started restoring it to its 1863 appearance. The house is named for Elon John Farnsworth, who was promoted to brigadier general on the eve of the battle. Soon after the failure of Pickett's Charge on the third of July, Farnsworth's regiments were ordered to charge the right flank of Longstreet's position on Ceme-

More than 100 bullet holes can be seen in the south-facing brick wall of the Farnsworth House, testimony to the in-town fighting that was waged during the Battle of Gettysburg.
KATE HERTZOG

tery Ridge. In this ill-fated charge, Farnsworth and 65 of his men perished.

If you enjoy talking about the Civil War, the Farnsworth House is full of opportunities to do so. The owner is very knowledgeable on the subject, and he knows the history of the house in detail. Movie fans will also want to visit the Killer Angel Tavern on the grounds, which has a great assortment of clothing and props from the movie *Gettysburg* displayed.

ered deck that overlooks the garden. A deck overlooking the gatehouse weather vane is accessible from the third floor. All guest rooms have a private bath, central air-conditioning, and in-room cable TV and phones. There are three levels of rooms at the inn, with three rooms in each level. Standard rooms have a queen-size bed, and their private baths have stall showers. Superior rooms have a queen-size bed, a fireplace, and a private bath with a spa, which is a 5-foot-wide shower that has two molded seats and converts to a steam bath at the touch of a button. You're given a choice when choosing between the Deluxe rooms—either a queen-size bed and a fireplace in the bedroom and the bathroom, which has a double-wide Jacuzzi, or a king-size bed or twin beds, a fireplace, a convertible love seat in a sitting area, sliding doors onto a deck that overlooks the gardens, and a spa in the private bath.

A full gourmet breakfast, served on the brick patio in nice weather, is included with your stay, and guests often gather on the front porch in the afternoon for snacks and refreshments. Ample parking is located behind the inn. Innkeepers Becky and Mike Hanson set themselves apart by their hospitality and attention to details. Every guest receives an orientation to the area, and Becky and Mike will provide personalized itineraries, arrange private tours, chill your wine, whatever they can do to make your stay with them perfect.

Gettystown Inn $$$
89 Steinwehr Avenue
(717) 334-2100
www.dobbinhouse.com

You can truly gaze upon where history has been made when you stay at the Gettystown Inn—three of its suites overlook the National Cemetery. And the inn is adjacent to The Historic 1776 Dobbin House Tavern, Gettysburg's oldest house. Centrally located within walking distance of the National Military Park Visitor Center, Gettystown Inn has lots of room choices, beginning with which of its three Civil

War–era houses you want to stay in. Accommodations in all three houses feature air-conditioning, antique-filled rooms, and private baths. The Victorian House has the Lincoln Suite, a three-room suite that comes with a king-size canopy bed, a private sitting room with a cherry daybed, a full kitchen with a table that seats six, a private porch, and two cable TVs.

The Remembrance House has the Gettysburg Address Overlook Suite, a second-floor two-room suite whose bedroom windows overlook the National Cemetery. This room has a queen-size cherry-carved four-poster bed, a private sitting area, a small refrigerator, and two cable TVs. Aunt Holly's Garden Suite is also in the Remembrance House, and it's named for the abundance of rhododendron planted around the suite's porch, which were transplanted from the innkeeper's Aunt Holly's garden. This is a two-story, two-room suite, with a first-floor sitting room complete with a sleeper sofa, a second-floor bedroom with a queen-size black-iron bed, an iron claw-foot tub in the bathroom, and two cable TVs.

The Leister House has one two-room suite and four other guest rooms, each named for a Civil War commander and each outfitted with a queen-size bed and a small refrigerator. The Steinwehr, Stuart, and Reynolds Rooms are on the second floor, and the Meade Room is a large first-floor room that has a private entrance and a private porch for you to enjoy. The Lee Suite features an 18th-century clothes closet called a cas and a porch off its sitting room. It also has cable TV.

Your included country breakfast is served at the Dobbin House, which is also open to the public. (For more on the Dobbin House, see the Restaurants chapter.) Breakfast includes fresh-baked breads, fresh fruits, cereals, juice, and eggs or a hot entree. The Gettystown Inn also has plenty of free parking available to its guests. To complete your experience at this historic site, there's also a tavern and a gift shop on the grounds.

Lightner Farmhouse
Bed and Breakfast $$–$$$
2350 Baltimore Pike
(717) 337-9508, (866) 337-9508
www.lightnerfarmhouse.com

Dennis and Eileen Hoover, also innkeepers of the Cashtown Inn (see subsequent write-up in this chapter), bought the Lightner Farmhouse Bed and Breakfast in March 2004, and their son, Jason, is the inn's manager. Eileen has already put her own personality into the new venture—she wrote and produced Murder Mystery weekends during the Hoovers' first winter season as innkeepers of this historic house.

The Federal-style brick building was built circa 1862 by Isaac Lightner, an Adams County sheriff and farmer. The 1st Corp of the Union Army used the house as a hospital in July 1863, and the property was used as a hospital area for five weeks following the Battle of Gettysburg. It sits on 19 acres of countryside only 3 miles from the center of Gettysburg, and it's truly amazing how such beautiful country-side can be only a five-minute drive from town. The house's original character is expressed through the wide molding, random-plank floors, and four fireplaces that have been preserved, and it has a Victorian parlor full of books and maga-zines. Guests gather to enjoy all sorts of videos and games as well as cable TV in the common room, where free refresh-ments are provided for guests.

Although this bed-and-breakfast pre-serves the spirit of 19th-century rural life, it has also embraced the modern world—wireless Internet is available in every room. The farmhouse has central air-conditioning, and each of the guest rooms, which are named after Pennsylvania's native trees, has a queen-size or king-size bed, private bath with shower, hair dryer, and small watercooler. Four guest rooms, the two-room Pine Tree Suite, and the two-floor Walnut Cottage are available. The cottage is ideal for romantic getaways. Guests are served a private breakfast in the breeze-way, and they can also relax on their pri-

The walking trails on the grounds of the Lightner Farmhouse Bed and Breakfast are available for guest exploration. Be sure to take along the Lightner Farm-house History and Natural Trail *guide on your walk; it was specially designed to help guests understand the farmhouse and surrounding countryside's historical and environmental significance.*

vate wraparound deck. Another attraction of the cottage is its beehive oven, where bread was baked for Union soldiers in 1863.

Between 8:00 and 9:00 A.M., guests gather in the dining room for a breakfast that consists of several courses. Along with coffee, tea, and juice, you'll be offered warm sweet bread or muffins followed by a fruit dish. The main entrees alternate daily between sweet fare and egg dishes, often served with sausage or bacon on the side. In the afternoon, guests relax in rock-ing chairs on the porch while afternoon tea is served.

EAST OF LINCOLN SQUARE

Aunt Pittypat's Bed & Breakfast $$–$$$
34 York Street
(717) 338-1832
www.americanhistoricalart.com

Located in the first block of York Street off Lincoln Square, Aunt Pittypat's Bed & Breakfast opened in late summer of 2005. It joins two other new businesses at this address—Aunt Pittypat's Tea Room and the American Historical Art Gallery & Framery, both of which opened in 2004. All three businesses are owned by Rodney and Tracy Cromeans, who purchased and began renovating the space in 2004. (See the Restaurants chapter for more on the tearoom and The Arts chapter for more on the gallery.)

The bed-and-breakfast offers four rooms on the second floor, where you'll also find a relaxing side porch. Although the rooms are modern and new, the building dates from the 1800s and the original woodwork has been retained throughout. Guests need to check in at the gallery when they first arrive, but the bed-and-breakfast has its own street entrance as well as an entrance that's between the tearoom and art gallery. The theme throughout is based on the *Gone with the Wind* novel. Aunt Pittypat was the aunt of Melanie and Charles Hamilton, and you can stay in the Scarlett Room, the Bell Watling Room, the Rhett Butler Room, or the Texas Room (the owners are originally from Texas).

As you enter the bed-and-breakfast, you climb a staircase to the second floor, where you'll find four immaculate rooms exquisitely designed. All rooms are equipped with a full bath, a TV/DVD combination (with free DVDs available), and a ceiling fan. Three rooms have fireplaces, two rooms have Jacuzzis, and three rooms have kitchenettes. Each room's climate can be individually controlled, and each has a dedicated hot water heater, guaranteeing you hot water any time of day. The showcase among the four rooms is the Rhett Butler Room. It sits at the front of the house and has a great in-town view as well as upscale amenities. The bedroom has a separate sitting area with a chaise lounge and a pullout full-size sleeper sofa, and the area boasts a see-through fireplace that you can admire from the sitting area or the bedroom. There's also a TV/DVD combination that swivels for viewing from either location, and the spacious bathroom has a Jacuzzi.

Brafferton Inn   **$$$**
44 York Street
(717) 337-3423, (866) 337-3423
www.brafferton.com
Built in 1786, this stone home is the oldest continuous residence in historic downtown. The inn also includes the carriage house, which was added to the stone house in the 1850s, and the annex at 42 York Street, circa 1850–1900. Listed on the

National Register of Historic Places, the house is known to many locals as the Codori House, after the family that lived here for 124 years. (See the Close-up on the Codori House in this chapter for more on the house's history.) The home was bought in 1984 and converted into a bed-and-breakfast in 1986. Innkeepers Joan, Brian, and AmyBeth Hodges purchased the inn in spring 2005.

You'll find antiques, stenciling, and colonial murals throughout the inn, and artist Keith Rocco has turned the parlor into a mini gallery of his works. There are nine rooms and five suites spread out between the three houses. With its original exposed stone walls, open-rafter cathedral ceiling, and wide pine floorboards, the third floor of the stone house brings the house's history to life. Here you'll find the Loft Suite, which is one large room that takes up about two-thirds of the entire floor. The suite includes a queen-size bed, attached tub and shower bathroom, comfy chairs, a small fridge and wet sink, and a primitive fainting couch. A wall-unit air conditioner allows you to control the room's temperature. The second floor of the stone house has three guest rooms or a suite to pick from. The Deck Suite has a private balcony that overlooks the inn's gardens and deck, a queen-size bed and antique maple bureau, a cable TV, an attached double-stall shower bathroom, and a window-unit air conditioner. If you want to stay in an original bedroom, the Olde Master Bedroom fits the bill. This large room boasts a stately hand-carved queen-size cherry rice poster bed, a walnut Victorian dresser, wingback chairs, a nonworking fireplace, and a window-unit air conditioner. The stall shower bathroom is across the hall but it isn't shared with any other guests. Robes are provided for trips back and forth. The Battle Room is also a good choice for the history buff; this is the room that has the minie ball lodged in its fireplace's mantel. The room also has a queen-size cherry sleigh bed, an Edwardian armoire with mirrors, a sitting chair and slipper bench, an attached stall shower bathroom, and a window-unit air conditioner. The third room on the second floor is the Thomas Hoke Room, a romantic little corner with an iron queen-size bed and a cherry bureau. The room has an attached full tub and shower bath and a window-unit air conditioner.

The Carriage House contains the bulk of the guest accommodations, with one suite and six guest rooms under its roof. Both the Lincoln and the Chamberlain Rooms in the North Wing have antique beds—one double and one twin each—antique dressers, comfy chairs for reading in, and window-unit air conditioners. The Brass Room's bathroom, with its stall shower, is located off the floor's hallway, and the full tub and shower bathroom for the Chamberlain Room is also located off the hallway. Although these bathrooms are not attached to the rooms, each is private to its room and not shared with other guests. The South Wing contains the Codori Suite and the Gettys Room, which is a smaller room with a queen-size colonial pediment bed, a butter-print Victorian dresser, reading chairs, an attached double-stall shower bathroom, and a window-unit air conditioner. The spacious Codori Suite has a sitting room that contains a queen-size sofa bed, comfy chairs, cable TV, and a master bedroom that has a queen-size bed. The suite has an attached full tub and shower bath and central air. Both the Garden and the New Rooms are near the house's flower gardens and deck. These quiet rooms have queen-size beds, antique bureaus, comfy chairs, and attached full tub and shower bathrooms. The Garden Room has central air, and the New Room has a window-unit air conditioner. Completing the carriage house lodgings is The Nook, a cozy economy room for a single traveler with an antique bed, one-person shower stall bathroom, and window-unit air conditioner.

The Annex is the home of the North and South Suites, both on the second floor. As you enter the South Suite through its private entrance, you'll discover a sitting room with a sofa bed, comfy chairs, a card table, and cable TV. The master bedroom reveals a handpainted queen-size bed and a marble-top bureau, and the attached full tub and shower Jacuzzi bathroom is another door down within the suite. You'll also find window-unit air conditioners throughout the suite. The North Suite has an inviting sitting room with a queen-size sofa bed, comfy chairs, and cable TV as well, but it also boasts a writing desk and a gas fireplace. Its bedroom has a queen-size cherry colonial pediment bed and a matching bureau. The full tub and shower Jacuzzi bathroom is down the hallway within the suite, and there are window-unit air conditioners throughout.

Your stay includes a full breakfast served in the dining room, where the four walls are covered by a folk mural by artist Virginia Jacobs McLaughlin that depicts the area's history. As you admire this unique piece of art, you'll enjoy treats such as stuffed french toast or crab and asparagus quiche. If you get to breakfast early, enjoy the classical music playing in the living room every morning and settle in to read the newspapers delivered daily. Afternoon refreshments, with accompanying music, are also enjoyed in the living room. Some of the rooms of the inn can accommodate children age eight and older. Parking is located behind the inn at the parking garage.

Keystone Inn Bed & Breakfast $$
231 Hanover Street
(717) 337–3888
www.virtualcities.com

Flowers are in their full glory at the Keystone Inn Bed & Breakfast. You'll find them outside in the garden, and inside they can be found throughout the house. The five guest rooms of this late-Victorian three-story brick house are decorated with flowers and lots of ruffles and lace, and flowers of soft pastel decorate the rooms' wallpaper and sheets. Built in 1913 by Clayton S. Reaser, a local furniture maker, the first thing you notice as you approach the inn is its leaded-glass front door and high-columned wraparound front porch.

CLOSE-UP

The Codori House

The Brafferton Inn got its name from Jim and Mary Agard, who opened the home as a bed-and-breakfast in 1986. They named it after Brafferton Hall at the College of William and Mary in Williamsburg, Virginia. But many locals will always think of this place as the Codori House, after the family that made it their home for more than a century.

The home dates from 1786, making this the oldest deeded house in Gettysburg. Michael Hoke was a tanner who worked with the Gettys family, and he purchased the lot the house sits on for "3 pounds, 15 shillings of real gold." In 1796 he transferred ownership of the house to his brother Henry, and since neither Hoke brother had sons who could inherit the property, it was eventually sold out of the family. Nicholas Codori purchased the home in 1843 for $1,600. Codori was a local butcher who had 11 children, thereby needing a large house, so he also bought the property on either side of the house. Behind the house, he built a carriage house and also set up his meat market. Nicholas was a good businessman, and at the beginning of the Civil War, he purchased a farm on Emmitsburg Road that he used to raise livestock and as a slaughterhouse. This farm would become famous during the Battle of Gettysburg; it sits in the middle of the area known as Pickett's Charge.

The Codoris were at their house, not the farm, during the battle. They hid in the basement as bullets whizzed through the floors above them. One of the rooms of the house still has a minie ball embedded in its fireplace mantel. After the battle,

Once inside, be sure to take note of the original chestnut and oak gleaming throughout the house—there's an oak and chestnut staircase, chestnut in the high-ceilinged rooms of the first floor, and natural oak in the rest of the house. Each guest room has a private bath, individually controlled air-conditioning, a comfy chair, and a reading nook. Grandpa's Room has a full Reaser bedroom suite. A queen-size iron bed is featured in Aunt Faye's Room, while Uncle Eby's Room boasts an antique, hand-carved, queen-size oak bed. Viewing the battlefields from your private veranda is a perfect ending to the day when staying in Uncle Art's Room. And Aunt Norma's Suite is great for a family or friends traveling together—its interconnected rooms can accommodate four persons, and it's equipped with a TV, fridge, and microwave.

A full country breakfast is served to guests in the dining room. You might choose from fruits, muffins, juices, coffee, tea, Denver French toast, waffles made from scratch, pancakes, scrambled eggs, oatmeal, and a variety of meats. Innkeepers Wilmer and Doris Martin are also able to accommodate special diets. The Martins offer afternoon lemonade on the front porch in summer and hot drinks in the dining room in winter. The inn has cable TV and a courtesy phone available to guests, and many visitors have whiled away some quiet hours perusing the reading choices found in Aunt Weasie's Library.

The Codori House, now operating as the Brafferton Inn, is the oldest deeded house in Gettysburg, dating from 1786. KATE HERTZOG

the home was used as the Catholic chapel since the church was occupied with wounded soldiers.

The Codoris resumed their peaceful existence after the battle, and the house was passed down through generation after generation of Codoris, until it was eventually sold out of the family. The house is still often referred to as either the Hoke-Codori House or just the Codori House. The farm retains the name Codori, and it's a stop on the battlefield tour.

Red Bud Inn
at the historic Isaac Miller Farm $$
240 Cavalry Field Road
(717) 334-1909
www.red-budinn.com

The Red Bud Inn sits on 13 acres only minutes east of Gettysburg. The grounds border the East Cavalry Field battlefield, and during the Battle of Gettysburg this small farm was turned into a Confederate hospital for Stuart's cavalry. Be sure to enjoy a leisurely stroll around the tranquil grounds and visit the barn, where there are six horse stalls for overnight horse stabling.

The addition to the farm was added in 1989. You'll find two guest rooms, each with a queen-size bed, private bath, and walk-in closet. A three-bedroom suite is in the original house. There's also a common room, where you can read or watch TV. Innkeepers Peggy and Dennis Bear welcome children age 14 and older. For breakfast, which is included in the daily rate; guests receive gift certificates to Dunlop's, a local family restaurant.

WEST OF LINCOLN SQUARE

Cashtown Inn $$$
1325 Old Route 30, Cashtown
(717) 334-9722, (800) 367-1797
www.cashtowninn.com

The Cashtown Inn was built around 1797

as the first stagecoach stop west of Gettysburg. It's located 8 miles west of Gettysburg on Old Route 30, and in 1863 the inn was used by Gen. A. P. Hill as his Confederate headquarters while the 22,000 men of his Third Corp camped throughout town. If you think the inn looks familiar, it very well might. It has appeared in the movie *Gettysburg* and in the Mark Nesbit book and video *Ghosts of Gettysburg*. It's also been featured on the cover of *Blue and Gray* magazine, in the video *Haunted Gettysburg,* and in the book *Haunts of the Cashtown Inn.* Civil War artist Dale Gallon also depicts the inn in his limited-edition print *Serious Work Ahead,* which shows Confederate generals Lee and Hill meeting on July 1, 1863. This is the same scene created by artist Mort Kunstler in his 1998 painting *Distant Thunder.*

Innkeepers Dennis and Eileen Hoover entered the bed-and-breakfast world when they acquired the Cashtown Inn in March 1996. The Hoovers certainly enjoy the bed-and-breakfast experience; they also purchased the Lightner Farmhouse Bed and Breakfast in March 2004 (see earlier listing). They've decorated the inn and its fine-dining restaurant and tavern with Civil War art and antiques, and the guest rooms are original to the 1797 house. The most famous guest room is the Heth Room, with its double four-poster bed. The other three rooms have queen-size beds, and you can choose between an iron bed in the Pettigrew Room, a four-poster bed and a view of South Mountain in the Imboden Room, or a lace canopy and a view of the village of Cashtown in the A. P. Hill Room. The inn has three two-room suites in addition to its four guest rooms. All accommodations come with private bath, clock radio, and air-conditioning. The General Lee Suite is located under the eaves on the inn's third floor. Outfitted with a TV, VCR, refrigerator, and queen-size sleeper sofa in the living room, this suite has a king-size iron bed with a pillow-top mattress that's bound to have you dreaming pleasant dreams all night. The Pender and Anderson Suites are identical and next door to each other at

the rear of the inn. You'll be very comfortable in either suite, with a private entrance and porch, a queen-size four-poster bed in the bedroom, and a queen-size sleeper sofa in the living room. Groups of four to eight can rent both suites for a private retreat. Children age 12 and younger are welcome only in the Pender and Anderson Suites.

You certainly won't go hungry at the Cashtown Inn. A full breakfast included with your stay, lunch fare at the tavern, and a delicious dinner await you at the inn. Lighter fare and a more casual ambience are served up in the tavern, while the formal dining room is the perfect spot for an elegant evening. For a full description of the inn's culinary delights, see the Restaurants chapter. Guests are welcome to walk off their meals in the inn's gardens, where the chefs pick the fresh herbs used in the restaurant's dishes. Many a guest has found relaxation by sitting and swinging on the front porch while admiring the beautiful vistas around the inn. For guests who wish to have a weekend of activity, the Hoovers offer many packages and theme weekends, such as murder mystery weekends and ghost hunters weekends.

The Fairfield Inn 1757 $$$
15 West Main Street, Fairfield
(717) 334-8868, (717) 642-5410
www.thefairfieldinn.com
The Fairfield Inn was built in 1757 to serve as the Mansion House of Squire Miller, an original founder of the town of Fairfield. It was believed that the Mansion House first began welcoming guests when it became an inn and stagecoach stop in 1823. But in November 2004, a colonial-era tavern license for the inn dated 1786 was discovered, making this one of the oldest taverns still operating in America. The inn has welcomed such famous Americans as Patrick Henry, Thaddeus Stevens, Gen. Robert E. Lee, Gen. Jeb Stuart, and Ike and Mamie Eisenhower.

When the fighting at Gettysburg ended, the Confederate army retreated west through the town of Fairfield, and many homes, including the Mansion House, were used as field hospitals. The Fairfield Inn was operating as an inn, so General Lee and other Confederates stopped here for food. And the house was also a stop on the Underground Railroad. With all this history, it's no wonder that the Fairfield Inn is on the National Register of Historic Places.

Innkeepers Joan and Sal Chandon, who previously owned The Doubleday Inn (see The Doubleday Inn entry earlier in this chapter), began an extensive renovation to the inn in February 2003. Two years later, Joan and Sal are thrilled with the results—four of the six guest rooms are completed and hosting guests. All of the inn's guest rooms and suites have private baths, air-conditioning, and cable TV. And there are plenty of places to warm up—the inn has eight fireplaces.

Breakfast is served in the restaurant in the original Mansion House. The inn's two chefs and their staffs present mouthwatering meals that can be enjoyed beside a blazing fire in the winter months or on the patio garden off the restaurant in warmer weather. To satisfy your culinary needs throughout the day, luncheon and dinner vouchers are included for the Squire Miller Tavern and the Mansion House Restaurant. (See the Restaurants chapter for more on the Mansion House Restaurant.) The tavern is on the first floor of the Mansion House, and it too has been extensively renovated. With seating for about 25, the Squire Miller Tavern serves as the restaurant's smoking section. The inn also offers dinner theater, where you can hear ghost stories and see a re-creation of a Civil War séance (see the Gettysburg Civil War Era Dinner Theatre entry in The Arts chapter).

Gettysburg Pond View Farm Bed & Breakfast $
530 Carr Hill Road
(717) 642-9493, (877) 888-1957
www.bbonline.com/pa/pondview
Innkeepers Peter and Karen Samuels welcome you to their Civil War–era brick

farmhouse. This cozy bed-and-breakfast has central air-conditioning and three guest rooms. Each has a queen-size bed, with the Brass Room having a brass bed and the Canopy Room having—you guessed it—a canopy bed. Both rooms come with a private bath. The Corner Room has a very large private bath that is down the hall from the room.

Because the bed-and-breakfast is small, Peter and Karen can give guests special attention. One fabulous way they do this is by serving a breakfast of lox and bagels, muffins, or omelets in the guest's room. Now, that's pampering.

Also due to the size of the farmhouse, Peter and Karen do not allow guests younger than age eight. This farm 15 minutes from Gettysburg is surrounded by countryside. Take time to walk the grounds and enjoy the serenity of the pond. And be sure to admire the horses, the sheep, and Coco, the goat. If you're bringing your horse, overnight horse boarding in open pasture may be available.

Herr Tavern & Publick House $$$-$$$$
900 Chambersburg Road
(717) 334-4332, (800) 362-9849
www.herrtavern.com
Thomas Sweeney built a tavern and publick house on this site in 1815. In 1828 the establishment was sold to Frederick Herr, and the business was run by the Herr family for almost 40 years, and sometime during this time the house was a stop on the Underground Railroad. The ridge the house stands on came to be known as Herr's Ridge, and the Battle of Gettysburg began in the fields around the tavern buildings. The publick house was used as the first Confederate hospital during the battle, and much of the house was converted into operating rooms. After the war, it became a boardinghouse for the many visitors to the battlefields. After that it became an operating farm, and then rental property, which is what it was when current owner Steven Wolf bought it in 1977. Steven researched the history of the house and restored it to its original pur-

pose, opening for business in May 1978. Everything went well until June 1987, when the original house was nearly leveled by a windstorm that hit Gettysburg. Today the house, which is on the Register of Historic Places, has been faithfully restored to its 19th-century appearance.

But Steven didn't stop at restoration. In 1997 he added a banquet room and seven more guest rooms, and in 2001 he purchased an adjacent property and added an annex. The annex is home to four unique guest suites, and this sprawling bed-and-breakfast has a total of 16 luxurious guest rooms. Suites 1 through 5 are in the original historic building, Suites 6 through 12 are in the wing built in 1997 off the original building, and Suites 14 through 18 are in the adjacent annex. If you're wondering how 16 rooms are numbered 1 through 18, there isn't a number 13 suite and Suite 12 is the massage room, where you can be pampered by the in-house masseuse. Each suite is decorated with period pieces and has a private bath, fireplace, cable TV, air-conditioning, and telephone with answering machine, and most have a queen-size bed, double Jacuzzi tub with shower, and sitting area. The romantic Garden Room has an oversize round bed. Room 14 has a ground-level entrance and is wheelchair accessible.

But some of the rooms here boast more than fine furniture and accoutrements. Some of the rooms are haunted. It's no wonder when you realize what hospitals were like in the days of the Civil War. It was reported that amputated limbs were thrown out a window into a waiting wagon for burial. Sterilization techniques didn't exist, and there were few painkillers. Who knows how many spent their last days or hours during the wretched heat of July 1863 at this spot. There are numerous stories of ghost sightings here by Steven, by the staff, and by the guests. Ask around and you'll hear lots of firsthand ghostly encounters, such as things moving, voices heard when there's no one there, and lights turning on and off, just to give a few examples. Be prepared if you stay in rooms 1, 2, 3, or 4—they seem to have the most ghostly activities.

Your included breakfast is served at the posted time, and continental breakfast is available at other times as needed. The inn does not accommodate children younger than age 12, and there is a strict no-smoking rule—you'll be charged a $75 service fee if you smoke in the rooms. The Herr Tavern and Publick House offers gourmet dining in one of five dining areas in the main house, and each room accommodates 20 to 35 diners. There is an extensive wine cellar, and guests of the inn may arrange to dine privately amongst the 3,000–bottle collection. (For more on the Herr Tavern restaurant, see the Restaurants chapter.) The Livery is a casual-atmosphere tavern where you can get food inside or outside on the deck (see the Nightlife chapter).

James Gettys Hotel $$$
27 Chambersburg Street
(717) 337-1334, (888) 900-5275
www.jamesgettyshotel.com

With red awnings covering each window, the James Gettys Hotel looks as it did in the 1920s. As you enter this fully renovated circa-1804 four-story historic hotel, you're gazing upon its original chestnut staircase, which has been impeccably restored. Ring the bell at the desk if you don't see anyone around—one of the owners is also co-owner of Lord Nelson's Gallery, an art gallery next door. (For more on Lord Nelson's Gallery, see The Arts chapter.) A chair and a table with selected brochures on it complete the lobby.

A climb up the magnificent chestnut staircase will lead you to 11 suites, each with a sitting area, a kitchenette with a full-size refrigerator, stove, and microwave,

The lobby of the James Gettys Hotel is one of the few places in town where you'll find a brochure for Gettysburg's self-guided walking tour.

a bedroom with a queen-size or full-size bed, and a private bath. Each suite is named for a business that existed in or near the building in the past 200 years. Guest-room amenities are sure to please even the most discriminating guest. They include complimentary fresh-ground coffees and imported British teas, fine toilet soaps, fresh-cut seasonal flowers, additional pillows, and Egyptian-cotton bath towels. Guests also receive evening turn-down service, and morning begins with continental breakfast served in your suite. The hotel staff will also make your travel and tour arrangements, and same-day laundry and dry-cleaning services are available upon request. And here's a real benefit to readers who will be traveling with children—there's no charge for children younger than age 12 who are sharing a room with parents. There is, however, a maximum of four persons per suite, depending on the suite you choose. The hotel also offers long-term rates and extended-stay vacation packages.

This building is on the National Register of Historic Places, and it does indeed have a full and varied history. It was originally known as the Union Hotel, and it served as a hospital for the wounded during the Battle of Gettysburg. By April 1888, Gettysburg had become a popular tourist spot, and the City Hotel, as it was then named, readied for the influx of visitors for the battle's 25th anniversary by expanding to accommodate 250 guests. Sometime after this the hotel was renamed the James Gettys Hotel, and it enjoyed a thriving business until the 1960s, when motels gained in popularity and the hotel closed its doors. The building functioned as an apartment house until the 1980s and then served as a youth hostel for 10 years. The current innkeepers bought it in 1995, revived the name, and began the hotel's transformation back to its 1920s look. Besides Lord Nelson's Gallery, the Blue Parrot Bistro (see the Restaurants chapter for more information) is also located within this historic building.

GUESTHOUSES

Canter Berry Trails Apple Ranch
989 Center Mills Road, Aspers
(717) 677-8900
www.farmstay.us

This fully furnished, 10-room, 4-bedroom, 1½-bath 1822 center-hall colonial farmhouse, which is owned by Ted and Sandy Abahazy, can be rented for $550 for two nights on a weekend to $1,200 for a full-week stay. Once you check in, the run of the house is yours; no one enters the house until you check out. Sitting on an apple orchard surrounded by 35 acres and located only 8 miles north of Gettysburg, the house is often rented by Gettysburg College alumni for reunion weekends.

The house is beautifully furnished with antiques in a country colonial motif, and each of the four bedrooms has a theme. The North Room, with stenciling throughout, has a four-poster queen-size bed, and the South Room has a canopy queen-size bed. Both the North and South Rooms have mannequins outfitted in ladies' dresses from the Civil War era. The Garden Room has a full bed and is filled with all things related to gardening. A three-quarter bed (a little shorter than a full-size bed) is in the Hunting and Fishing Room, which is often used as a child's room. In addition to the modern kitchen and baths, you'll also find a living room, dining room, laundry room, and game room, which has chess, lots of board games, and a record player that actually plays 45s and 33s (records are supplied also—you can give the kids a history lesson while you're being nostalgic). Don't worry about doing laundry—towels left in the laundry basket on the front porch are replaced by fresh ones daily, and one extra set of sheets is also available. You don't need to bring any essentials except food, and Ted and Sandy will be glad to direct you to the local grocery. The house comes with a TV with basic cable and a phone for local calls only. It also has central air-conditioning with separate controls for the upstairs and downstairs levels of the home.

If you're feeling adventurous, be sure to ask to see the alpacas that are raised on the neighboring farm by Ted and Sandy's daughter. Or visit the hen house and retrieve a few eggs for your morning meal. Guests may also pick their own apples, with the first bushel being free of charge. Corn and pumpkins are also available for harvesting.

Little House Guest House
Rear 20 North Washington Street
(717) 334-3940
www.gettysburgaddress.com

Originally a brick carriage house that was built in 1870, the Little House Guest House is 1 block west of Lincoln Square. This guesthouse can sleep four persons and it's open year-round. The rate is $125 a night, a rate that's reduced if you decide to rent the house for more than one night. Weekly rates are also available. When you arrive, owners Beverly and Ed Ruggles will welcome you with wine, fruit, cheese, and flowers and then leave you to enjoy your privacy. The Ruggles come in only every three days for housekeeping. Downstairs you'll find a living room with a wrap-around sofa that converts to a queen-size sleeper, a TV with cable, and a small modern kitchen. The kitchen is stocked with coffees, teas, and bagels, and you can cook your own meals with food you bring in. Wooden beams adorn the living-room ceiling while the kitchen has a refurbished tin roof. The bedroom is on the second floor, and it's outfitted with an iron antique double bed, marble-topped dresser, and antique lamp and nightstand. Also upstairs is a small sitting room with a vintage working washbasin and stained-glass windows. The bathroom, which has a shower, is adjacent to the sitting room.

Ed and Beverly Ruggles have been running the Little House since 1992, and they live close by in a separate building. They have the house fully outfitted with sheets, towels, and the like; guests only need to bring food. But please don't bring your four-legged friend—pets are not allowed. Smoking is also prohibited. A phone is provided for guests to make local calls. Payment is by check or cash; credit cards are not accepted.

Quaker Valley Orchards & Guest House
315 Quaker Valley Road, Biglerville
(717) 677-7351
www.quakervalleyorchards.com

This fully furnished guesthouse is attached to the owners' 1882 brick home that sits on a 220-acre fruit farm 10 miles north of Gettysburg. The owners are Winn and Winifred Schulteis, and the farm has been in the Schulteis family for more than 40 years. The guesthouse sleeps six, and the rate is $90 per night with a two-night minimum, or it can be rented for $575 per week. To reach the guesthouse, head north from Lincoln Square on Route 34 (Biglerville Road). At the traffic light in Biglerville at York and Main Streets, continue straight 2 miles north and turn left onto Quaker Valley Road. Quaker Valley is the first farm on the right.

The air-conditioned guesthouse was added on to the original home in the 1980s. It has its own private entrance, and inside you'll discover a large living room with a queen-size sleeper sofa and a spacious bedroom with two double beds. There's also a bath and kitchen, and the house's TV has an outdoor antenna and a VCR. Besides linens, the Schulteises provide you with an iron and ironing board, a hair dryer, a clock radio, and coffee and teas. All guests need to bring is food, and you're invited to pick some of the farm's fresh fruit and vegetables. The farm has three ponds, and one is a fishing pond. There's also a phone that guests can use for local calls. Smoking and pets are prohibited, and credit cards are not accepted.

CAMPGROUNDS AND RV PARKS

Camping around the Gettysburg area offers you the chance to sleep under the same starlit skies that Civil War soldiers gazed upon so many years ago. Here you can imagine yourself among those men, waiting for dawn so the day's battle could begin. This is especially easy during June, when the campfires of Civil War reenactors illuminate the grounds.

Along with this chance to reconnect with history, Gettysburg campgrounds and RV parks offer affordable lodging with all the modern amenities. You'll find full-facility restrooms, including hot showers, and laundry facilities, and each campground and park offers a pool, a game room, and a playground in addition to a myriad of recreational activities. Camp stores are there in case you forgot anything, with gift shops to round out your shopping expedition. Bus tours to the Gettysburg battlefield and to Washington, D.C., are offered, and there are planned activities every weekend in season. But don't think that the campgrounds are interchangeable—each is unique, and each has something special to offer.

None of the campgrounds is more than 6 miles from Lincoln Square, with Artillery Ridge and Round Top to the south, Gettysburg, KOA, and Granite Hill to the west, and Drummer Boy to the east. Pets are welcome at the campgrounds but not in the rental units.

The rates listed are for the 2005 season. Expect to be required to stay a minimum of two nights during the summer season, and sometimes a three- or four-night minimum might be in effect.

Artillery Ridge Campground & National Riding Stables
610 Taneytown Road
(717) 334-1288, (717) 334-5596, (877) 335-5596 (toll-free), (866) 932-2674 (toll-free)
www.artilleryridge.com

Artillery Ridge, which is open April through November and located about a mile south of town on Route 134 (Taneytown Road), is the home of both the National Riding Stables (see the Gettysburg National Military Park chapter) and the Gettysburg Miniature Battlefield Diorama (see the Attractions chapter).

Here you'll find 135 hookup sites, 45 nonhookup sites, and 3 cabins to rent. If you have access to the Internet, the Web site has a great map of the campground. Rates are for two people at one camping site. A site without hookups is $27.50 a night or $165.00 a week. If you want a site with water and electric, the cost is $35.50 a night or $213.00 a week. If you also want sewer hookup, the price is $38.50 a night or $231.00 a week. There are large open tenting grounds with some secluded sites, and every tent site has a picnic table and a fire ring. Internet access is available. The log cabins have a double bed and one set of twin bunk beds, air-conditioning, electric, water, a porch and chairs, a picnic table and fire ring, and a driveway. They rent for $55 a night or $330 a week.

Since this is also the site of the National Riding Stables, you can bring your own horse or rent one. The campground offers a two-hour battlefield tour on horseback that covers the history of the three-day battle.

Recreational activities here include fishing (no license required) or paddle-boating on the property's pond and playing horseshoes, basketball, or volleyball. There are also pony rides for the little ones and church services on Sunday. You might find bingo being played at the pavilion or maybe you'd rather catch that night's movie. And be sure to check out the planned activities if you're staying over the weekend—maybe you'll take a hay ride, attend an ice-cream social, or lose yourself in a Western- or 1950s-themed weekend.

Drummer Boy Camping Resort
1300 Hanover Road
(717) 334-3277, (800) 293-2808
www.drummerboycamping.com

Drummer Boy is the largest campground in the area: It has more than 400 sites, 75 of which were added in 2005. But you won't feel crowded here—the tent sites, deluxe full-service cottages, and camping cabins sit on 90 acres of woodlands. The place is so big that you can rent a golf cart in order to zip around the campground during your stay.

Open the first Friday in April until the last Sunday in October, Drummer Boy also added a swimming-pool complex with water slide in 2005, and high-speed wireless Internet can be accessed from your site. Good old-fashioned fun is also at your fingertips, with volleyball, horseshoes, basketball, minigolf, and a walking trail available. There are nightly movies in the minitheater from June through September, and fishing (no license required) at the pond. There's also a snack bar, and church services are held on Sunday. The Web site has a great map of the campground, so check it out if you get a chance.

A site without hookups is $37 a night or $224 a week; one with water and electric is $41 a night or $252 a week, and a site with water, electric, sewer, and cable is $45 a night or $280 a week. Rates are for two people at one camping site. For $65 a night or $420 a week, you can rent a one-room camping cabin, with a double bed

and one set of twin bunk beds, electricity, a dorm-size refrigerator, and heating and air-conditioning. A two-room camping cabin costs $80 a night or $525 a week and comes with a double bed and two sets of twin bunk beds, electricity, a dorm-size refrigerator, and heating and air-conditioning. There are six one-room and six two-room cabins, none of which have cooking facilities. Outside each cabin is a charcoal grill, picnic table, and water faucet.

Drummer Boy also has 20 full-service cottages for rent at $130 a night or $875 a week. The main room has a queen-size bed, a dining table, and seating, and a separate bedroom has two sets of twin bunk beds. There's also a bathroom, kitchenette, heat, air-conditioning, and cable TV. A kitchenette is equipped with a dorm-size fridge, two-burner stove top, microwave, and coffeemaker. Your dishes, pots, pans, and utensils are included; just bring bedding and towels.

Depending upon when you're camping at Drummer Boy, your weekend planned activities might be a Crab Feast weekend, a NASCAR weekend, or a Mardi Gras weekend. Wednesday and Friday nights, the campground organizes a downtown Ghost Tour, and on Sunday mornings the camp historian conducts a downtown historical tour.

Gettysburg Campground
2030 Fairfield Road
(717) 334-3304
www.gettysburgcampground.com

Gettysburg Campground is located on Marsh Creek, the western boundary during the Battle of Gettysburg. It's also located adjacent to the Black Horse Tavern, a historic landmark that was used as an inn and hospital during the Civil War years. In June you can be transported back to those days as you observe Civil War reenactors camping on the grounds.

Open April through November, the campground has 250 sites and offers RV repairs on-site. While staying here, you're a mere 10 miles from the South Mountain Fairgrounds, home of the South Mountain Fair and the National Apple Harvest Festival (see the Annual Events and Festivals chapter). There's also a daily shuttle bus to downtown Gettysburg during the summer.

When you want to relax at the campground, you can enjoy the ice-cream parlor or take in a movie. For those who want more activity, there's a ball field, shuffleboard, minigolf, fishing in the stocked creek (no license required), volleyball, and horseshoes available. Planned weekend activities such as a sock hop, a night of ghostly stories, a fishing contest, or a chili cookoff are sure to round out your stay.

All sites have a picnic table and a fire ring. A site without hookups is $29.70 a night or $158.40 a week; a site with water and electric is $34.70 a night or $188.40 a week. Having a site with water, electric, and sewer will run you $36.70 a night or $200.40 a week, and if you want 50-amp electric, there's a $4.00 fee per day. Rates are for two people and two children at one camping site.

There are also two cabins and two cottages available for rent. Outside of each is a picnic table and a fire ring for cooking, and you supply your own linens. The cabins are $48 per night and they have one full-size bed and one set of bunk beds in one room, a small refrigerator, and a small table with two stools.

The cottages rent for $100 per night. One cottage has a full-size bed and the other has a queen-size bed. Both cottages have heat, air-conditioning, two sets of bunk beds in a separate room, full private bathroom with shower, refrigerator, stove top, microwave, coffee pot, toaster, dishes, pots and pans, and utensils.

Gettysburg KOA Kampground
20 Knox Road
(717) 642–5713, (800) 562–1869
www.gettysburgkoa.com
Open April through October, the Gettysburg KOA Kampground has 100 private wooded sites as well as air-conditioned cottages and cabins. Be sure to check out the Kamper Kitchen, which is located at the pavilion and outfitted with a stove, sink, and counter space. You might also want to head to the pavilion to take advantage of the inexpensive all-you-can-eat pancake breakfast that's held every summer weekend. Campers will also find minigolf, horseshoes, bike rentals, shuffleboard, and nature trails to fill up their days. A history film is shown nightly, and a shuttle to and from town is available twice a day at $5.00 per person round-trip. Weekly planned activities include a Civil War–era fashion show, candlelit ghost walks through the campground, and the chance to experience living history by observing Civil War encampments.

A campsite without any hookups is $20 to $39 per night; a site with water and electric is $26 to $44 a night, while a site with water, electric, and sewer will cost $30 to $52 per night. Rates are for two adults and two children younger than age 13 at one camping site.

The campground's 16 one-room and two-room Kamping Kabins, which rent for $50 to $85 per night, are equipped with air-conditioning, heat, a porch swing, a picnic table, a fire ring with grill top, and a charcoal grill. Pets are allowed in the cabins for a $10 fee. There are also four Kamping Kottages. The basic camping cottages have all the amenities the cabins have plus a bathroom, and they rent for $70 to $97 per night. The Deluxe Kamping Kottages also have a bathroom with shower; a propane fireplace; a kitchenette with refrigerator, stove top, coffeemaker, toaster, microwave, pots and pans, dishes, cooking and eating utensils, and dish towels; and a dining area with a log table and chairs. The deluxe cottage is $100 to $149 per night. No pets are allowed in the cottages, and there's a two-night minimum stay.

There are also two Kamping Lodges available for rent. Each has a complete bathroom with shower; a kitchenette with refrigerator, stove top, coffeemaker, toaster, microwave, pots and pans, dishes, cooking and eating utensils, and dish towels; a dining area with log table and chairs; wood-framed beds; air-conditioning and ceiling fans; heat; a porch swing and a picnic table; and a fire ring with a grill top. Renting a lodge will cost you $100 to $149 per night. No pets are allowed, and there's a two-night minimum stay.

Granite Hill Campground and Adventure Golf
3340 Fairfield Road
(717) 642-8749, (800) 642-TENT
www.granitehillcampground.com

Granite Hill sits on a farm that was granted from Penn's Charter in the late 18th century and was called the Drais Farm. The owner at the time of the Battle of Gettysburg was Felix Drais, who was wounded while fighting in the Wheatfield on July 2. The bank barn that sits on the property was used to shelter wounded soldiers during the battle, and General Lee's retreat on July 4 passed directly by Granite Hill on what is now Route 116. The Drais Farm became the property of the Cornett family in 1972 and is the only Gettysburg Civil War farm to become an RV park.

Open April through October, the campground has 300 sites on 150 acres of woodlands, meadows, and rolling hills, where you can camp in your own RV or tent or stay in one of their rustic cabins. This is the site of the Gettysburg Bluegrass Festivals, which are held in May and August (see the Annual Events and Festivals chapter). Adventure Golf is an 18-hole state-of-the-art minigolf course sculpted from a stone mountain overlooking the campground's Bass Lake (for more on the Adventure Golf, see the Kidstuff chapter). The golf is challenging, fun for kids and adults, and open to the public. Kayaks and paddleboats are also available for rent at Bass Lake, and there's a trout pond for fishing (no license required). Shuffleboard, tennis, softball, horseshoes, volleyball, and basketball add to your recreational

choices, and there's also a snack bar available for when you need to refuel your energy. Wireless Internet service is available and there's a "Safari Area" for club camping. Planned weekend activities run the gamut from hay rides to a trout derby to ice-cream socials and hoedowns to pig roasts.

A site without any hookups is $28 a night or $143 a week, and one with water and electric runs $33 a night or $175 a week. A site with water, electric, and sewer costs $36 a night or $192 a week. Rates are for two people at one camping site. There is also a two-room cabin available that rents for $70 a night or $400 a week. It has one double bed and two sets of bunk beds and comes equipped with a heater, fan, picnic table, and outdoor grill.

Round Top Campground
180 Knight Road
(717) 334-9565
www.roundtopcamp.com

This is the only Gettysburg campground that is open year-round. When you camp here, you're on the battlefield at the south end of Big Round Top. The campground has 260 sites as well as cabins and a cottage and a trailer for rent. Permanent sites are also available. The rentals have heat and air-conditioning, and the lodge has a lounge for you to relax in. For your convenience, liquid propane gas is sold here. When you want to relax, you can play basketball, shuffleboard, tennis, or minigolf on the one-acre 18-hole course. You'll also find a snack bar and pavilions, and church services are held on Sunday during the season.

Campsites without hookups go for $18.00 a night or $108.00 a week; one with water and electric will cost $29.50 a night or $177.00 a week. Sites with water, electric, and sewer are $31.50 a night or $189.00 a week. There are also sites with water, electric, sewer, and cable, which are $33.50 a night or $201.00 a week. Water, electric, sewer, cable, and a 50-amp hookup at your site will run you $35.50 a night or $213.00 a week. Rates are for two adults at one camping site. The two cabins at the Round Top cost $50.00 a night or $300.00 a week.

There are three cottages available for rent. One sleeps four people with a double bed and a pullout couch, and the rental rate is $99 night or $594 a week. The other two cottages have a double bed and two sets of single bunk beds. They rent for $120 a night or $720 a week. The trailer that's for rent is the park's model, and the rate is $99 a night or $594 a week.

RESTAURANTS

One thing's for sure about dining in Gettysburg—there are lots of choices. You can get dressed up and head out for a five-course meal one night and the next night grab something at whatever casual place is nearby when hunger strikes. Dressy casual is the most dressed up you need to be in any of the restaurants, and all the finer restaurants except The Cashtown Inn also have a tavern or more casual dining area on the premises. But that's not to say you can't put on your best outfit if you're so inclined, especially if you plan on dining at Herr's Publick House or Centuries on the Square. At most restaurants you'll find a varied menu that aims to please many different tastes. Pasta, chicken, seafood, and beef dishes, as well as sandwiches and lighter fare, appear on most menus. If you like to try ethnic fare, you can sample Italian, Greek, Asian, and Irish cuisines.

Some of the dining establishments are housed in historic landmarks, making dining there about much more than enjoying excellent food. For instance, the Farnsworth House housed Confederate sharpshooters during the Battle of Gettysburg, and the Dobbin House and Herr's Tavern were stops on the Underground Railroad. You really shouldn't miss these places, and you might want to try their dishes that are representative of the Civil War period.

The southern end of town contains the most concentrated area of restaurants, probably because many tourist sights are also in this part of town. Gettysburg doesn't have many chain restaurants—a McDonald's and a Friendly's are in the southern end of town, and a Ruby Tuesday, an Arby's, a Perkins Family Restaurant, and another McDonald's are along York Street east of the square.

Most of the restaurants described in this chapter are within the borough limits.

Although this makes them conveniently located by attractions and shopping, it also sometimes leads to congestion. If you can, leave your car behind and walk. I'll mention if a place has lots of parking available; otherwise, assume there's either no customer parking or very little parking available, often behind the restaurant. If you're driving, be prepared to have to find a spot on the street and feed the meters. There's also a parking garage on Race Horse Alley behind the Gettysburg Hotel on the square.

When asked, most establishments claim to be wheelchair accessible, but this often means coming in a back door or the staff putting down a ramp for easier access. My best advice to those needing special assistance is for you to call ahead and speak about the facilities directly with someone from the restaurant.

Gettysburg is a tourist town, so most places accept credit cards. But there are a few exceptions, which I'll note in those restaurants' write-ups. Reservations are often accepted only at the fine-dining establishments, and waiting for a table is a common experience. Many tourists seem to break for lunch late, about 1:00 to 1:30 P.M., so don't think you'll outsmart everyone by delaying lunch—you'll just be hungrier while you wait.

Entries in this chapter are arranged geographically from the focal point of Lincoln Square and then listed alphabetically.

PRICE CODE

Prices represent the average cost for two dinner entrees, excluding appetizers, desserts, refreshments, tax, and tip. If you have a large party, check whether a gratuity is automatically added to your bill. And check the rate of the gratuity—it might range from 15 to 20 percent.

$	Up to $15
$$	$16 to $25
$$$	$26 to $40
$$$$	$41 and higher

LINCOLN SQUARE

Centuries on the Square   **$$$$**
McClellan's Tavern
Best Western Historic Gettysburg Hotel
1 Lincoln Square
(717) 337-2000
www.hotelgettysburg.com
The Gettysburg Hotel, then known as
Scott's Tavern, was established in 1797. The
hotel basks in this history, as evidenced
by the name of its restaurants, Centuries
on the Square and McClellan's Tavern.
(William McClellan, a local sheriff, bought
the tavern in 1809.) Open for breakfast and
dinner, Centuries on the Square offers you
smoke-free fine dining as you enjoy its
colonial decor. For dinner, you'll find elegant beef, chicken, and seafood dishes.
Prime rib of beef is available on Friday and
Saturday evenings; the salmon is filleted in-
house to ensure its fresh quality. A children's menu is available, and your server
will be attired in period dress.

McClellan's Tavern is open for lunch
and lighter fare during the evening. As you
enter the pub, you're sure to notice the
gleaming mahogany bar before you. This
turn-of-the-20th-century Van Tromp Bar
was imported from Brick Lane in England,
and it's a beauty. The bar stools are
mahogany and soft, soft leather that you
can't help but caress. Cozy tables sit
around the bar area, and there's a separate
dining area to the right that features a
large fireplace. Gourmet sandwiches dominate the menu, which also has a good
selection of appetizers.

Hard Bean Cafe   **$**
17 Lincoln Square
(717) 338-0929
www.17onthesquare.com
This small smoke-free cafe has a few
tables and some stools at a counter. Open

daily from 8:00 A.M., the shop offers
brewed coffees and teas, pastries, cakes,
muffins, and homemade ice cream and
cookies. This is a great spot to take a
break and watch the activity on the
square. As you refresh with a steaming
cup of tea and a scrumptious homemade
dessert, take a look at the paintings that
adorn the walls. The art is by local artists
and for sale at very reasonable prices.
(See The Arts chapter for more on the
artwork.)

---

*Some establishments have separate
entrances for the dining area and the
bar area, often within a few feet of each
other.*

The Plaza Restaurant and Lounge **$$$**
2-8 Baltimore Street
(717) 334-1999
Open seven days a week for lunch and
dinner, The Plaza has gyros, ke-bobs, sou-
vlaki, and other Greek dishes as well as
more traditional dishes featuring fresh-cut
steaks, seafood, chicken, chops, and bar-
becued spare ribs. Grilled deli sandwiches,
such as the grilled reuben, are featured at
lunchtime, which also finds many cus-
tomers ordering the homemade soups.
Favorite Greek dinner dishes are the Gyro
Platter and the Chicken Ke-Bob Platter,
which are served on pita bread with
tzatziki (Greek garlic sauce) and accom-
panied by a small Greek salad and fries or
a potato. The barbecued spare ribs, crab
cakes, and lamb chops also are frequent
dinner choices. The menu includes kids'
meals reasonably priced for children age
12 and younger.

The Plaza has two entrances, one that
opens onto the bar area and one that
takes you directly into the dining room.
The entrance to the bar is on the square
while the restaurant entrance is a few
steps down Baltimore Street. The bar area
serves as the Plaza's smoking area, and the
dining room has booths along its perime-

ter and tables in the middle. You'll find a casual atmosphere here, with good views of the square from the bar area.

The Pub & Restaurant $$$
20–22 Lincoln Square
(717) 334-7100
www.the-pub.com
This upscale restaurant and pub offers a full-service menu with something for everyone. You'll find appetizers, salads, soups, pitas, strombolis, nachos, burgers, sandwiches, pasta, steaks, seafood, and desserts. The Pub is known for its generous portions and for its burgers and chicken sandwiches. The restaurant is on one side and the pub is on the other. The dark wood booths and tables on the smoke-free restaurant side add to the old-world ambience, as does the abundance of dark wood on the pub side. And the view of the square can't be beat. The pub side has tables as well as the bar seats, and there are a few arcade games to keep the kids busy as you wait for your meals. There's also a kids' menu available for children age 10 and younger, with prices in the $4.00 to $5.00 range. You'll find a wide range of cocktails, wines, and beers here. There are 12 drafts on tap, one of which is always Guinness.

The Pub is open for lunch and dinner daily, and it serves dinner until at least 10:00 P.M. during the week and until 9:00 P.M. on Sunday. The place closes during the first week of January but is open the rest of the year. If you're visiting The Pub for a drink, it serves until 1:00 A.M. Monday through Saturday and until 11:00 P.M. on Sunday.

The Pub gets really crowded sometimes, so be aware . . . there are two sets of restrooms, one downstairs on the pub side and one upstairs. The upstairs ladies' room also has a changing table.

NORTH OF LINCOLN SQUARE

Deliso Pizza, Pasta and Subs
Restaurant $$
829 Biglerville Road
(717) 337-9500
Located on Route 34 (Biglerville Road) and just a bit more than a mile from the square, Deliso's has been around since 1995. Since the parking lot encircles the building, parking isn't a problem here. Open seven days a week and smoke-free, Deliso's has a wide variety of menu selections. Besides such Italian fare as pizza, subs, strombolis, calzones, and Italian dinners, the menu also offers burgers and a few fish choices. Or you can order a gyro or honey-dipped chicken. Beer and wine are available to accompany your meal, and Deliso's also sells six-packs of beer for carryout.

Deliso's decor is similar to many pizzerias, with booths and a few tables available for those who wish to eat inside the restaurant. Deliso's also advertises their fast pick-up service.

Distelfink Drive-in $
2710 Old Harrisburg Road
(717) 337-3665, (717) 337-9636
Distelfink Drive-in has been in operation since 1952, but it's no longer a true drive-in. Instead, you can either eat inside or order at a walk-up window. Open daily for breakfast, lunch, and dinner, Distelfink is located 4 miles north of town along U.S. Business Route 15 (Old Harrisburg Road). Besides soups, salads, sandwiches, pizza, and subs, you can also find 50 flavors of soft-serve ice cream and milk shakes as well as soft pretzels. While you're at Distelfink, you can also pick up some fresh produce, flowers, and crafts.

Lincoln Diner $
32 Carlisle Street
(717) 334-3900
The Lincoln Diner is open 24 hours a day, 7 days a week. It's a block off the square, across the street from the Lincoln Train

Station, which is being renovated and will eventually serve as a welcoming center. The Lincoln is also beside the Flying Bull Saloon, and some patrons of the saloon stop at the Lincoln on their way home.

When you enter the Lincoln, you'll first be struck by just how like a diner it is. Booths line one side and the other side has a long, long lunch counter. This is the smoking section. Beyond this room is another room that serves as the smoke-free dining room. Here you'll find mostly tables and a few more booths. The menu at the Lincoln covers the spectrum. Depending on your hunger level, you can choose from homemade soups, sandwiches, burgers, salads, seafood, steaks, chops, chicken, and pasta. There's also an inexpensive kids' menu for children age 10 and younger. The diner's on-site bakery creates delicious desserts, and the Lincoln is especially known for its cheesecake.

The Lincoln Diner does not take credit cards or personal checks. Cash is the name of the game here, although they will take a traveler's check.

SOUTH OF LINCOLN SQUARE

The Avenue Restaurant $$
21 Steinwehr Avenue
(717) 334-3235
www.theavenuerestaurant.com

This nonsmoking casual restaurant has been locally owned and operated since 1958, and the couple who bought the place in 2005 are only the fourth owners. The Avenue offers homestyle cooking daily for breakfast, lunch, and dinner, and its location puts it right in the heart of everything. The inside of the restaurant is set up like a diner, with a counter to the left and lots of booths throughout the large dining area. Everyone in your group will find something that appeals here, from sandwiches to chicken to beef to seafood. Be sure to try their old-fashioned milk shakes.

Brigades Food, Wine & Spirits Restaurant & Lounge $$$
Holiday Inn Battlefield
516 Baltimore Street
(717) 334-6211

Located within the Holiday Inn Battlefield, Brigades serves breakfast Monday through Sunday and dinner Monday through Saturday. The lounge is also open Monday through Saturday evenings. When you enter the Holiday Inn, Brigades is to your left, and the focal point of the large dining area is the huge brick fireplace at the back of the restaurant. A rich mauve rug complements the blue, plastic tablecloths, and casual is the attire of choice here. There is plenty of off-street parking for patrons at the side of the hotel, and the menu is extensive and varied. Brigades is popular with locals from the area as well as hotel guests.

Dino's Pizza, Pasta & Subs $$
226 Steinwehr Avenue
(717) 337-3453

Dino's serves lots of pasta, which is accompanied by garlic bread and a salad, and if you don't want the salad, they'll take a dollar off your bill. They also offer a kid's spaghetti that is served without the salad at an even more reduced rate. You'll find Greek touches throughout the menu, such as the tzatziki sauce (Greek garlic sauce) and the Zorba the Greek Pizza, which has tomatoes and steamed spinach leaves and feta cheese crumbs in an olive oil garlic sauce atop a blend of mozzarella and cheddar cheese. Dino's tops their fresh pizza dough with their family-recipe tomato sauce and a blend of mozzarella and cheddar cheese, and their hot subs are served toasted on freshly baked Italian rolls. Their Italian meatballs are homemade, and besides having them with pasta or in a sub, you can get them as a side order.

This full-service restaurant is open daily, and they also offer carryout and delivery. Dino's serves beer and wine to accompany your meal, and six-packs of beer are available for takeout.

Dobbin House Tavern $$$-$$$$
89 Steinwehr Avenue
(717) 334-2100
www.dobbinhouse.com

Built in 1776, the Dobbin House is the oldest building in Gettysburg and is listed on the Register of Historic Places. Just a block from the Gettysburg National Military Park Visitor Center and across the street from the National Cemetery, the home served as a hospital for the wounded after the Battle of Gettysburg. The house's native stone walls, seven fireplaces, and hand-carved woodwork have been restored to their original 18th-century beauty and decorated with period antiques. (For more on the rich history of the Dobbin House, see the Close-up in this chapter.)

Here you can enjoy colonial and continental cuisine, either in the casual Springhouse Tavern or in the more formal Alexander Dobbin Dining Rooms. Both places are smoke-free, and in both you'll be served by waitstaff whose period clothing is completely authentic. The tavern is in the lower level of the house, and you are transported back in time the minute you enter. The room is dimly lit with a colonial candle on each table and hanging colonial lanterns, and the deep wood of the exposed wood beams and tall wooden booths gleams against the stone walls and brick floor. The trickling of the underground spring mingles with the Irish and colonial music that plays in the background. But atmosphere is not the only thing in abundance here. Good, hearty fare also awaits you. You'll find a variety of salads, burgers, and sandwiches, and there's also spit-roasted chicken, a grilled catch of the day, and char-grilled steak for those looking for a more filling meal. The tavern is open daily for lunch and dinner, and reservations are not accepted.

There are actually six separate dining rooms on the main level of the house, and each is decorated in a different colonial motif. My favorite is the cozy Library, complete with bookshelves and a fireplace. But perhaps you'd rather dine in the Dining Room, Parlour, Study, Spinning Room, or Bedroom. Yes, you read that right—you can actually dine in bed. The food here is exquisite—Dobbin House recipes have been published in *Bon Appetit* and *Cuisine* magazines. You'll find lots of choices, with beef, chicken, pork, and seafood dishes available. The restaurant makes its own breads, soups, and desserts; people rave about the onion soup. As you dine, the china and flatware you'll be using exactly match fragments that were uncovered during the reexcavation of the cellar. The dining rooms are open for dinner only, and reservations are a must.

After you've eaten your fill, be sure to check out the secret slave hideout behind the pantry shelf (see the Close-up in this chapter). The premises also house the Country Curiosity Store, a great gift shop; the Gettystown Inn (see the Bed-and-Breakfasts and Guesthouses chapter); and the Abigail Adams Ballroom. With all that's going on here, it's a good thing the Dobbin House has a large parking area.

The Dog House $
523 Baltimore Street
(717) 338-3494

Although this place is easy to miss—don't. Where else can you find the choice of more than 40 toppings for your hot dog? The Dog House shares a building with Rita's Italian Ice and the Gettysburg Cigar Company, and The Dog House sits in farthest from the street. Although small and open only seasonally, this is a fun place to grab a bite. Nothing on the menu is expensive, and the posters on the walls are from the owner's life as a DJ. Besides hot dogs, you can also enjoy quesadillas, chicken sandwiches, burgers, fries, salads, and ice cream. You have your choice of eating in the restaurant or at picnic tables outside, or you can carry your treats with you.

Farnsworth House $$$-$$$$
401 Baltimore Street
(717) 334-8838
www.farnsworthhouseinn.com

The Farnsworth House, which was built in

1810, has three locations for dining: the main dining room, where you can dine by candlelight and be served by period-dressed waitstaff; the open-air garden, where you choose from the same fine-dining menu as you relax beside a spring-fed stream that served as a water source for both the Confederate and Union armies; or the Killer Angel Tavern, which serves light fare with a touch of Pennsylvania Dutch cooking thrown in. The tavern also houses South Street Pizza (717-334-4419), home of the $6.00 16-inch cheese pizza and a variety of hoagies. (For more on the tavern, see the Nightlife chapter.) The Civil War is *the* topic of conversation at all the dining locations, which isn't surprising given the house's history during the Battle of Gettysburg. The house sheltered Confederate sharpshooters during the battle, and one of them is believed to have fired the wayward shot that killed Jennie Wade, the only civilian to perish in the three-day battle. More than 100 bullets holes can still be seen in the south wall of the building.

The Farnsworth House has been owned by the Loring Schultz family since 1972, and they are responsible for restoring the house to its 1863 appearance, complete with its original walls, flooring, and rafters. The house serves as a bed-and-breakfast, and many news stories have been written about the ghosts that supposedly reside here. (See the Bed-and-Breakfasts and Guesthouses chapter for more on the eerier side of the Farnsworth House.) The main dining room is smoke-free, but smoking is permitted in the tavern, which houses a unique display of *Gettysburg* movie props and uniforms.

Lunch and dinner are served here, and Civil War–period fare figures prominently on the menu. You'll be able to try game pie, peanut soup, spoon bread, and pumpkin fritters. For those with less adventuresome palates, steaks, chops, and fish are also available. A good selection of beer, wine, and cocktails accent your dining pleasure. The food at the Farnsworth House has many admirers—*Bon Appetit* magazine has described it as "History

never tasted so good." A children's menu, with entrees for less than $10, is available, and reservations are required for dining in the main dining room.

Plenty of parking is available behind the Farnsworth House, and Civil War buffs will definitely want to check out the Farnsworth House Military Impressions bookshop and the Gettysburg Quartermaster (see the Shopping and the Gettysburg National Military Park chapters), which are also on the grounds. During the summer, there's entertainment here on Friday and Saturday nights.

**General Pickett's
All-U-Can-Eat Buffets** $$
**571 Steinwehr Avenue
(717) 334-7580**
If your group has big appetites, these all-you-can-eat-buffets will satisfy everyone in your party. And those with smaller appetites will appreciate being able to order just the soup and salad bar for a reduced price. Although groups make up a large part of the business here, individuals are also welcome. It's open every day during the season but closed in January and open only on weekends in February. The lunch buffet begins at 11:00 A.M. Monday through Saturday, and the dinner buffet is served Monday through Sunday at 4:30 P.M. With room for 225 people and the bountiful buffet offered, it's easy to see why this place is so popular with tour groups. Because groups are often eating here, the dining room may be totally non-smoking on some days.

Be careful as you leave the Farnsworth House and cross the street that runs behind it to get to the parking lot. As you leave the trellised walkway, it's easy to forget that this alley is traveled by many cars. Stop at the end of the sidewalk on the side of the Farnsworth House and look both ways before stepping into the alley.

RESTAURANTS

CLOSE-UP

The Underground Railroad in Gettysburg

The Civil War comes to mind when you think of Gettysburg, not the Underground Railroad. But the railroad that helped slaves escape to freedom had a stop at the Dobbin House on Steinwehr Avenue. Now a restaurant, the Dobbin House was built in 1776 by Alexander Dobbin, an Irish minister who had come to the area in 1773 with his wife, Isabella. After the forming of Gettysburg, Alexander was a community leader, and he opened the first classical school west of the Susquehanna River in his home. He and Isabella had 10 children before her death in 1800, and before his death in 1809, Alexander married Mary Agnew, who had nine children of her own. Although town records show that Alexander owned slaves, the house would help many slaves obtain freedom.

You can view where slaves hid in the Dobbin House while journeying north to freedom. The hideout is along a staircase that leads from the main floor to the second floor, and a pane of glass has been installed so visitors can peer into the tiny and cramped space. Look closely to the left; the first time I looked I didn't see the slave hiding in the corner.

If you're dining in the main dining rooms, the staircase leading to the hideout is to the left of where the hostess will greet you as you arrive for dinner. If you're eating at the tavern, you can get to the hideout by going through the door to the left of the colonial bar, which was built in 1818 by the current owner's great-great-great-grandfather for his tavern near Dillsburg, Pennsylvania. As you step through the door, be sure to stop and admire the underground spring that you can see right ahead of you. (The spring is also visible in the tavern's dining area.) The original three springs, which have

---

The buffets feature down-home cooking in a family atmosphere. The soups, rolls, and desserts are handmade, and the dinner buffet features hand-breaded deep-fried catfish. Lunch features a selection of daily specials, such as baked chicken, meat loaf, and Salisbury steak. If you like, you can order an alcoholic beverage with your dinner. General Pickett's location across from the Gettysburg National Military Park is ideal, and their large lot makes parking a breeze. Although General Pickett's and the Gettysburg Battle Theatre (see the Attractions chapter) are located in the same building, they are not associated.

The Gingerbread Man $$$
217 Steinwehr Avenue
(717) 334-1100
www.thegingerbreadman.net
Known to locals as the G-Man, you'll find lots of casual ambience and lots of food and drink choices here. From the outside, it looks like someone's house, but when you enter the restaurant, you realize it's much larger than it looks. The front part of the main level has lots of tables, and the bar area is in the back, where you'll find more tables available. Upstairs is another room that can be used for private parties or overflow business.

This hideaway within the Dobbin House shows how slaves were smuggled to freedom on the Underground Railroad. KATE HERTZOG

been diverted into one area to help preserve the house, were used as a well (especially important during Indian attacks) and a refrigerator. After looking at the spring, go up the staircase and to the left there will be another door leading to another staircase. As you head up this staircase, the hideout is to your left. After viewing the hideout, continue up the steps and you'll enter into a room that has pictures of the Dobbin House in times past, and you can view some of the original stone of the house. This room also contains artifacts from colonial times. As you head back down the staircase, watch your step. The staircase is windy and the steps are narrow.

All the food served here except for the potato salad and coleslaw is homemade. For lighter fare, you can choose from soup, salads, burgers, sandwiches, and fajitas. Dinners, which are served beginning at noon, include beef, seafood, chicken, pork, and pasta selections. And don't overlook the Snacks, Treats, and Eats part of the menu—most of these are ample enough to serve as a meal. My husband is always stuffed after eating the Supreme Nachos from this part of the menu, and my cousin Teresa always orders the potato skins for lunch when she's in town visiting. My favorite selection for lunch or dinner is the English Style Roast Beef Sandwich, which is served with au jus for dipping.

The G-Man also offers an extensive kids' menu, ranging from a peanut butter and jelly sandwich to battered shrimp and fries, with prices in the reasonable $4.00 to $5.00 range.

Hunt's Cafe $-$$
61 Steinwehr Avenue
(717) 334-4787

Hunt's Cafe and Battlefield Fries was formerly known as Hunt's Battlefield Fries, but the name has been changed to reflect that there's a lot more than just fries here. Breakfast is available, and for lunch or dinner you can pick from cheesesteaks, hamburgers, wings, salads, and hot and cold sandwiches. There's also old-fashioned bottled soda, hand-dipped ice cream, fresh lemonade, milk shakes, and desserts, including whole pies.

You'll want to add the fries to anything you order—they're fresh cut, and owner Scott Hunt lets you jazz them up with lots of topping selections. Scott's proud of his fries and of his cheesesteaks—he has patrons that have driven from Philadelphia, home of the cheesesteak, just to get one!

Hunt's has been serving up great food since 2002, and the place opens at 8:00 A.M. every day during the season. (Hunt's is closed on Wednesday from November through April.) You can relax inside the smoke-free dining area or enjoy watching the world go by from your outside table. For now, you must pay cash for your meal, but Scott is planning on accepting credit cards as payment in the near future.

May Flowers
Asian Buffet & Restaurant $$
533 Steinwehr Avenue
(717) 337-3377, (717) 337-9998
www.themayflowers.com

May Flowers is set among chain restaurants, and its building actually looks like it used to be a fast-food restaurant. But inside, the smoke-free restaurant is spacious and beautifully decorated with tables with high-backed chairs and lots of plants. Featuring dishes of southern Chinese, Japanese, and American cuisine, all items on their extensive menu are available for takeout. You'll find everything from shrimp egg rolls to filet mignon to lobster to Peking duck. If you can't manage to limit your choice to one item on the menu, you can always try the lunch or dinner buffet. May Flowers has special dishes for dieters, and they will gladly steam most items on the menu if you're watching your calorie intake.

Open seven days a week for lunch and dinner, May Flowers has ample parking. It also has a drive-through for take-out orders. Be sure to check out their lunch specials, which are served Monday through Saturday to 3:00 P.M.—they're great bargains.

Olivia's Mediterranean Grille $$$
3015 Baltimore Street
(717) 359-9357, (717) 359-9857

Although Olivia's is 4.5 miles south of Lincoln Square, the short drive is well worth it. When you pull into the parking lot, the place looks small and not overly impressive, but the inside is quite a different story. The large dining room has clusters of booths and tables, and some tables sit in a private alcove. Lots of plants and accents contribute to the Mediterranean-cafe feel of the place. Olivia's is named after the daughter of owner Harry Tassou. And this is definitely a locally owned and run restaurant—Harry lives across the street, and the last time I stopped by he was preparing chocolate-covered strawberries for Valentine's Day dining.

The dinner menu is a mix of fresh seafood, hand-cut steaks, and Greek and Italian cuisine. Olivia's also serves lunch, and breakfast is available on the weekend. Food is served here every day but Monday. Bottled domestic and imported beer, wine, and spirits are available to complement your dinner, and there's entertainment occasionally on the weekends. If you like beef, many customers especially enjoy the Jack Daniels steak. Olivia's has been recommended by the *Washington Post,* and although the atmosphere is casual, reservations are suggested.

O'Rorke's Family Eatery and Spirits $$$
44 Steinwehr Avenue
(717) 334-2333

This is a lively place, and you'll often see reenactors in full garb enjoying good food, beer, and conversation here. The finer casual cuisine includes soups, salads, burgers, seafood, steaks, and a few Irish entrees. I especially like the Guinness Beef Stew, a rich combination of beef, potatoes, carrots, and a hint of Guinness served in a bread bowl.

O'Rorke's, which opened in March

2003, is named for Patrick O'Rorke, an Irish-born American soldier who was killed on the western slope of Little Round Top during the Battle of Gettysburg. A monument to the colonel stands on the spot where he died. O'Rorke's is open daily for lunch and dinner, and they host entertainment on Friday and Saturday nights. There are six beers on tap, including Guinness and Harp, wine by the glass, and cocktails, including a variety of martinis. You can dine outside on the patio in season, but be sure to take a trip inside to admire the two walk-in fireplaces you'll find there.

Pike Restaurant & Lounge $$$
985 Baltimore Pike
(717) 334-9227

Located just up the road from the Battlefield Military Museum, Pike Restaurant is open for lunch and dinner daily, and sometimes for breakfast on the weekends. You have three choices for dining ambience here. The nonsmoking dining room has a family atmosphere, the large deck out front is great for kicking back and relaxing, and the sports lounge features a big-screen TV and is open until 2:00 A.M. (For more on the lounge, see the Nightlife chapter.) Casual dining at all three locations includes homemade soups, sandwiches, wraps, quesadillas, Angus burgers and steaks, and pasta dishes. Lunch and dinner specials are offered daily, and a bountiful breakfast buffet is served on summer weekends. The kids' menu offers those age 10 and younger meals for less than $5.00.

There's plenty of parking available at the Pike, and it's better to drive here rather than walk from town. Although it's located at the edge of town, the sidewalk stops at the Evergreen Cemetery, and I don't advise walking along the berm of this busy road.

Ping's Cafe $$
34 Baltimore Street
(717) 334-2234

Ping's Cafe serves Japanese and Chinese cuisine, and it's the only restaurant in

Don't assume that the cheesesteak you order in Gettysburg will be made the same way it is in your hometown. It might be made with beef, onions, provolone cheese, and tomato sauce, or with beef, onions, provolone cheese, lettuce, tomato, and mayo, or with just beef and Cheese Whiz, or . . . well, you get the idea. So clarify what a cheesesteak is to you before you order; most likely, the place can make it just the way you like it.

town where you'll find a sushi bar, let alone one with a professional sushi chef. As you enter Ping's, the sushi bar is in the back, and booths round out the rest of the area. To the left is a large room that has lots of tables available. Ping's has more than 30 varieties of rolls, but these aren't the type you slather butter on. You might want to try their Spicy Tuna Roll, or the Dream Roll, which has smoked salmon, eel, caviar, cucumber, and seaweed salad. Lunch specials are combinations of rolls, and they're served until 3:00 P.M. There's also Japanese ice cream for dessert. Ping's is smoke-free and open for lunch and dinner Tuesday through Sunday (closed Monday).

Ross's Coffeehouse & Eatery $
65 West Middle Street
(717) 337-9034

Ross Hetrick owned this coffeehouse for eight years, and when he sold it to Brian and Mary Eastman in October 2004, they didn't change the name. They also didn't change this place's relaxed, living-room atmosphere. Two tables and a wraparound couch are the only seating you'll find in this small space. But you will find many ways to tempt your taste buds. This smoke-free eatery offers sandwiches, salads, and stuffed pitas in addition to gourmet coffee and specialty drinks. The place opens at 6:00 A.M. so you'll also find breakfast fare, including oatmeal, breakfast sandwiches, and bagels. Ross's is open daily for breakfast and lunch, and if you're lucky, you might get to watch an artist at work. The artwork in progress fills one wall, and the artists stop by and paint as the mood strikes them.

Spiritfields Pub & Fare and Poe's Patio $$
619 Baltimore Street
(717) 334-9449
www.spiritfield.com

Spiritfields opened its doors in May 2005, and it serves daily year-round from 11:00 A.M. to 11:00 P.M. Everything on the menu is made on the premises according to owners Tami and Ed Reese, including the hand-pattied burgers. Among the specialties are Maryland seafood dishes prepared according to secret family recipes, ale-soaked and seasoned briskets of beef served up in sandwiches, and the daily Chef's Whimsy. A full bar, specialty drinks, and wine and beer are available to complement your meal. The full menu is also available on the outside deck, Poe's Patio, which features evening entertainment on occasion.

Tommy's Pizza $$
105 Steinwehr Avenue
(717) 334-4721, (717) 334-8966

Tommy's has been family owned and operated and serving pizza to the community since 1973. Its location is convenient to all the sites on Steinwehr Avenue and Baltimore Street, and there is parking available on-site. Tommy's gives you the choice of pizza, stromboli, hoagies, salads, and wings seven days a week, but you won't find full pasta dinners here. The nonsmoking dining area can seat quite a few people, with booths and tables available. Delivery service is available, and there's also a drive-through pick-up window for customers who call their order in for carryout. If you like a beer with your pizza, Tommy's can accommodate you. They also have six-packs of beer available for takeout only.

EAST OF LINCOLN SQUARE

Aunt Pittypat's Tea Room $$
34 York Street
(717) 338-1832
www.americanhistoricalart.com

This is the new tearoom in town, having opened in 2004, and it's located at the back of the American Historical Art Gallery & Framery (see The Arts chapter). The name comes from the character of Aunt Pittypat in *Gone with the Wind*. Aunt Pittypat, the aunt of Melanie and Charles Hamilton, fainted from shock several times a day while Scarlett was living with her in Atlanta.

Open for tea and light fare Wednesday through Sunday, this is a delightful addition to the tearooms of Gettysburg. The large room is decorated in shabby chic, and little girls love the area full of hats, costume jewelry, and the like. Here they get to add the perfect touches to their outfits, making afternoon tea a fun dress-up affair. Owners Tracy and Rodney Cromeans are charming and attentive hosts, and the scones served here are already getting a reputation for their size as well as their taste. Reservations are not required, but they are recommended.

Civil-La-Tea $$
39 York Street
(717) 334-0992
www.civil-la-tea.com

Tea and light sandwiches and salads are served here Thursday through Monday (closed Tuesday and Wednesday) in a vintage tea parlor and on the veranda of this Civil War house during nice weather. Enjoying tea on the veranda is particularly lovely because you sit back from the street, allowing you to observe the crowds passing by without being a part of them. Civil-La-Tea opened in 1997, and when you enter the house from the veranda, you step into a beautiful gift shop filled with handcrafted items, jewelry, and antiques. The tearoom is located beyond the gift shop. The shop offers theme teas, for which reservations are required. At other times, reservations are recommended but not required.

Eastside Lounge and Restaurant $$
1063 York Road
(717) 337-0118

The Eastside sits along U.S. Route 30 in front of the Hilton Garden Inn. Here you'll find a varied menu available for breakfast, lunch, and dinner seven days a week. But don't come here for an early breakfast— they open at 10:00 A.M., and breakfast is served until noon. For lunch you can choose from homemade soup, hot and cold sandwiches and subs, fish, chicken, and hamburgers. If you're really hungry, try the Eastside Nightmare—ham, roast beef, turkey, American and Swiss cheeses, lettuce, tomato, onion, and ranch dressing served on a roll and big enough for two to share. Crab cakes are the house specialty, and the prime rib, broasted chicken, and barbecue spare ribs are also favorites. Other dinner selections include steaks, pasta dishes, ham, and seafood.

There's a large parking area beside the Eastside, and there are separate entrances for the lounge and restaurant. The restaurant entrance opens onto a casual dining room decorated with green chairs and matching plastic tablecloths. The lights above the tables are illuminated candles placed inside upside-down bushel baskets, a tribute to the area's orchards. The lounge, which you can also enter through the dining area, has a large bar, a few tables, and a game room with three pool tables.

Gettysbrew Restaurant & Brewery $$$
248 Hunterstown Road
(717) 337-1001
www.gettysbrew.com

Gettysbrew offers casual fine dining in a restored brick-end barn on the historic Monfort Farm, which was used as one of the largest Confederate field hospitals following the Battle of Gettysburg. Wounded soldiers were left at the farm when the Confederates retreated, and 47 men were buried here. Their bodies were later disinterred and moved to Hollywood Cemetery in Richmond, Virginia. Gettysbrew opened in 1997 as the area's largest brewery, and all beer, root beer, and ginger ale are crafted on-site. The beverages are also available for takeout in half-gallon glass jugs called growlers. If you bring your growler back for a refill, you get it at a reduced price. Wine is also available to complement your meal.

To get to Gettysbrew from Lincoln Square, take York Street about a mile and then bear left onto Hunterstown Road. Gettysbrew is on the left in about half a mile. Closed in January and February, Gettysbrew is open seven days a week the rest of the year, opening at noon on the weekends and at 4:00 P.M. during the week. Lighter fare includes piegga sandwiches, which are served hot and open-faced on piegga bread, which is folded focaccia bread with a hint of honey. Entrees feature seafood and steaks, and a children's menu is available for those age 12 and younger.

Gettysburg Family Restaurant $$
1275 York Road, Peebles Plaza
(717) 337-2700

Family owned and operated, Gettysburg Family Restaurant is located in Peebles Plaza along York Road. It's open seven days a week for breakfast, lunch, and dinner. Early risers can grab a bite beginning at 7:00 A.M. on Sunday and at 6:00 A.M. the rest of the week. And seniors receive discounts on dinner entrees after 2:00 P.M. If you like, you can also order an alcoholic beverage to go with your dinner.

Reminiscent of a large diner, the restaurant has a counter in the back and plenty of booths and tables. There are also plenty of choices on the menu, with homemade soups, sandwiches, broasted chicken, pasta dishes, meat loaf, ham, steaks, and seafood being among them. Children age 12 and younger can order from the children's specials, which are all priced less than $5.00, and some are less than $3.00. All items on the menu are available for takeout, and you can even order up to 25 pieces of broasted chicken, which is the house specialty.

La Bella Italia $$
402 York Street
(717) 334-1978

La Bella Italia is conveniently located downtown at Fourth and York Streets, and the restaurant has recently expanded to accommodate its many eager patrons. The restaurant's new building, completed in late 2005, seats about 100. The restaurant is divided into small alcoves and decorated like an Italian villa, with rounded archways, exposed bricks and beams, trellises, and bottles filled with assorted foods showcased in many wall inserts and ledges.

Finding something on the menu to please each person in your group is a snap at this family-owned and -operated business, which is entirely nonsmoking and open daily. You can choose from New York–style pizza, stromboli, calzone, subs, and salads to full dinners featuring pasta, chicken, veal, seafood, and steak. Low-calorie dinners are available, as is a kids' menu, which offers a wide variety of dinner choices that are priced in the $4.00 to $6.00 range. Bottled beer is available to accompany your meal, and you can also pick up six-packs of beer to go here. Everything on the menu is available for takeout, and LaBella also makes 4-foot subs and party trays for takeout.

New Garden Chinese Restaurant $$
20–44 Natural Springs Road
(717) 337-9995

The New Garden is tucked into the strip mall in Gettysburg Marketplace, which also houses a Giant grocery store among its tenants. Although New Garden appears miniscule from the outside, once you're inside, its size seems just right. There are lots of tables for four and a buffet area tucked away in the back. If the New Garden is your first foray into sampling Chinese food, you'll appreciate the descriptions of the dishes given on the

extensive menu and that hot and spicy dishes are clearly labeled. If you're adventurous but a little timid, you can also ask for a hot and spicy dish to come mild. Dishes that represent Szechuan, Hunan, and Cantonese cuisine are available at this nonsmoking restaurant.

New Garden has steamed dishes for dieters and a children's menu with items priced at less than $3.00 on it. If your children don't want Chinese, fried chicken nuggets and fried scallops are available. Lunch specials, always a great bargain, are available until 4:00 P.M., and the restaurant is open for lunch and dinner seven days a week.

WEST OF LINCOLN SQUARE

Appalachian Brewing Co. (ABC) $$$
401 Buford Avenue
(717) 334-2200
www.abcbrew.com

This restaurant and brewery serves lunch and dinner Wednesday through Saturday. ABC is an extension of the brewpub's original location in Harrisburg, Pennsylvania's capital, and free brewery tours are conducted on Saturday at 1:00 P.M.

You'll find plenty of parking at this restaurant, which sits at the crest of Seminary Ridge beside General Lee's Headquarters Museum (see the Attractions chapter) and the Quality Inn Larson's (see the Hotel, Motels, and Resorts chapter). The menu includes sandwiches, brick-oven pizza, bolis, burgers, steaks, fish, and pasta dishes. You'll find traditional fare, such as the crab cakes and New York strip steak, and not-so-traditional fare, such as General Lee's Sausage and Apples and Venison Osso Bucco, venison simmered with carrots, onions, tomatoes, and white wine served atop garlic mashed potatoes. If you're not sure which ABC brew will complement your entree selection, the menu conveniently lists the brewmaster's suggestion. Wine and cocktails are available as well.

ABC offers call-ahead seating on Friday and Saturday nights. Call at least an hour before you plan to arrive.

Blue Parrot Bistro $$$
35 Chambersburg Street
(717) 337-3739

This is another restaurant that isn't nearly as small as it seems to be from the out-side. If you peek in the window, you see only the lounge, which consists of an impressive wooden bar and a few tables. The lounge and dining room each has a separate entrance, with the dining room's entrance a few steps farther westward down the street. The dining room is actu-ally behind and to the left of the lounge, and a pool table occupies the space between the lounge and dining room. The intimate booths in the bistro are veiled from the lounge area by plants and adorned with cloth tablecloths and nap-kins. But you don't have to get dressed up to enjoy the food here; blue jeans or black-tie attire is accepted equally.

The bistro fare is varied, with beef, veal, pork, chicken, seafood, pasta, and vegetar-ian dishes available. Some of the dishes are adventuresome, such as the filet mignon topped with Brie cheese and a mushroom demi-glace, while others are deliciously familiar, such as the angel-hair pasta topped with marinara sauce and Parmesan cheese or the beef lasagna. The artwork by local artists that you'll find on the walls is for sale, and the selection is always changing. Closed on Monday, the Blue Par-rot Bistro has been serving lunch and din-ner since 1988. It shares space with Lord Nelson's Gallery and the James Gettys Hotel in a circa-1804 building that's on the National Register of Historic Places.

Brother's Pizza $$
1685 Fairfield Road
(717) 339-0599, (717) 339-0598

Brother's Pizza is a few miles from town, right before the entrance for the Gettys-burg Campground. (See the Camp-grounds and RV Parks chapter.) It sits in a small strip mall, and unfortunately Brother's is the only business there at this time. But think of it this way—it has plenty of parking! Besides round, Sicilian, and gourmet pizza, you'll also find salads, subs, sandwiches, strombolis, and pasta dinners. This smoke-free restaurant is open daily, and its decor is typical of a pizzeria, with booths and hanging plants.

Appalachian Brewing Co. donates $1.00 from the price of each New York strip steak it sells to the Trade Towers Orphan Fund—www.ttof.org.

Cashtown Inn $$$$
1325 Old Route 30, Cashtown
(717) 334-9722, (800) 367-1797
www.cashtowninn.com

Located 8 miles west of town on Old Route 30, the restaurant at the Cashtown Inn is closed on Monday. The tavern serves lunch Tuesday through Saturday, and dinner is served Tuesday through Sunday in the restaurant. Here you'll find elegant fine dining in a historic building that was used as Confederate headquar-ters during the Battle of Gettysburg. The inn has been featured in the movie *Gettys-burg*, and it has also graced the cover of *Blue and Gray* magazine.

Reservations for dinner are strongly recommended, and you'll find a full range of meals featuring beef and seafood in inventive dishes, as well as some chicken, veal, and pasta dishes. All salad dressing, all sauces, and most desserts are made in-house, and produce and herbs from the inn's garden are featured in many dishes. Although you'll dine at a table dressed with a cloth tablecloth and cloth napkins, your dress may be casual if you choose.

Dunlap's Restaurant & Bakery $$
90 Buford Avenue
(717) 334-4816
www.dunlapsrestaurant.com

Dunlap's is locally owned by Barry and Ruth Dunlap, and their son is often the host who greets and seats you. Open seven days a week for casual family dining for breakfast, lunch, and dinner, Dunlap's sits across from the post office and has a large parking lot for your convenience. The restaurant is much larger than it appears from the street, with leather booths, a counter, and tables for seating. Be sure to check out their daily dinner specials, which are very reasonably priced. And definitely feast your eyes on the desserts in the case beside the register—they're all homemade. You'll want to either save room for these delights or order a slice to go.

Besides the dinner specials, you'll also find a salad and soup bar, sandwiches, burgers, and wraps for lighter fare. Entrees include beef, pork, poultry, vegetarian, pasta, and seafood selections. Their crab melt sandwich is a house specialty, as is their filet mignon, veal parmigiana, seafood platter, and crab cake dinner. On the weekends, Dunlap's has a breakfast buffet, and kids can always order from their own menu.

El Costeño $–$$
51 West Street
(717) 339-0029

This delightful Mexican restaurant opened in April 2005 within the small shopping center beside the Dollar General store, taking the spot that was formerly occupied by Lupita's Mexican restaurant. The space has been completely refurbished and now has a fiesta theme, complete with waitresses dressed in traditional Mexican attire. The dining area is not large, but tables are spaced well enough apart that somehow the area doesn't seem as small as it is. Owner Arturo Gyento often adds to the restaurant's festive mood by visiting the seating area and interacting with the costumers.

Ernie's Texas Lunch really is reminiscent of a 1930s diner—its grill is in the restaurant's front window.

The menu is extensive, with selections ranging from salads, burritos, enchiladas, fajitas, and tacos to lunch specials, full meals, kids' meals, and desserts. Descriptions are given for all items, and the menu notes when a particular dish is especially spicy, so you can be sure of what you're ordering. The prices are right, too, with seven lunch platters that are each less than $5.50. El Costeño is open daily for lunch and dinner, and you're welcome to bring your own beer to accompany your meal.

Ernie's Texas Lunch $
58 Chambersburg Street
(717) 334-1970

Ernie's has been a fixture on Chambersburg Street since 1921, when the original Ernie opened a sandwich shop across the street from the restaurant's current location. Ernie moved his business to its present site in 1934, and Ernie's grandson, also named Ernie, now runs the place.

This 1930s-style diner serves breakfast, lunch, and dinner Monday through Saturday. Ernie's has only eight booths, one of which is family-size, and a lunch counter, so seating is often at a premium here. But the tables turn over quickly; the service is fast and efficient, just as you would expect in a diner. Ernie's is famous for its Texas Hot Weiner, the same sandwich the first Ernie opened his shop with. It's a hot dog in its natural casing that's topped with mustard, chopped onion, and chili sauce. Other hot dog concoctions are available, as well as hamburgers, hot and cold sandwiches, deep-fried chicken and fish, homemade soups, and salads. Bring cash when you eat here—Ernie's doesn't accept credit cards or checks.

The Fairfield Inn 1757
Mansion House Restaurant $$$$
15 West Main Street, Fairfield
(717) 642-5410, (717) 334-8868
www.thefairfieldinn.com

When you enter the Mansion House Restaurant at the Fairfield Inn, you step back in time. The inn dates from 1757, when it was the home of the founder of the town of Fairfield, Squire John Miller, and you can actually dine in the room that served as the home's downstairs. The Fairfield Inn is also a bed-and-breakfast (see the Bed-and-Breakfasts and Guesthouses chapter), and its Squire Miller Tavern is one of the oldest taverns still operating in America, with a license that's dated 1786.

Besides providing lodging for many famous Americans, the Fairfield also served General Lee chicken and biscuits as the Confederates stopped throughout the town of Fairfield on their retreat from Gettysburg. You can order this dish just as General Lee did almost 150 years ago; the restaurant serves more than two tons of it annually. But the restaurant's signature dish is The St. Michael, jumbo lump crab cake, shrimp, breast of chicken, and scallops baked in a dill cream sauce. Other menu selections include grilled and roasted game, pasta, seafood, and steaks. Your meal will be served in one of several dining areas, with tables throughout dressed in linen tablecloths and napkins. (The ambience is elegant, but casual dress is perfectly okay.) If you're interested in knowing the historic significance of the room you're dining in, the inn has a great brochure that takes you on a history tour of the inn. The tour also shows the hidden attic room that served as a stop on the Underground Railroad.

The Mansion House Restaurant serves lunch and dinner Tuesday through Saturday and brunch on Sunday. Squire Miller Tavern is the restaurant's smoking section, with seating for 25 in addition to the seats at the bar itself. Fireplaces are featured throughout the house, and a patio garden filled with flowers and privacy hedges makes for perfect outdoor dining in nice weather. On the first and third Fridays of the summer months, the inn hosts a culinary concert series, where dinner is highlighted by live bands playing Celtic music and music of the 18th and 19th centuries.

Herr Tavern & Publick House $$$$
900 Chambersburg Road
(717) 334-4332, (800) 362-9849
www.herrtavern.com
Established in 1815, the Herr Tavern and Publick House offers gourmet dining in five dining areas that each seat 20 to 35 guests, and reservations are a must on the weekends. Located about 1.5 miles from Lincoln Square, the restaurant is in the same building as the bed-and-breakfast located here, and diners are invited to walk throughout the house to enjoy the decor. (See the Bed-and-Breakfasts and Guesthouses chapter for more on the lodging here.)

Herr's is open Monday through Saturday for lunch and dinner and Sunday for dinner. Eating here is an elegant affair, with fine-dining ambience. Lunchtime fare includes sandwiches, burgers, and light entrees, such as the Scampi Saute and the Raspberry Chicken Salad. Dinner selections are highlighted by the chef's weekly specials and seasonal entrees, such as Crab and Lobster Imperial and grilled beef tenderloin.

If linen tablecloths and candles are beyond your dining plans, The Livery tavern across the parking lot is available for lighter fare and casual dining. The Livery opens at 3:30 P.M. during the week and at noon on the weekends. The menu consists of sandwiches, burgers, steaks, chicken, and seafood. For your entertainment, The Livery has dartboards, foosball, touchscreen video games, and a black-light poolroom.

Hong Kong $$
28 Springs Avenue
(717) 338-9954, (717) 338-0948
Hong Kong entered the Gettysburg restaurant scene in 2005. It's located in the Gettysburg Shopping Center, which is 3 blocks up Chambersburg Street from Lincoln Square. The dining room is not large, but it is nicely decorated with tables and high-back chairs. Serving Szechuan,

Hunan, and Cantonese cuisine, Hong Kong is open seven days a week for lunch and dinner, and lunch specials are available until 3:00 P.M. The menu has dishes especially for dieters and a wide selection of lunch specials and combo platters. Don't forget to order your fortune cookie!

Mamma Ventura's Restaurant $$$
13 Chambersburg Street
(717) 334-5548

This Italian restaurant offers lots of pasta dishes and dishes featuring poultry, veal, and seafood. But beef eaters be warned—beef dishes are not on the menu. The front part of Mamma's has booths and tables, and there's a cozy bar at the back of the room. To the left of the bar are many more seats that travel down a long hallway, so don't assume that there aren't any seats if the front part of the restaurant is full. Mamma's serves lunch and dinner Monday through Saturday and is closed on Sunday.

Ragged Edge Coffeehouse
& Jasper's Juice Works $
110 Chambersburg Street
(717) 334-4464
www.raggededgecoffeehs.com

The apartment building next door to Ragged Edge had a fire in January 2003, and the coffee shop sustained smoke, water, and fire damage. The decision was made to completely renovate, and the Ragged Edge reopened in December 2004 with a new layout, new lighting, and new floors. The second floor now has a stage, which is used for live performances. Open seven days a week from morning to late evening, Ragged Edge offers breakfast, sandwiches, and salads in addition to Jasper's juices, smoothies, and supplement drinks. You'll also find hot and cold Ragged Edge specialty drinks, such as Italian or French sodas and mochas, and the smell of delicious baked goods fills the air.

You'll find lots of room to spread out here. Besides the counter where you order, the downstairs has two large rooms, and the room in the back has a computer available for your convenience. Up the stairs you'll find a nice-size room with a stage and seating, and another room has groups of tables comfortably arranged. When the weather is warm, seating is also available outside in the back of the coffehouse.

GETTYSBURG NATIONAL MILITARY PARK (GNMP)

Gettysburg National Military Park measures 6 miles by 7 miles, and its 1,400 monuments and markers and 400 artillery pieces along 35 miles of scenic avenues pay homage to the 51,000 men who became casualties upon this battlefield in July 1863. A $95 million project managed by the nonprofit Gettysburg National Battlefield Museum Foundation is under way to restore the battlefield to its 1863 appearance, wiping out landscape changes that have occurred between then and now. Controversy swirls around the benefit of this project, which could not move forward until it had raised $75 million of its $95 million goal, an amount that was raised about 10 years after the initial proposal of the project. Groundbreaking for a new visitor center began on June 2, 2005, and the foundation hopes to have the new facilities open to the public by early 2008. For now, the visitor center is located at 97 Taneytown Road (717–334–1124; www.nps.gov/gett/home.htm).

When complete, the refurbished park will have a 139,000-square-foot visitor center containing an artifact museum and a cyclorama gallery in buildings near the intersection of Hunt Avenue and Baltimore Pike, about 2/3 of a mile southeast of the existing visitor center and Cyclorama building. The new museum and visitor center will be designed as a Civil War–era Pennsylvania farmstead, and it will sit on land that saw no major fighting in the battle. The center will also include two film theaters, a book and museum store, a 250-seat period-themed snack bar, and triple the parking capacity at the current center. Once the new center is open, the Gettysburg National Battlefield Museum Foundation, currently based in Washington, D.C., will move to Gettysburg and operate it for 20 years; after that time the buildings and land will be donated by the foundation to the federal government.

The current visitor center has an electric map presentation and is the site of the Gettysburg Museum of the Civil War, which holds one of the largest collections of Civil War artifacts in the world. It also contains a large bookstore that has books on many aspects of the war as well as artwork, memorabilia, and gifts associated with the Civil War. Tickets to Eisenhower National Historic Site are sold at the center, which is also where the tours depart from. The visitor center is open daily from 8:00 A.M. to 5:00 P.M., and the park is open from 6:00 A.M. to 10:00 P.M. April through October and to 7:00 P.M. November through March. The park also has an amphitheater located off West Confederate Avenue near the Seminary Ridge area, where each evening a park ranger gives a presentation on a different Civil War subject that usually lasts about 45 minutes. You can visit the battlefield on foot, on bicycle, on horseback, in your car, or by bus. It's up to you whether you want to explore on your own or

Start your exploration of the battlefield by attending either the electric map program at the visitor center or the multimedia presentation at the Gettysburg Battle Theatre (or both). These programs give an essential historical and geographical orientation to the park.

whether you'd like someone to help interpret the events of July 1863.

**Gettysburg National Battlefield
Museum Foundation**
P.O. Box 4224
Gettysburg, PA 17325-4224
(866) 889-1243
www.gettysburgfoundation.org
This nonprofit educational organization
works with Gettysburg National Military
Park to restore, preserve, and enhance the
consecrated ground of the Gettysburg
battlefield. The foundation, along with
park officials, is the driving force behind
the current changes being made to the
battlefield, including the relocation of the
visitor center and the cyclorama painting.

**Friends of the National Parks
at Gettysburg (FNPG)**
(717) 334-0772
www.friendsofgettysburg.org
The mission of the Friends of the National
Parks at Gettysburg is to honor, support,
protect, and enhance the resources associated with the National Parks at Gettysburg, the Battle of Gettysburg, and the
Eisenhower National Historic Site. The
Friends was started in 1989 by a small
group of concerned citizens and today
has grown to include close to 25,000
members and supporters throughout the
world. One of its prominent endeavors is
the Rupp House History Center located on
Baltimore Street. (See the Attractions
chapter.)

---

i *With 1,400 monuments and markers, the
Gettysburg National Military Park has
the largest collection of outdoor sculpture in the country. Monuments and cannons, which number 400, were placed
to mark positions of regiments and to
honor the sacrifices made by the men
who fought here. The park requests that
you not sit, stand, climb, or hang on any
sculptures.*

TOURING GETTYSBURG NATIONAL MILITARY PARK

Auto Tours

**Auto Tour Using GNMP Official Map
and Guide Brochure**
GNMP Visitor Center
97 Taneytown Road
(717) 334-1124
www.nps.gov/gett/home.htm
This free brochure is available at the information desks within the visitor center. It
follows the three days of the battle in
chronological order on an 18-mile tour
that has 16 stops. A map guides you along
the way, and brief descriptions of the
action that occurred at each stop are
included.

Auto Tour Using Audio Cassettes or CDs
GNMP Visitor Center Bookstore
97 Taneytown Road
(717) 334-1124
www.nps.gov/gett/home.htm
The bookstore in the visitor center sells
audio tapes that you use in your own car
to tour the battlefield. Tours vary from
two to four hours in length, and some
include maps and photos. Some are very
detail oriented, and some are dramatized
with sound effects. The top-selling audio
tour is the *Gettysburg Field Guide,* narrated by Wayne Motts. Wayne is a historian at the Adams County Historical
Society who served as a Licensed Battlefield Guide. His field guide has historic
photos and detailed battle maps along
with the audio tour. Wayne also offers the
Gettysburg Expedition Guide, which has all
that the field guide offers and a CD-ROM
for home use.

**Auto Tour with a Licensed
Battlefield Guide**
GNMP Visitor Center
97 Taneytown Road
(717) 334-1124
www.nps.gov/gett/home.htm
Battlefield guides are tested and licensed

by the National Park Service, and they must meet park service standards for accurately interpreting the Battle of Gettysburg and the American Civil War. They will accompany you in your car for personalized two-hour tours on a first-come, first-served basis beginning at 8:00 A.M. at the visitor center. Operating since 1915, this is the nation's oldest professional guide service. Tours are customized to your need and level of knowledge; cost is $40 for up to six people per vehicle.

The bookstore at the GNMP visitor center has a wide variety of audiocassettes and CDs for sale that you use to tour the battlefield in your own car. Many stores throughout town also carry these audio tours—usually at a higher price than the exact same thing sold at the visitor center.

Bike Tours

GettysBike Tours
240 Steinwehr Avenue
(behind Flex & Flannigan's)
(717) 752-7752
www.gettysbike.com

This outfit began operations in the summer of 2005, and it can team you up with a Licensed Battlefield Guide who specializes in bike tours of the park. You'll travel on two wheels to see Little Round Top, Devil's Den, The Peach Orchard, The Angle, and the High Water Mark. Gettys-Bike arranges everything for you, including, of course, the bikes. The tours last approximately 2.5 hours and cover 8 miles of the park. If you want you can rent the bikes for additional time after the tour for reduced rates and explore the park on your own. All rentals include a helmet, and all bikes are equipped with bottle racks to carry a drink. Escorted trips to the highlights of the battlefield that are led by one of the GettysBike employees are also available. Or you can simply rent a bike from them and explore on your own. Children 4 feet 6 inches or taller who are competent on a bike may ride their own bike, and toddlers and small children may accompany a parent or guardian on a trailer carrier or trailer tandem (child trailers that attach to an adult bike). Gettys-Bike is open Wednesday through Sunday beginning at 8:00 A.M. and on Monday and Tuesday by reservation only. The cost to rent a mountain bike is $7.00 per hour or $30.00 per day for an adult and $5.00 an hour or $25.00 a day for a child. A tour with a Licensed Battlefield Guide is $35.00 for an adult and $25.00 for a child, and reservations are requested.

Gettysburg Bicycle & Fitness
307 York Street
(717) 334-7791
www.gettysburgbicycle.com

At Gettysburg Bicycle & Fitness, you can rent a bike and explore the battlefield on your own. The outfit has been in business since 1990, and with advance notice they can arrange a tour of the battlefield with a licensed guide on a case-by-case basis. Cost to rent two wheels is $7.00 per hour or $25.00 for the entire day. All rentals include helmets, locks, rear racks, and bungie cords. On busy weekends and holidays, every bike in their large inventory is usually rented, so you should reserve your bike in advance if possible. Serious cyclists gather at this location every Wednesday at 6:00 P.M. for a two-hour ride, and Gettysburg Bicycle & Fitness also sponsors bike races around the area. The shop is open every day but Sunday, and parking is available at the rear of the building.

Bus Tours

Gettysburg Tours
Gettysburg Tour Center
778 Baltimore Street
(717) 334-6296
www.gettysburgbattlefieldtours.com

Gettysburg Tours offers a two-hour battle-field bus tour, with your choice of either a dramatized stereo tour aboard a double-decker bus for $19.95 per adult and $12.35 per child or a Licensed-Battlefield-Guide-led tour aboard an air-conditioned motor coach for $21.95 per adult and $14.90 per child. The main office for Gettysburg Tours is listed above, but you'll find satel-lite offices throughout town. The business has been operating year-round since the 1960s, and tours begin throughout the day. If you plan on visiting other attrac-tions in addition to the battlefield, the package plans offered here are a great bargain. You get unlimited use of the Get-tysburg Town Trolley and, depending on which plan you choose, admission to two, four, or all of the following seven attrac-tions: the Hall of Presidents, the Soldier's National Museum, the Jennie Wade House Museum, the Lincoln Train Museum, the Gettysburg Battle Theatre, the American Civil War Museum, and the Lincoln Room Museum.

Historic Tours
55 Steinwehr Avenue
(717) 334-8000
If you want to tour the battlefield in a bit of history, Historic Tours is the place for you. Tours are given in a 1933 modi-fied school bus and two modernized 12-passenger 1936 and 1937 Yellowstone buses. The Model 706 Yellowstone buses were developed specifically for sightseeing within the western national parks, and the Yellowstone buses were used in Yellow-stone National Park from 1936 to the mid-1960s.

As you tour in style, an audio CD tells the story of the entire three days of the battle as you travel the battlefield. The driver has the ability to stop the CD and start it again, and both of the drivers/tour guides are extremely knowledgeable about the battle. The 2.5-hour tour runs twice a day Monday through Saturday and once on Sunday. Advance reservations are encouraged but not required. Cost is $16.95 for adults and $11.00 for children

age 7 to 11; children age 6 and younger ride for free with a paying adult.

Horseback Tours

Hickory Hollow Farms
219 Crooked Creek Road
(717) 334-0349
www.hickoryhollowfarm.com
Hickory Hollow Farms offers one-hour scenic rides on the battlefield for $40 an hour, two- to four-hour scenic rides on the battlefield for $35 an hour, or a two- to six-hour historic ride on the battlefield with a Licensed Battlefield Guide for $50 an hour. The scenic rides are just that—scenic; they're led by wranglers, not bat-tlefield guides, and they don't provide a history of the battle. Tours are kept to small groups of six to seven riders, and children must be eight years old to ride. Riders have a 250-pound weight limit, and helmets must be worn by children younger than age 16. When calling, ask for Pam or Jackie. Riding lessons are also available here, and you can board your own horse if you'd like (see the Recreation chapter). Hickory Hollow Farms is open seven days a week.

National Riding Stables
Artillery Ridge Campground
610 Taneytown Road
(717) 334-1288
(877) 335-5596 (toll-free)
www.artilleryridge.com
On the "Ride into History" tour offered here, you can relive the Gettysburg battle while on horseback. A two-hour ride reviews the entire three-day battle, and you ride across the sites involved on the second and third days of the battle. A CD by a Licensed Battlefield Guide pipes the history in through headsets that you wear. You can either rent one of their horses or bring your own; Artillery Ridge Camp-ground offers box stalls and corrals. The cost to rent a horse is around $60 per person, and some restrictions apply. Rid-ers must be at least eight years old, no

Cyclorama Center

At the time this book is published, the Cyclorama Center will no longer be open to the public. The distinctive round building that housed the "Battle of Gettysburg" cyclorama was closed in November 2005 to complete the removal and restoration of the painting in order to ready it for its new home—the visitor center off Hunt Avenue that is scheduled to open in 2008.

The "Battle of Gettysburg" is a 360-degree circular oil-on-canvas painting that depicts Pickett's Charge, the famous charge of 12,000 Confederates who were attempting to overtake the Union troops on Cemetery Ridge on the final day of the battle. Cycloramas were very popular in the late 1800s; they have a three-dimensional effect that makes the viewer feel as if he is in the center of the scene depicted on the canvas.

The new visitor center will display the 1884 painting more effectively in a safer environment for the canvas. There will also be an accompanying sound and light program that will re-create the scenes of the battle and highlight points of interest on the painting. The panorama is 359 long, 27 feet high, and weighs an estimated 3 tons. Once the new center is open, the round building that held the cyclorama since 1962 is scheduled to be demolished, part of the restoration project that intends to return the battlefield to its 1863 appearance, a project that not everyone in town agrees with.

The building was built by architect Richard Neutra in 1961, and it has been said that this was Neutra's greatest public commission and the finest example of his work east of the Mississippi. In September 1998 the Cyclorama Center was determined to be eligible for the National Register of Historic Places, and in December 1999 the Association of Architectural Historians nominated the building as a National Historic Landmark—the highest honor a building can receive. Neither action was able to save the building, and when the new visitor center opens, the round building will be demolished—and a piece of history will be gone forever.

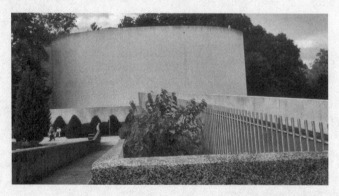

The Cyclorama Center housed the circular "Battle of Gettysburg" painting from 1962 to 2005; the building is scheduled to be torn down as part of a battlefield restoration project. KATE HERTZOG

more than one rider is allowed on the horse, and a weight limit of 240 pounds applies to riders. Also, riders age 15 and younger must be accompanied by an adult, and riders younger than age 18 must have a parent or guardian sign a waiver in order to ride. Tours are offered several times a day seven days a week. Reservations are required, and they usually need to be made well in advance if you want a weekend ride on this popular tour.

Walking Tours

Park Rangers
GNMP Visitor Center
97 Taneytown Road
(717) 334-1124
www.nps.gov/gett/home.htm
Park rangers offer many free guided walks and tours of the battlefield during the summer. Programs range from about half an hour to three hours. You can get a guided tour of the National Cemetery, explore the importance of Little Round Top in the battle, accompany a ranger on a hike of the battlefield, or enjoy a myriad of other activities. For a full schedule of all the free programs offered, check at the information desk at the visitor center or visit the Web site. There are also programs specifically tailored for children; see the Kidstuff chapter for details.

MILITARY MEMORABILIA SHOPS

South of Lincoln Square

Arsenal of the Alleghenys
141 Steinwehr Avenue
(717) 334-1122
www.arsenalofthealleghenys.com
Arsenal of the Alleghenys owners Jay and Melody Thomas travel to more than 20 Civil War and antiques shows each year to find

unique artifacts to sell out of their store. Jay focuses on artifacts from the Civil War and the Indian War period while Melody specializes in Victorian-era items. All items they offer are guaranteed to be authentic relics that are considered investment-grade quality. Military memorabilia might include weapons, clothing, journals, corps badges, and medical items, and you can usually also find some Indian-related memorabilia and antique silver, glassware, and porcelain from the Victorian era. The shop is open every day but Monday, and it's located at the southern end of Steinwehr Avenue.

Dirty Billy's Hats
20 Baltimore Street
(717) 334-3200
www.dirtybillyshats.com
Dirty Billy's motto is "Historical Artwork You Can Wear," and this shop is full of hats, hats, and more hats. You'll find hats representing the ranks of the North and South as well as ladies' bonnets, straw hats, and tall top hats such as Lincoln wore. The hats are precise replicas that Billy creates from examining pictures and artifacts. Billy's attention to authentic details has resulted in his hats being worn by Martin Sheen and Sam Elliott in *Gettysburg*, Patrick Swayze in *North and South*, and Tom Berenger in *Rough Riders*. Dirty Billy's is open on Friday, Saturday, and Sunday and by appointment the rest of the week

Gettysburg Gift Center
297 Steinwehr Avenue
(717) 334-6245, (800) 887-7775
www.e-gettysburg.cc
Although it's located in the lobby of the American Civil War Museum (see the Attractions chapter), this store, with more than 3,000 square feet of space, is anything but tiny. It has a complete selection of gifts and souvenirs, including books, hats, flags, shirts, and limited-edition art. On display are miniature statues by Chilmark and George Fund, reproductions of handpainted photographs of Civil War

generals, White House china, numerous Mort Kunstler items, and many more interesting collectibles. The back of the store is where you'll find souvenir-type items, the middle of the store has military memorabilia, and a section at the front of the gift center has a nice selection of Americana gifts. On my last visit, I was especially intrigued by the earrings that were made from hair—and you could have a set made out of your own hair if you'd like! The Gettysburg Gift Center is open daily.

Gettysburg Miniature Soldiers
200 Steinwehr Avenue
(717) 338-1800

This store doesn't just appear small from the outside—it is small. But how big does a store that carries historical miniatures and toy soldiers need to be? This one-room store manages to stock thousands of metal and plastic soldiers, and that's all you'll find here. Open daily, this tiny gem shares a building with the Gettysburg Tour Center; the entrance is around the corner on the right when you're facing the building.

Gettysburg Quartermaster
419 Baltimore Street
(717) 334-8838
www.farnsworthhouseinn.com/
quartermaster.html

Located on the Farnsworth House Complex, the Gettysburg Quartermaster has thousands of items for the Civil War collector. Here you'll find fine original military relics from the Revolutionary War to the war in Vietnam, with an emphasis on Civil War and WWII items. Cases of museum-style shelves are filled with rare artifacts, photographs, and military correspondence, and collectors come here to buy, sell, trade, and broker consignments. Browsers who wish to peruse the goods will also find much to interest them. Among the many great finds here are a McClellan saddle and military memorabilia posters. You'll also be surrounded by rack upon rack of WWII fatigues, helmets, uniform badges and buttons, as well as bayo-

nets and a variety of guns on display. The Gettysburg Quartermaster has been in business since 1972, and it's open on Monday, Thursday, and Saturday afternoons.

Horse Soldier
Old Gettysburg Village
777 Baltimore Street
(717) 334-0347
www.HorseSoldier.com

If you love admiring military goods but dislike the cramped spaces that often accompany such excursions, plan a visit to the Horse Soldier. Since the Small family opened their business in 1971, it has grown, and grown, and grown . . . and grown. It now fills eight spacious rooms within its location in Old Gettysburg Village. This is the largest store featuring military antiques and memorabilia in Gettysburg, and you can find items dating from the Revolutionary War to WWI, with an emphasis on Civil War items. Artillery, currency, bottles, guns, swords, soldiers' letters, documents, autographs, prints, musical instruments, medical instruments, 19th-century civilian and military photographs, and a myriad of other intriguing items are housed here. Military-related books (old and new), music, and videos are also available.

Be sure not to miss the two cases filled with Gettysburg-related items. The Horse Soldier displays items from the John Plank Geiselman Museum Collection, the last major grouping of Gettysburg artifacts assembled and documented by a local resident. In many instances, Geiselman noted not only the source of the Gettysburg relic and the date of its recovery but also the part of the battlefield it came from. All items at the Horse Soldier are guaranteed to be authentic, and the staff also conducts appraisal and soldier research services. The store is open daily except on Wednesday. Adjacent to the Horse Soldier on the Baltimore Street entrance is Hallowed Ground, also owned by the Small family, where you can get Gettysburg T-shirts and Horse Soldier hats.

The Regimental Quartermaster
49 Steinwehr Avenue
(717) 338-1864
www.regtqm.com
The Regimental Quartermaster makes the most of its limited space. In the front of the store you'll find Civil War reproductions, muskets, swords, leather goods, equipment, accessories, books, and manuals. Toward the rear of the store are period civilian wear and military uniforms, including one of the largest collections of shoes from the era. The Jeweler's Daughter (see the Shopping chapter) is located in the middle of the store. Reenactors can find everything they need in this one spot to completely outfit themselves appropriately.

Stoneham's Armory
5 Steinwehr Avenue
(717) 337-2347
www.tbhabitat.com
Stoneham's fills the ground floor of its early 20th-century Prairie-style brick building with a wide assortment of historically authentic reproduction swords, revolvers, muskets, and memorabilia from the Civil War through the WWII time frame. Pewterware, copperware, tinware, books, CDs and DVDs, flags, and Civil War chess sets complete the upscale ambience. Up the stairs are five more rooms where you'll find tea sets, Irish gifts, period candles, sculptures, and clocks. Stoneham's and the two shops beside it, Camelot and Habitat, are owned by the same couple, and their good taste is evident throughout the three shops.

Tarbox Toy Soldiers
Arbor House
76 Steinwehr Avenue
(717) 338-1865
This miniature "wax museum" of historical figures includes Civil War military figures and dioramas, and owner Charlie Tarbox purchases some of the collectibles from Russian miniature dealer Sergei Ilyashenko, of the company Lead Army. Charlie is as much a reason to visit as his beautiful pieces of art. He's known as Gettysburg's

resident historian, and his knowledge of the Civil War and Gettysburg is truly remarkable. Charlie taught at Gettysburg College for many years, and he currently gives historical presentations at the Patriot Point Theatre (see The Arts chapter) and at the Battlefield Bed & Breakfast Inn, which he owns with his wife, Florence.

The Union Drummer Boy
13 Baltimore Street
(717) 334-2350
www.uniondb.com
The Union Drummer Boy shows off its collection of authentic Civil War artifacts in glass cases within this spacious shop. Every item within the place is guaranteed to be authentic, and the owners attend more than 20 Civil War and military shows yearly throughout the country, where they buy and sell Civil War artifacts. Among the treasures are muskets, revolvers, carbines, uniforms, canteens, photos, leather goods, letters, artillery shells, documents, flags, autographs, swords, and relics. You can also have your Civil War goods appraised here. The Union Drummer Boy is open daily.

East of Lincoln Square

Fields of Glory
55 York Street
(717) 337-2837
www.fieldsofglory.com
Fields of Glory is filled to the brim with Civil War relics. As you enter, it's hard to decide whether to start at the original Civil War muskets and swords hanging along the left wall or at the glass cases full of memorabilia that line the wall on the right. There's also a room to the left and a room in the back, both filled with authentic Civil War–era items. You'll find tintype photographs, buttons, medical supplies, soldier accessories, uniforms, drums . . . the list never seems to end. Fields of Glory is open seven days a week.

GETTYSBURG ANNIVERSARY CIVIL WAR BATTLE REENACTMENT

Held on the weekend closest to the Fourth of July, this annual three-day event features battle reenactments, sutlers, entertainment, special guests, living-history events, and educational demonstrations. The reenactment takes place in conjunction with Gettysburg Civil War Heritage Days, more than a week of events happening throughout town. (For more on Heritage Days, see the Annual Events and Festivals chapter.) This is definitely the event of the year for area tourism and those who want to commemorate the Battle of Gettysburg. Reenactments that take place on five-year anniversaries of the battle usually draw 15,000 to 20,000 reenactors, while the in-between years usually draw 3,000 reenactors and 25,000 to 30,000 visitors. In 2003 the reenactment to commemorate the 140th anniversary of the battle drew 60,000 attendees. Call (717) 338-1525 or visit www.gettysburgreenactment.com for updates about the current year's reenactment.

The first thing you need to know about the reenactment is that it's not held on the hallowed ground of Gettysburg National Military Park, where the actual Battle of Gettysburg unfolded. Instead, it's held at a site near the town, usually at an area farm. Every yearly event is unique, but you can expect to see battle reenactments and mortar fire competitions each day, and every reenactment culminates in the battle of Pickett's Charge. Throughout the three days there are also living-history demonstrations, and visitors are welcome to tour the military camps and meet the reenactors. Sutlers showcase their military goods to the reenactors, just as they did when they followed the soldiers during the war, and visitors can find food, beverage, and souvenir stands.

Two types of tickets are available to visitors. A general admission ticket admits you into the reenactment site and includes

Each weekend from April through October, reenactors camp within Gettysburg National Military Park at Spangler's Spring, Pitzer Woods, and the Pennsylvania Monument. Anyone is welcome to stop by and see what camp life was like for soldiers at Gettysburg. For more information, contact Gettysburg National Military Park at (717) 334-1124, ext. 446.

all activities and demonstrations. You may bring lawn chairs or blankets and view the reenactments from the grounds, with spaces on a first-come, first-served basis. A grandstand ticket, which is bought in addition to the general admission ticket, includes admission to grandstand seating on bleachers that are located to give the best view of field events and demonstrations. Grandstand seating is limited, and your ticket guarantees you a seat in the grandstand, not a particular seat.

Tickets may be purchased for one, two, or all three days of the event, and you can buy them in advance or at the gate on the day you wish to attend. Tickets are nonrefundable and cost less if you purchase them in advance. Advance tickets are sold by phone, via the Web site, and at many area stores. The reenactment is subject to weather conditions, and although it's rare for the event to be rescheduled, it has happened—in 2003 it was moved to August because the farmland was too wet from a particularly soggy spring. Grandstand seating usually sells out prior to the event, and grandstand seats cannot be ordered without also purchasing general admission tickets. In 2005 advance ticket prices were $20 for one day, $35 for two days, and $48 for three days for those age 13 and older, and $10 for one day, $18 for two days, and $24 for three days for those age 6 through 12. Children younger than age six are admitted to the event free of charge, but a grandstand seating ticket must be purchased if they're going to sit in the grandstand. At the 2005 event grandstand seating was $8.00 per day for all ages. Tickets purchased at the gate are higher, but not exorbitantly—my ticket in 2005 was $25 at the gate when I went on the third day to see the reenactment of Pickett's Charge.

Most people don't realize that the reenactors also have to pay to partake in the event. They pay a registration fee rather than having to buy a ticket. The registration fees for the 2006 event are $5.00 for reenactors who register before February 28, $10.00 for those who register before April 15, $15.00 for those who register before June 1, and $20.00 for reenactors who register later than June 1.

Attending a battle reenactment is an exciting way to make history come to life. All the descriptions in the world don't compare to actually witnessing the smoke from the guns or hearing the Rebel Cry as Pickett's Charge begins. It's also enlightening to talk to the reenactors, who often are walking historians about their units.

REENACTORS

Contributing a large part to the Gettysburg experience are the reenactors you see around town, who bring the Civil War and the Battle of Gettysburg to life through their hobby. Most casual observers don't see much beyond someone dressed in military or period-style clothing, but reenactor dress varies from beginners who may not realize their uniform was made in Pakistan to those who are wearing an outfit that is authentic down to the number of threads used and the thread's country of origin. Although

If you're a fresh fish (new recruit) and you don't want to commit a farby—a Civil War–reenactment term for anything not typical of the period—visit www.cwreenactors.com for lots of information on how to get started in the hobby.

the level of authenticity varies, most reenactors agree that all you really need to enjoy the hobby is a love of the Civil War era. But becoming a reenactor is not quite as simple as that.

Reenactors usually do a great deal of research to ensure they make the most realistic impression they can. Civilians don't just put on a period-style dress; they also research the correct hair style, accoutrements, and jewelry being worn at the time. Most military reenactor groups are set up to parallel military life, with new recruits entering as privates and working their way up the ranks, with promotions based on how authentic their portrayals are. Looking the part doesn't come cheap—a basic Union soldier outfit with rifle, tent, clothes, belt, and ammo pouch can easily run $1,200 to $1,500.

Groups dedicated to Civil War reenacting have members throughout the states and even in some foreign countries. Often the love of reenacting is passed down from generation to generation, and many hobbyists love that reenacting is something the entire family can enjoy together.

Civil War Clothing and Accessories

Abraham's Lady
25 Steinwehr Avenue
(717) 338-1798
www.abrahamslady.com
Owner Donna Abraham has been making Civil War–era clothing and accessories for ladies since 1991, and she's especially known for making beautiful Garibaldi red shirts. Everything Donna makes is authentic to the Civil War period. You'll find skirts and dresses, underclothes, jewelry, accessories, and shoes—everything needed to outfit you completely for your trip back in time. Lots of period-authentic patterns for women, men, and children are also available for those who prefer to make their own clothes.

A Civil Affair
100 Baltimore Street
(717) 338-1565
www.acivilaffair.com

From ball gowns to camp clothing and clothes for every occasion in between, A Civil Affair has what you need to be an authentically dressed Civil War–era lady. Their garments are produced on the premises, or you can choose from their patterns and make your own clothes. And you can complete your outfit with all the appropriate accessories, including period wigs and hairpieces, hats and hat pins, period jewelry, Victorian fans, and lots more. While you're picking out your outfit, you can shop for Victorian goods at Battlefield Baskets & Gifts, also at the same location (see the Fine Gifts and Home Accents section of the Shopping chapter). A Civil Affair is open every day but Tuesday.

Beth's Place
2215B Fairfield Road
(717) 337-3172

Beth is considered by many reenactors and sutlers to be the premier maker of ladies' reenactment clothing in Gettysburg, and more than one person told me they can always spot Beth's exquisite dresses at an event. Her small shop is located on the left side of the building that houses Needle & Thread Fabrics (see separate entry within this chapter); there's no sign but it's easy to find. Beth stocks a few ready-made items, such as undergarments and shoes, and all the accessories a proper lady of the time could want are here also. Cases hold antique original jewelry while their tops are adorned with reproduction jewelry, and there's also a nice selection of redware pottery on display. Beth's Place is open on Friday and Saturday only, and it's reached by traveling Route 116 West (Fairfield Road) for about 3.5 miles from the square. Turn in at the parking lot for Needle & Thread Fabrics.

Gettysburg Sutler
1180 Hanover Road
(717) 337-9669
www.gettysburgsutler.com

The Gettysburg Sutler has appropriate Civil War–period clothing for civilian as well as military reenactors, male and female, adult and child. A room in the front of the shop is filled with ladies' clothing and accessories, including jewelry, bonnets, and patterns for those who like to make their own clothes. The main room contains uniforms for officers and enlisted men, as well as clothing for civilian men and boys. You'll also find equipment and accessories, including weapons, canteens, medical supplies, and much more. The Gettysburg Sutler is located just west of the Hanover Road interchange with U.S. Route 15, and the store is open daily.

Highland Rose Civil War Sutlery
Old Gettysburg Village
777 Baltimore Street
(717) 339-0660

Open mainly on the weekends, this compact store offers attire for those who want to dress as one did during the Civil War. You'll find garments on the rack to choose from, which can be altered, or you can have an outfit custom designed. Liz, the owner, also does beautiful work on period wedding gowns, with lots of hand beading being her forte. The shop is located in the courtyard of Old Gettysburg Village.

Sutlers, civilians licensed by the government to follow the armies in wagons and sell luxury goods to the soldiers, were more prevalent among Union than Confederate troops. Today many stores within Gettysburg still call themselves sutlers; unlike their historical ancestors, they carry goods for reenactors from both sides of the war.

Lady Beneath the Veil and Victorian Costume Rentals
141 Steinwehr Avenue (second floor)
(717) 357-0518

Owner Maggie Abbott Ward opened Lady Beneath the Veil in November 2005, and her enterprise shares the upstairs space at 141 Steinwehr Avenue with Somewhere in Time, a similar shop. (See the separate listing on Somewhere in Time later in this section.) The first floor of the building is occupied by Arsenal of the Alleghenys, a military memorabilia shop. (See the Military Memorabilia Shops section of this chapter for more on Arsenal of the Alleghenys.)

Lady Beneath the Veil has two focuses. First is custom-made historical clothing from the mid-1800s, especially wedding and formal attire. The second is renting Union and Confederate military clothing and Civil War–era civilian clothing for men. With more than 20 years of historical costuming experience, Maggie infuses a lot of knowledge into her clothing creations and rentals, and her respect for historical accuracy shows in her clothes. The shop consists of two rooms, one where Maggie works and one where she displays her various outfits. The store is open every day except Wednesday.

Memories Past Historical Outfitters & the Captain's Lady
230 Steinwehr Avenue
(717) 334-9712, (717) 334-7482
(800) 438-8971
www.memoriespast.net

Although not actually connected, these two stores share an address and they're run by the same group of people. Memories Past is geared toward male reenactors while the Captain's Lady carries fashions for women reenactors. The Captain's Lady actually fronts on Taneytown Road, but you want to park on Steinwehr Avenue or in the small parking lot between the two stores that's behind Memories Past. The three owners are reenactors themselves, as are many of the staff, so it's no surprise that both stores carry a full array of clothing and accoutrements that should satisfy the needs of any Civil War living-history reenactor. Dresses at the Captain's Lady vary from day dresses to fancy gowns, with an entire room set aside to display the wide variety of "underthings" the store carries. Memories Past also displays its goods in a spacious setting, and it sells Civil War weapons as well as clothes. Both stores are closed on Tuesday and Wednesday.

Mrs. Mellie's Mercantile
45 Steinwehr Avenue
(717) 334-7470
www.geocities.com/mrs_mellies

This small shop specializes in creating handmade Civil War-era civilian clothing for men, women, and children. Opened in April 2005, Mrs. Mellie's is owned by Terry and Melanie Whittington, who create the clothing themselves, which keeps the cost low. Both have been reenactors since 1995 and sutlers since 2000, so they know what 19th-century fashion should look like. Mrs. Mellie's has clothes for all levels of reenactors, from beginners to experts. And if you're a beginner and you don't want to invest too much into your new hobby right away, used clothing is also for sale.

Needle & Thread Fabrics
2215 Fairfield Road
(717)334-4011

Sewers and quilters will be in heaven at this shop, which fills its large building with bolt after bolt of Civil War–style patterns and fabrics. Everything you need to complete your outfit also can be found here, as well as notions, quilting and sewing supplies, smocking supplies, foam rubber, cross-stitch, and much, much more. Needle & Thread also stocks everything needed to make curtains, quilts, tablecloths, place mats, and more. With all that's within this store, your only limit is your own imagination. Needle & Thread is about 3.5 miles west of the square right along Route 116; the shop is closed on Tuesday and Sunday.

CLOSE-UP

Zouave Units in the Civil War

The Zouave uniform, which consists of baggy trousers, a braided jacket, and a tasseled fez, is modeled on the uniform worn by French colonial troops. Elmer Ellsworth organized the first American Zouave unit, the Chicago Zouaves, and he drilled them in tactics adopted from French manuals. Ellsworth and 50 of his best Chicago Zouaves toured the country in 1860 on a 6-week, 20-city tour to challenge other state militias in a drill competition. The unit's precise drills not only won them the competition hands down but also awed thousands of spectators. Before long, dozens of new Zouave companies were formed throughout the country.

The fighting skills, precise maneuvers, and colorful Zouave uniforms of the 5th New York Volunteer Infantry, known as Duryee's Zouaves, made them one of the most renowned regiments of the Civil War. General George Sykes was quoted as saying, "I doubt whether it had an equal, and certainly no superior among all the regiments of the Army of the Potomac."

In the 1970s several Civil War reenactors decided to organize a living-history unit that would pay homage to the Zouave units of the Civil War. Company A, 5th New York Volunteer Infantry, is cur-

Tim Sheads, who began reenacting at the age of four, displays his Zouave uniform outside his S&S Sutler shop on Buford Avenue.
KATE HERTZOG

rently active in living-history programs, encampments, and battle reenactments. Members dress in full Zouave regalia and pride themselves on their military skills.

Octagon Ladies' Repository
330 Baltimore Street
(717) 334-7688
www.OctagonLR.com
This shop is geared toward the lady reenactor although children's and men's civil-

ian period clothing is also available. Run by a mother-and-daughter team who are part of a family that has four generations involved in Civil War reenacting, Octagon specializes in Civil War clothing and accessories, patterns, and needlework.

They sell booklets on ladies' hair styles and patterns for knit and crochet accessories. They also publish *Past Reflections* magazine, a quarterly publication for the lady reenactor. Ladies may also make an appointment to have their hair done in an appropriate style of the time. As is true of most of the sutleries in town, this shop is very small, but it makes good use of its space. Octagon is open on Friday, Saturday, and Sunday from late morning to early evening.

S&S Sutler
331 Buford Avenue
(717) 338-1990
www.ss-sutler.com

This delightful shop is owned by Tim and Debbie Sheads, both originally from Gettysburg and both a wealth of information on the life and mind-set of reenacting. After years of working for the state and raising a family in nearby Bendersville, Tim and Debbie decided to move back to Gettysburg and open a sutlery. Their first shop was on Steinwehr Avenue, but they moved to their current location across from the Lutheran Theological Seminary when the home of an ancestor of Tim's became available. The Carrie Sheads House was built in March 1862, and it certainly saw fighting on the first day of battle. A projectile is embedded in its front wall, and three soldiers etched their names in one of the house's windows. The Carrie Sheads House is listed on the National Register of Historic Places, and the sutlery is located in a converted garage at the rear of the house.

Tim put on his first reenactment uniform when he was four years old. As an adult, he's been a reenactor since 1969, and today he is an active member of the 5th New York Duryee Zouaves (see the Close-up on the Zouaves in this chapter). Debbie is also an avid reenactor, and both Tim and Debbie strive to offer the most historically correct garments and equipment at the best prices. Here you will find only authentic goods that are of good quality and value, and many are hand-crafted. They stock uniforms, military goods, and civilian accessories. The sutlery is open Friday through Monday and other days and evenings by appointment.

Somewhere in Time
141 Steinwehr Avenue (second floor)
(717) 337-2143

This small shop opened in November 2005 and shares the second floor of a house with Lady Beneath the Veil and Victorian Costume Rentals. (For more on Lady Beneath the Veil, see the listing earlier in this section.) The first floor of the house is occupied by the military memorabilia shop Arsenal of the Alleghenys (see the listing earlier in this chapter). At Somewhere in Time, the emphasis is on historical clothes—primarily clothing of the Civil War era—handmade with impeccable quality. The shop consists of only two rooms, one where the clothes are made and displayed and one containing various accoutrements, including underclothing and handmade and reproduction jewelry. Somewhere in Time is open during the day except on Wednesday, when the shop is closed.

Stitch-n-Place
155 Plank Road
(717) 334-2895

When you are admiring the more than 20 beautiful custom and Civil War–era reproductive quilts for sale at a wide range of prices in the studio here, you're also standing in what was a summer kitchen that was used as a field hospital after Pickett's Charge during the Battle of Gettysburg. Glenda Shetter is the proprietor of Stitch-n-Place, and she also conducts lectures on and demonstrations of quilts used as codes for the Underground Railroad. Glenda's hours are by appointment or by chance, so call ahead to be sure she'll be home when you wish to visit. To reach the studio, take Fairfield Road (Route 116) west and turn left onto Black Horse Tavern Road. At the Y intersection, veer right; Stitch-n-Place is located in the fourth house on the right.

ATTRACTIONS

O f course, the number one attraction in Gettysburg is the Gettysburg National Military Park (GNMP), and this site of the three-day battle in July 1863 that many feel was the turning point of the Civil War is usually what brings travelers to Gettysburg. Many people feel one trip to the battlefield isn't enough; in fact, some visit time and again, and others move here to be nearer the battlefield. Gettysburg and the battle are so intertwined that an entire chapter of this book is devoted to the Gettysburg National Military Park and the role of reenactors in the Gettysburg experience.

This chapter covers the other attractions that Gettysburg has to offer, and it's split into three categories—historical, general, and ghostly attractions. Since most visitors here are interested in history, the chapter begins with that category. Around town there are many attractions that help one interpret the battle and the entire Civil War. Since President Lincoln made his famous address here, you'll also find attractions dedicated to Lincoln. And another president, Dwight D. Eisenhower, who made a farm near Gettysburg his home, also shares the historical attractions spotlight.

If you need to take a break from all this historical knowledge, check out the general attractions Gettysburg has to offer. You can visit a winery, take a scenic train ride, or visit some of the fruit orchards in the area. After all, Adams County is the leading fruit-producing and -processing county in the state of Pennsylvania. There are also tours available that take you on walks in town, drives through the countryside, and romantic jaunts around town and the countryside in horse-drawn carriages.

I doubt many visitors leave Gettysburg without taking a ghost tour. At times it seems the ghosts are as big an attraction as the history that was made here. There are numerous tours to pick from that will satisfy your curiosity about the spirit world.

PRICE CODE

Prices represent the cost for one adult admission. Most places reduce the price for children and senior citizens, but each establishment sets its age ranges differently, so be sure to ask about prices for specific ages. Many attractions allow children younger than a certain age to be admitted for free, and I'll mention this when it applies.

$	$2.00 to $5.50
$$	$5.51 to $7.50
$$$	$7.51 to $15.00
$$$$	More than $15

HISTORICAL ATTRACTIONS

Gettysburg Tours offers package plans that combine a bus tour of the Gettysburg National Military Park with attractions in town. See the Bus Tours section of the Gettysburg National Military Park chapter for details.

Lincoln Square

Lincoln Room Museum $
The Wills House
12 Lincoln Square
(717) 334-8188
www.gettysburg.com/lincolnbedroom
The Lincoln Room Museum is within the Wills House, the home where Lincoln stayed the night before he gave his famous Gettysburg Address. David Wills was a local attorney who owned the house from 1859 to about 1895, and he was the one who invited Lincoln to say a few words at the dedication of the National Cemetery.

The tour presentation takes place in the actual bedroom where President Lincoln slept, which is also where he worked on the speech's final draft. A display room shows copies of the Gettysburg Address and Lincoln memorabilia. The Lincoln Room Museum opened in the Wills House in 1938, and the borough sold the house to GNMP in March 2004 for $550,000. The National Park Service has begun a $6.5 million restoration that will turn the Wills House, which is on the Register of Historic Places, into a downtown museum and orientation center for visitors. The Park Service plans to restore the exterior of the house to its 1863 appearance and to renovate its interior to include exhibits and a bookstore on the first floor, galleries and the restored Lincoln bedroom on the second floor, and administrative offices and a resource center on the third floor. The museum has been able to remain open during the initial renovations, but it will close in the future and reopen sometime in 2007. It's probably best to call the number above for an update on where the renovations stand at the time you are visiting. Currently, the museum is open daily, and children age five and younger are admitted for free.

South of Lincoln Square

American Civil War Museum $
297 Steinwehr Avenue
(717) 334-6245
www.e-gettysburg.cc

Many return visitors may know this museum as the National Civil War Wax Museum, which was its name for about 40 years until 2003, when the name was changed to better represent the museum. Whatever you call it, this is the number one private attraction in Gettysburg. Dioramas of life-size wax figures tell the story of the Civil War from its beginnings through to its conclusion. At the end of the dioramas, you view a digitally enhanced audio-visual presentation that includes more than 200 life-size figures highlighting Pickett's Charge and a finale that has an animated President Lincoln delivering the Gettysburg Address. There's always something going on in front of the museum, too. Reenactors are camped outside as part of the living-history programs that are held on weekends April through November, and there are special activities for children most Saturdays from June through August (see the Kidstuff chapter for details). This is also the home of the Gettysburg Gift Center (see the GNMP chapter). The museum is open daily from 9:00 A.M. to 6:15 P.M., with the gift shop open until 7:00 P.M. Children younger than age six are admitted for free.

Battlefield Military Museum $$
900 Baltimore Pike
(717) 334-6568

George Marinos spent more than 60 years collecting military artifacts, all of which are on display at the Battlefield Military Museum, a large building at the south end of town that usually has a major piece of military equipment sitting out front. George and the rest of the Marinos family have been operating the museum at this location since the 1960s, and they claim to have the largest collection of authentic military artifacts in Gettysburg, with 10,000 items. More than 7,000 of the war relics are from the Civil War, and they include uniforms, weapons, photos, flags, medical kits, and more. Many pieces of the Civil War collection are from the Gettysburg struggle, including the medical kit of Gettysburg's only doctor at the time, Dr. Tate. The main floor is dedicated to the Civil War, while items downstairs are mainly from WWI and WWII, with a few displays of items from the Korean and Vietnam Wars. Here you can see gas masks from WWI, the WWII uniforms of actor Jimmy Stewart and Gen. Hap Arnold, and a letter an American soldier wrote home on Hitler's personal stationery. All displays are behind glass, and the museum is open daily. An inviting gift shop greets you as you enter the building, where some relics, Gettysburg memorabilia, and other cool stuff can be purchased. Children younger than age six are admitted to the Battlefield Military Museum for free.

Eisenhower National Historic Site $
97 Taneytown Road
(717) 338-9114
www.nps.gov/eise/
This was the home and farm of Gen. Dwight D. Eisenhower, 34th president of the United States, and his wife, Mamie. The Eisenhowers bought it in 1950 at the end of Ike's 30-year military career, and the site is preserved as it was during their time here. Once Ike was elected president in 1952, he used the farm as a weekend retreat and "temporary White House," and he and Mamie retired to the home in 1961.

Access is gained by taking a shuttle bus from the visitor center at the Gettysburg National Military Park to the site; arrangements may be made on a first-come, first-served basis at the center. You begin your adventure into the past with a 15-minute orientation tour of the farm and grounds. The Reception Center traces Eisenhower's life through exhibits and a video, and you can tour the first floor of the house, which features some of the Eisenhowers' original furnishings. There are also three self-guided walks that cover the grounds, the farm, and the skeet range. You can also attend 20-minute ranger-conducted walks and talks that focus on facets of Eisenhower's life, such as his military career, his presidency, his hobbies, his relationships with other world leaders, and more.

Much of Ike's presidency is defined by the Cold War, and there's a program where kids can become Junior Secret Service Agents (see the Kidstuff chapter). There are also special events held throughout the year, such as the 50s and the World War II Weekends (see the Annual Events and Festivals chapter) and the decking out of the house for Christmas as the Eisenhowers had it, including some original decora-

tions and Christmas cards. The site is open daily except for New Year's Day, Thanksgiving, and Christmas. Admission is free for children younger than age six, and holders of National Park passes and Golden Age passes receive a reduced admission fee.

Winston Churchill, Charles de Gaulle, and Nikita Khrushchev are just three of many world leaders who were guests of President Eisenhower and his wife, Mamie, at their farm outside of Gettysburg.

Evergreen Cemetery
799 Baltimore Street
(717) 334-4121
www.evergreencemetery.org
Evergreen Cemetery was established in 1854, and its grounds hold the graves of some of the most famous names in Gettysburg history. Encompassing 30 acres, this is the final resting place of Jennie Wade, the only civilian killed during the Battle of Gettysburg, and John Burns, a 69-year-old Gettysburg citizen who took up arms against the invading Confederates. Elizabeth Thorn is also buried here. Elizabeth was acting caretaker during the Battle of Gettysburg, and she personally dug the graves for 91 casualties of the fighting while six months pregnant. The Gettysburg Civil War Women's Memorial, which sits about 50 feet southwest of the gatehouse, is a 7-foot bronze statue of a six-month-pregnant Elizabeth leaning on a shovel as she takes a rest from her burial duties. The memorial was created by famous Civil War sculptor Ron Tunison in 2002, and it honors all the women who served in various capacities before, during, and following the Battle of Gettysburg. Another of many famous people buried here is the founder of Evergreen Cemetery, David McConaughy. You can visit the McConaughy History Room inside the gatehouse to learn more about this historic figure.

If you'd like to visit the graves of these and many other famous Gettysburg natives, your best bet is to buy the book *Beyond the Gatehouse: Gettysburg's Evergreen Cemetery*, which contains summaries of the lives of many of the notable people buried in Evergreen and an overview of the history of the cemetery. The book includes a map so visitors can easily find gravesites. It's written by Brian Kennell, the eighth and current superintendent of Evergreen Cemetery, who is a native of Gettysburg and who has lived at the cemetery gatehouse since 1976. The book is available at many bookstores in town, including the one at Gettysburg National Military Park Visitor Center.

All visitors to the cemetery are asked to remember where they are and to act accordingly. This is the final resting place for many, and respect should be paid to all who lie here and all who visit loved ones here. Evergreen is still an active cemetery—please visit with silence and respect.

Gettysburg Battle Theatre $$
571 Steinwehr Avenue
(717) 334-6100
www.gettysburgbattlefieldtours.com
Located next to the field that was the site of Pickett's Charge and adjacent to the GNMP Visitor Center, the Gettysburg Battle Theatre puts on a multimedia presentation of the three days of the battle and the events leading up to it. The theater is open daily, and the presentation runs every 45 minutes from 9:00 A.M. to the last showing at 8:15 P.M. There's also a gift shop filled with Gettysburg gifts and collectibles on-site. And if you decide it's time to satisfy your stomach as well as your brain, General Pickett's Buffet (see the Restaurants chapter) is located downstairs. (The restaurant and theater share a building, but they're not affiliated.) Children younger than age four are admitted for free.

Gettysburg Miniature Battlefield Diorama $
Artillery Ridge Campground
610 Taneytown Road
(717) 334-6408
www.artilleryridge.com
Consisting of about 20,000 handpainted soldiers, cannon, horses, and buildings, the Gettysburg Miniature Battlefield Diorama is one of the largest military dioramas in the United States. It allows you to visualize the entire three days of the Battle of Gettysburg at once, leaving a lasting impression of the magnitude of the conflict. The diorama is accompanied by a light and sound show, adding to the realism. You'll also see the entire battlefield as it appeared in 1863, before nature and time changed some of the vistas. Gettysburg Miniature Battlefield Diorama is located at Artillery Ridge Campground, about 1 mile south of town, and it's open every day. Children age five and younger may view the diorama for free. (See the Campgrounds and RV Parks chapter for more on Artillery Ridge Campground.)

Gettysburg National Cemetery
(717) 334-1124
This is the burial site of 3,512 Union soldiers killed in the Battle of Gettysburg, and its dedication was the reason Lincoln came to Gettysburg and delivered his Gettysburg Address on November 19, 1863. The cemetery consists of 17 acres on Cemetery Hill, part of the battleground near the center of the Union line. It was designed by landscape architect William Saunders, founder of the National Grange. Saunders placed the Soldiers National Monument at the center of his design, and the Union graves were arranged in a series of semicircles around the monument. A space 2-feet wide was allocated for each body, and the bodies were laid with their heads toward the center. The headstones are uniform in size and contain the name, regiment, and company, if obtainable, of each soldier. Graves are grouped by state, with one section for unknowns.

The cemetery was completed in March of 1864 when the last of 3,512 Union dead were reburied. It became a National Cemetery on May 1, 1872, when control was transferred to the U.S. War Department. Today it is administered by the National Park Service and contains the remains of more than 6,000 individuals who served in a number of American wars. The cemetery also contains other monuments in addition to the Soldiers National Monument, including the New York Monument, the first statue to Maj. Gen. John F. Reynolds, and the monument to Lincoln's Gettysburg Address.

You might wonder what happened to the Confederate dead who were buried in makeshift graves on the battlefield. The removal of these bodies was only undertaken seven years after the battle. From 1870 to 1873, 3,320 bodies of Confederate soldiers were disinterred and sent to cemeteries in southern cities for reburial.

Gettysburg National Cemetery is open daily from 6:00 A.M. to 10:00 P.M., and there is no entrance fee.

Hall of Presidents   **$$**
789 Baltimore Street
(717) 334-5717
www.gettysburgbattlefieldtours.com
Wax figures tell the story of America at the Hall of Presidents, which sits beside the main entrance of the National Cemetery. Each president tells his own story, often in his own voice. A Smithsonian collection of First Ladies' Inaugural Gowns is authentically reproduced in the Hall of First Ladies, and the "Eisenhowers at Gettysburg" exhibit highlights the years Ike and Mamie spent at their farm in Gettysburg. Books on the presidents as well as on the Civil War and Civil War- and Gettysburg-related souvenirs can be found in the gift shop. Children younger than age four are admitted for free. A tour takes about an hour, and the tours run daily. Tours begin every 15 minutes from 9:00 A.M. to the last tour, which begins at 7:45 P.M. Although informative, this attraction could use a bit of

updating—President Bush doesn't even mention 9/11.

Jennie Wade House Museum   **$$**
528 Baltimore Street
(717) 334-4100
www.gettysburgbattlefieldtours.com
Jennie Wade was the only civilian killed during the Battle of Gettysburg, and this is where she died while visiting her sister, who had just given birth. Only minor changes and repairs have been made to the house since the battle, and the house is authentically furnished from cellar to attic. Jennie was struck by a stray bullet while baking bread, and the actual bread tray that she was using is on display.

The house opens daily at 9:00 A.M., and tours begin about every 20 minutes, with the last tour starting at 7:00 P.M. The average time people spend on the tour is about half an hour, and children younger than age four are admitted for free. A docent begins the tour by giving you a short overview of Jennie's story, and then you tour the house on your own. Your self-guided tour begins in the kitchen, where an animated soldier describes the fighting and Jennie's death and its aftermath. After his story is done, you walk through the upstairs of the house, through a wall to the other side of this double home, and down to the home's cellar, where evidence of ghostly happenings at the house is displayed. When you're done in the cellar, you must exit the tour through the Jennie Wade Gift Shop, which features lots of Jennie Wade–related souvenirs. You'll also find Gettysburg souvenirs, Amish goods, and a nice selection of Civil War–related books on display. Tickets for the Ghostly Images of Gettysburg ghost tours are sold at the counter (see this chapter's Ghostly Attractions section).

Lincoln Train Museum   **$$**
425 Steinwehr Avenue
(717) 334-5678
www.gettysburgbattlefieldtours.com
This museum is home to the Lincoln Train

Ride, where you accompany President Lincoln aboard the Presidential Train as he travels from Washington, D.C., to Gettysburg to dedicate the National Cemetery in November 1863. It's also the home of the Lincoln Toy Train collection, a truly impressive array of more than 1,000 pieces that consists of toy trains from the 1800s to present day, with some of the trains displayed within operating layouts. One layout goes around the top of the museum and the adjoining train shop, chugging along on tracks above your head. You'll find trains of all gauges, HO to Z, and you can have fun running some of the trains and admiring the railroad memorabilia found here, such as the train menu from 1911 and some collectibles from the 1830s. There are also dioramas illustrating the role of the railroad during the Civil War, and the Stations Masters Gift Shop has an extensive selection of railroad memorabilia and Gettysburg souvenirs. The Lincoln Train Museum is open daily 9:00 A.M. to 9:00 P.M., and children younger than age four are admitted for free.

Mr. Lincoln Returns to Gettysburg $$
Gettysburg Battle Theatre
571 Steinwehr Avenue
(717) 334-6049
www.gettysburg.com/gcvb/lincoln
James Getty, a resident of Gettysburg but no relation to the founding father of the town, portrays Abraham Lincoln at the Gettysburg Battle Theatre. When he arrives on stage, you would swear he really was Mr. Lincoln come back to life. His 45-minute presentation covers Lincoln's entire life, and there's time at the end for questions from the audience. You can also have your picture taken with him. Mr. Getty also portrays President Lincoln during other events held by the town as well as putting on shows throughout the country. Children younger than age four are admitted for free.

National Shrine Grotto of Lourdes
Mount St. Mary's University
Emmitsburg, MD
(301) 447-5318
www.msmary.edu
The National Shrine Grotto of Lourdes is one of the oldest American replicas of the revered French shrine, dating from about two decades after the apparitions at Lourdes (1874). Sitting on a mountainside overlooking Mount St. Mary's campus, the grotto, which draws more than 55,000 visitors a year, is about 10 miles south of Gettysburg off U.S. Route 15. The grotto turnoff is on the right just beyond Mount St. Mary's College and Seminary, and there are plenty of signs to follow.

The grotto marks the site of a church built on the hill in 1805 by Father John DuBois, who was the founder of Mount St. Mary's College and Seminary. Today it overlooks the Shrine of Saint Elizabeth Ann Seton, who often prayed at the grotto. Mother Seton founded the Sisters of Charity in the United States, and she was canonized on September 14, 1975, becoming America's first native-born saint.

This is a peaceful place for prayer and reflection, and attending Mass here is a special event. The area is full of rugged beauty, with rocks and streams and plenty of wildflowers, and retreats and pilgrimages are held here throughout the year. If you want to take home a remembrance of the grotto, limited-edition prints of Frederick, Maryland, artist Harry Richardson's painting of the grotto are available only at Mount St. Mary's College and Seminary.

Ronn Palm's Museum
of Civil War Images $
229 Baltimore Street
(717) 337-1867
Civil War photographs are what this museum is all about, and Ronn Palm has amassed a collection of about 2,000 images. They're displayed within the second-oldest house in town, and Ronn has papers showing the owners of the

house from 1802 onward. Ronn's passion is collecting and identifying photos of Civil War soldiers, and his photos have been used in numerous books and films. Most of the photos at the museum are of Pennsylvania soldiers, and the layout is arranged by regiments. The display cases in the front room have photos that are for sale, while the museum is in the back. If you had a relative who served in a Pennsylvania unit, you have a good chance of finding a picture of him in the museum. The Museum of Civil War Images is open only on Friday night, Saturday, and Sunday.

Rupp House History Center
451 Baltimore Street
(717) 334-7292
www.friendsofgettysburg.org
The Rupp House opened in 2003 as a project of the Friends of the National Parks at Gettysburg (FNPG), a group dedicated to preserving and providing education on the battlefield and the Eisenhower National Historic Site. Interactive exhibits and hands-on displays relay the battle as seen through the eyes of John and Caroline Rupp, who lived at this address at the time. (The Rupps' original house was heavily damaged during the fight for Cemetery Hill; the current structure was built in 1868.) Both the military and civilian experiences during the battle are highlighted, and visitors can imagine what it was like for both soldiers and townspeople during the battle through sight, sound, touch, and even smell. You tour the house, which is divided into parlors dedicated to each day of the battle and its aftermath, at your own pace. The Rupp House is open March through December, and there's no entrance fee, although there are donation jars throughout the center if you choose to contribute to the work of the FNPG. A walking tour that highlights the events that happened on Baltimore Street during the Battle of Gettysburg is sponsored by the Rupp House every Saturday. It departs from the center at 8:00 A.M.

The stench of death from the Battle of Gettysburg could be smelled as far away as Harrisburg from July until the first frost. Locals put peppermint oil under their noses to cover the odor. A period peppermint oil pump is just one of the many interactive displays at the Rupp House History Center that takes you back to those times.

Schriver House Museum $$
309 Baltimore Street
(717) 337-2800
www.schriverhouse.com
The Schriver House tour relays the experiences of one family during the Battle of Gettysburg. You are escorted on an informative half-hour tour that tells the story of George and Hettie Schriver and their two daughters, occupants of the house during the battle. George had already enlisted in the Union army, and Hettie gathered the children and went to her family's farm for safety once fighting broke out along Baltimore Street. Hettie made it to her family farm, the Weikert farm at Little Round Top, which turned out to be the site of some of the bloodiest fighting of the battle. Wounded soldiers streamed in almost from the moment they arrived at the farm. Meanwhile, Confederate soldiers moved into the house on Baltimore Street and set up a sharpshooter's position in the garret for two days. Several bullet holes can still be seen in the walls of the garret and along the house's outside wall. When the current owners, Del and Nancie Gudmestad, bought the place and started renovations in 1996, they found live Civil War bullets and medical supplies in the floorboards of the garret. Also found throughout the house were a pair of eyeglasses that date from the late 1800s, a child's shoe (putting a shoe in the floorboards was considered good luck back then), and a 1960s-era *Mad* magazine. These items and more can be seen on the tour, which covers all four floors of

the house and is free to children younger than age six. The Schriver House is open daily, and the last tour is given at 4:30 P.M.

Soldier's National Museum $$
777 Baltimore Street
(717) 334-4890
www.gettysburgbattlefieldtours.com
When you tour this museum, keep in mind that the building you're in has historical significance. It was used by General Howard as his headquarters during the Battle of Gettysburg, and from 1866 to 1877 it served as the Soldiers National Orphanage, where children orphaned as a result of the war resided. Here you'll find a large collection of artifacts and memorabilia that tells the story of the wars that have been waged throughout time. After you peruse this history lesson, you continue through the museum by passing through a life-size narrated Confederate encampment and then viewing miniature dioramas of 10 major conflicts of the Civil War. At the end of the tour, you enter the gift shop; go up the steps and view the Charlie Weaver Museum of the Civil War, which tells the story of those orphaned by the war. The basement, which many believe to be haunted by the souls of the unfortunate children who were often mistreated here, is a stop on the Ghostly Images of Gettysburg ghost tour (see the entry within the Ghostly Attractions section of this chapter). The Soldier's National Museum is open daily 9:00 A.M. to 9:00 P.M., with the last tour beginning at 8:30 P.M. Children younger than age four may tour for free.

Fifteen-year-old Tillie Pierce accompanied Hettie Schriver to the Weikert farm on Little Round Top and kept a diary of her experience there. **At Gettysburg or What a Girl Saw and Heard of the Battle** *is considered one of the best personal accounts of the time. The book is still in print, and it's available at the Schriver House gift shop.*

U.S. Christian Commission Museum
Patriot Point, 241 Steinwehr Avenue
(717) 337-0080
www.usccgettysburg.org
This small museum, which opened in spring of 2005, is a new addition to Patriot Point minimall. Through artifacts and historical documentation, it tells the story of the U.S. Christian Commission, which was formed in 1861 by the YMCA. The commission consisted of 5,000 Christian volunteers who served the spiritual and temporal needs of Civil War soldiers on both sides of the battle lines. The museum doesn't charge an entrance fee.

West of Lincoln Square

Adams County Historical Society $
111 Seminary Ridge
(717) 334-4723, ext. 201
www.achs-pa.org
The Adams County Historical Society resides in Schmucker Hall on the campus of the Lutheran Theological Seminary. It contains primary and secondary resource material for researching county history, and it has about 8,000 feet of display space. Nearly 3,000 feet are occupied by museum galleries on three floors, and about 4,200 cubic feet are occupied by manuscripts. Self-guided tours are available any time the society is open, and guided tours of the museum are available by appointment. Among the collections are a Civil War Gallery, fossilized dinosaur footprints, and 1823 wooden water pipes. Free parking is available across the street from Schmucker Hall, which is accessed by stairs and therefore not wheelchair accessible. The society is open during the day on Tuesday, Wednesday, and Saturday and on Thursday evenings.

General Lee's Headquarters Museum $
401 Buford Avenue
(717) 334-3141
www.civilwarheadquarters.com
General Lee occupied the eastern side of

this stone house at the top of Seminary Ridge and used it as his personal head-quarters during the three-day battle at Gettysburg. Built in 1834 and owned by famous abolitionist Thaddeus Stevens, the house was probably a duplex at the time of the battle, and Mrs. Mary ("Widow") Thompson lived there with her daughter-in-law. While visiting the museum, you can stand in the very room where Lee met with his generals during the Gettysburg campaign. The museum also contains arti-facts from the house, Civil War–related items, and photographs from the time. Opened to the public as the Lee Museum in 1922, the museum has been in continu-ous operation ever since, making it one of the oldest museums in Gettysburg. The stone house has a nice gift shop on one side and the museum on the other, and you get your ticket for the museum at the gift shop. Lots of Lee memorabilia fills the gift shop, as well as Civil War–related books, gifts, artifacts, and memorabilia. General Lee's Headquarters is open daily, and it's part of the Quality Inn complex along Chambersburg Road. Guests of the inn and those younger than age 16 can tour the museum for free.

GENERAL ATTRACTIONS

Adams County Winery
251 Peachtree Road, Orrtanna
(717) 334–4631
www.adamscountywinery.com
This is Gettysburg's only winery, and its grapes cover about 10 acres of land 9 miles west of Gettysburg off U.S. Route 30. Signs direct you from US 30 down country lanes for the 3 miles you travel off the main road to reach the winery. Once you arrive, you enter a world of relaxation. The winery gift shop is within a 130-year-old bank barn where you're invited to sample the wine. If you wish, you can bring a picnic lunch, buy some wine to go with it, and enjoy your feast on the winery land. Free summer concerts are held every Saturday afternoon, and free tours of the

winery are available. Adams County Win-ery is open weekends only from January through March and daily the rest of the year. The winery took part in the first annual Gettysburg Wine and Music Festi-val held in September 2005 at Gettysburg Recreation Park (see the Annual Events and Festivals chapter), and it's also repre-sented at wine festivals throughout the region. Adams County Winery holds its own Art at the Winery Fest on its grounds in October, where they host several winer-ies. This event lets you enjoy good wine, food, and music while admiring the art of local and regional artists.

Allstar Events Complex   **$$**
2638 Emmitsburg Road
(717) 334–6363, (888) 497–9386
www.allstarpa.com
Allstar is located 4 miles south of Gettys-burg on Emmitsburg Road, and it func-tions as a 50,000-square-foot expo center (with parking for 2,000-plus cars) that's available for trade shows and group activ-ities. Individuals can also enjoy the fun here, but to avoid long waits, it's best to call ahead to make sure a large group isn't already filling up the place. See the Kid-stuff chapter for a full rundown of activi-ties available here for kids of all ages, such as go-kart tracks and minigolf.

Boyds Bear Country
75 Cunningham Road
(717) 630–2600, (866) 367–8338
www.BoydsBearCountry.com
Boyds Bear Country is open daily, and the 120,000-square-foot store is the home of 70,000 Boyds bears, hares, and other friends. The stuffed animals are grouped together and posed in adorable ways. Live entertainment goes on in the atrium on the first floor, and store displays change each season. The store has three display floors and a downstairs that's devoted to feeding hungry bears. See the Kidstuff chapter for information on making your own bear and the Shopping chapter for more information on the store.

Mr. Ed's Elephant Museum
6019 Chambersburg Road, Orrtanna
(717) 352-3792

17 on the Square (candy only)
(717) 339-0017
www.mistereds.com

Ed Gotwalt received his first elephant in 1967 as a good-luck gift on his wedding day. In 1975 his collection of all things elephant had grown so large that his wife made him open a museum so she could regain her house. His free museum contains more than 6,000 elephant collectibles from throughout the world, and they're made from just about every substance known to man. In addition to the selections of elephants, Ed has added a store that sells fresh-roasted peanuts and other nuts, fudge, classic candies from the 1950s through the 1970s (remember candy necklaces and penny candy?), sugar-free candy, and T-shirts and unusual gifts that relate to the museum collection. Mr. Ed's Elephant Museum appeared on *Good Morning America* on July 5, 2005, as part of a story on unusual attractions across America. The museum and candy shop are open daily; to get there, head west on US 30 (Chambersburg Road) for 12 miles. Between the many signs and the life-size elephant in front of the place, it's hard to miss.

National Apple Museum $
154 West Hanover Street, Biglerville
(717) 677-4556
www.nationalapplemuseum.com

If you're out taking in the area orchards on a Saturday or Sunday, this is a great place to stop and learn more about the history of the fruit industry and how it contributed to the development and growth of Adams County. The National Apple Museum is owned and operated by the Biglerville Historical and Preservation Society. Opened in 1990, it's housed in a restored pre–Civil War bank barn, and exhibits include a re-created 1880s farm kitchen and General Store and collections of farming implements, apple peelers, and fruit labels. The museum is open weekends only April through October. Guided tours are given at 10:00 A.M., noon, 2:00, and 4:00 P.M. Self-guided audio tapes are available if you prefer to tour on your own. There's also a museum gift shop, with most items having an agricultural or orchard-related theme. To reach the museum from Lincoln Square, take Route 34 (Carlisle Street) north from Gettysburg until you reach Route 394 (West Hanover Street) in Biglerville. Make a left, and the museum is about a quarter mile up the road.

Pioneer Lines $$$–$$$$
106 North Washington Street
(717) 334-6932
www.gettysburgrail.com

Formerly known as the Gettysburg Scenic Railway, Pioneer Lines offers a variety of train rides. You can pick from rides that offer great scenery, rides that are accompanied with food and entertainment, and rides that take you ghostly places. The Scenic Train Rides are an hour long, and they cover 16 miles of the Adams County countryside. They leave the station July through October at 1:00 P.M. on Friday, Saturday, Sunday, and Monday. On certain Saturdays from July through October, the three-hour Evening Paradise Dinner Train also takes on passengers. Dinner is served family style, and you share your table with other riders, but a private table is available for an additional cost. Pioneer Lines also offers a Conductor's Bagged Lunch Train Ride, where you get to enjoy the scenery while munching on your lunch. The three-hour Murder Mystery Train Ride and the one-hour Ghost Train Ride were introduced in 2005. The Ghost Train departs on Friday and the Mystery Train departs on Saturday evenings from Memorial Day throughout the summer. Special Event Weekends, such as the Pioneer Polar Days, Civil War Train Raids, and Fall Foliage Festival Days, are also offered. All trains but the Scenic Train Rides require you to make reservations in advance; reservations are requested but not required for the Scenic Train Rides.

The trains have limited access for

patrons with disabilities. Call the number above if you have questions about handicap accessibility.

GENERAL TOURS

Gettysburg Carriage Co. $$$$
(717) 337-3400
Gettysburg Carriage Co. offers two tours that take you along the battlefield and one town tour. The battlefield tours last about 90 minutes and go to either Culp's Hill or West Confederate Avenue, near where Pickett's Charge took place. These are scenic tours that relate stories of the battle as you enjoy the ride. The town tour runs about 35 minutes, and you get to see some of the older buildings in town and hear stories of what happened within the town during the Battle of Gettysburg. Reservations may be made if you like, but most people just show up where the carriage is parked along Baltimore Street by the Farnsworth House. Gettysburg Carriage Co. and Windmill Carriage (see entry within this section) alternate sides of Baltimore Street daily, and each company has a sign out to let you know who's who.

Guided Historic Walking Tours $$$
(717) 337-3491
www.gettysburgpa.org/mainstreet.html
Begun in summer 2005, the guided historic walking tours bring to life what it was like for the civilians of Gettysburg during the Battle of Gettysburg. For 90 minutes, tour guides take you down either Baltimore or Chambersburg Street and relay the impact those three days had on the people who lived here. Much of the information given during the tours is based on diary entries, personal accounts, and letters of the townspeople who were here during the battle, as well as drawings and photographs of the time. Tour guides must pass a test, and the tours are the creation of Main Street Gettysburg, a nonprofit organization dedicated to preserving and highlighting Gettysburg's rich history. (For more on Main Street Gettysburg, see The

Arts chapter.) Tours depart from Historic Christ Church, 30 Chambersburg Street, Thursday through Monday at either 10:30 A.M., 1:30, or 7:30 P.M. All three tours are available on Friday and Saturday; the morning and afternoon tours are given on Thursday and Monday; and only the afternoon tour is available on Sunday.

Historic Church Walking Tours $
(888) 882-1541
These tours emphasize town churches that were turned into emergency hospitals during and after the Gettysburg battle. Eight churches host performances that portray the events of those days through narratives, plays, and music, with four churches featured each Wednesday evening during the summer starting in early June. Churches on the East Tour are St. James Lutheran, United Church of Christ, United Methodist, and Gettysburg Presbyterian, while on the West Tour are Christ Lutheran, St. Paul's AME Zion, Prince of Peace Episcopal, and St. Francis Roman Catholic. The East and West Tours alternate each Wednesday night, and all tours begin at 6:00 P.M. in front of the Gettysburg Presbyterian Church at Baltimore and High Streets. Tours are conducted by volunteer docents, and children age 12 and younger tour for free.

Historic Conewago Valley Tour
Gettysburg Convention
& Visitors Bureau
102 Carlisle Street
(717) 334-6274, (800) 337-5015
www.gettysburgcvb.org
Covering 40 miles east and northeast of

Hike with Ike Walks are held every Thursday from mid-June through mid-August. A National Park Ranger takes you around downtown and tells you about the Eisenhowers' life in the community. The walk begins at the Race Horse Alley parking-garage plaza at 7:15 P.M., and it's free. Call (717) 338-9114 for more information.

CLOSE-UP

Covered Bridges of Adams County

Pennsylvania has the most covered bridges of any state (212), and Adams County has two covered bridges that are still open to the public. The Sachs Bridge crosses Marsh Creek on Water Works Road 3 miles southwest of town, and Jack's Mountain Bridge crosses Tom's Creek in Fairfield about 8 miles west of town. The Sachs Bridge, built by David Stoner in 1852, is 91 feet long and 15 feet wide and uses a truss system designed by Connecticut architect Ithiel Town. The bridge was used by both Union and Confederate troops during the Battle of Gettysburg and is listed in the National Register of Historic Places. Although you can't drive across it, walking across is allowed. To reach Sachs Bridge from Lincoln Square, travel Baltimore Street and turn right onto Steinwehr Avenue, which

is called Emmitsburg Road once you leave town. Turn right onto Millerstown Road (there's a sign on the left for the Peach Orchard). Continue straight on Millerstown Road when it intersects with West Confederate Avenue, and in a bit the road name changes to Pumping Station Road. About a mile later you'll cross a bridge that spans Marsh Creek, where you can see Sachs Bridge about 200 yards downstream on the left. Immediately after the bridge, make a left onto Scott Road to explore the bridge.

The Jack's Mountain Bridge was constructed by Joseph Smith in 1894 and is still used for daily motor vehicle traffic. It's a Burr truss covered bridge that spans 75 feet with a width of 14 feet, 6 inches. To reach the bridge, travel south from the square and make a right onto West Mid-

Gettysburg, the Historic Conewago Valley Tour takes you by the East Cavalry battlefield, working farms, country churches, and the quaint towns of New Oxford and East Berlin. There's a lot of history along the way, especially in East Berlin, which was designated a Pennsylvania Historic Site in 1985. The town was laid out in 1764, and 52 structures that appear on an 1856 map of the town are still standing, including a house once owned by Thaddeus Stevens, a Pennsylvanian representative and famous abolitionist of the time. Many of the churches seen along the way date from the 1800s, and quite a few bank barns are also on the route. The tour is named for the Conewago Creek, which

meanders through the eastern half of Adams County. Touring is done in the comfort of your car, and the approximate driving time is two hours. The route is clearly marked with signs, and the free brochure that's available from the Gettysburg Convention & Visitors Bureau explains what you're seeing and shows a good map of the tour. As the tour brochure emphasizes many times, this is a country tour, with steep hills and twisty roads. The tour route crosses busy roads, sometimes at places where visibility isn't always ideal, so careful driving is a must. Follow the brochure when it says to slow down, and pay attention if it says to proceed with caution at an intersection.

The Sachs Bridge, built in 1852, carried both Union and Confederate troops across Marsh Creek during the Battle of Gettysburg. KATE HERTZOG

dle Street (Route 116). Travel this road, which will change its name to Fairfield Road once you leave town, through the town of Fairfield. Follow Fairfield Road at the Y intersection with Iron Springs Road, and follow Jacks Mountain Road at the next Y intersection. You'll soon be cross-ing the covered bridge. Jack's Mountain Bridge carries a good deal of traffic, so be aware of other vehicles as you admire the bridge. There is a very limited area for parking if you want to get out and explore a bit.

Historic Gettysburg Walking Tour
Gettysburg Convention & Visitors Bureau
102 Carlisle Street
(717) 334-6274, (800) 337-5015
www.gettysburgcvb.org
You can view more than 100 restored buildings as this self-guided walking tour takes you through the downtown area. The free tour brochure, available at the Gettysburg Convention & Visitors Bureau, contains a brief description of the tour's 32 stops and a corresponding map. Your adventure begins at the Gettysburg Lincoln Train Station off Carlisle Street, and you travel to Lincoln Square, up and down the first block of York Street, down Baltimore Street all the way to its intersection with Steinwehr Avenue, and back up to the square. Baltimore Street has the most stops along the way, and after returning to the square you tour up and down the first block of Chambersburg Street, and the tour ends a block off the square, on Carlisle Street. Estimated to last about 90 minutes, the walking tour integrates the wayside markers located along the route, which relay in-depth information about the Battle of Gettysburg and its aftermath.

Scenic Valley Tour
Gettysburg Convention & Visitors Bureau
102 Carlisle Street
(717) 334-6274, (800) 337-5015
www.gettysburgcvb.org

Thirty-six miles of beautiful countryside can be seen on this self-guided drive through Adams County. The drive's accompanying free brochure, which has a map of the route, is available from the Gettysburg Convention & Visitors Bureau. Scenic Valley Tour signs mark the entire route, and the brochure gives you clear directions to the start of the tour from either the tourist bureau or Lincoln Square. Approximate driving time is two hours, and along the way you'll visit the Seminary Ridge area of the Gettysburg National Military Park and take in some fabulous scenery. Easy detours from the route take you to a mid-19th-century covered bridge and a tavern where George Washington slept. (See the Close-up in this chapter for more on covered bridges in Adams County.)

Windmill Carriage $$$$
(717) 677-6852, (717) 253-3732 (cell)
Windmill Carriage has two in-town locations; you can begin your horse-drawn carriage ride from the Dobbin House on Steinwehr Avenue or from Baltimore Street by the Farnsworth House. For a town tour that lasts half an hour, you can just walk up and make arrangements right when you want to leave. A battlefield ride is an hour long, and it's a scenic journey to Spangler's Spring and Culp's Hill, not a tour of the battlefield or the events of the battle. Although you can also walk up and request this tour, it's probably better to make reservations. Carriage rides are available daily, weather permitting. On Baltimore Street, Windmill Carriage and the Gettysburg Carriage Co. (see entry within this section) alternate sides of the

Besides the Convention & Visitors Bureau on Carlisle Street, brochures for the self-guided downtown walking tour can be found in the lobby of the James Gettys Hotel, just up the block from the square on Chambersburg Street.

street daily, and each company has a sign out so you know which company the beautiful horses and carriages belong to.

GHOSTLY ATTRACTIONS

Civil War Hauntings $$
240 Steinwehr Avenue
(717) 752-5588 (cell)
Located next to Flex & Flannigan's store, you'll recognize Civil War Hauntings by the skeleton out front. The skeleton is where you buy your tickets and meet for candlelight ghost walks led by an experienced guide in Civil War–period dress. Tours are given seasonally Thursday through Sunday at 8:00 and 9:30 P.M. They last an hour and cover about half a mile, and the area toured is where some of the bloodiest fighting occurred during the Battle of Gettysburg. Civil War Hauntings includes the free use of an electronic ghost finder on its tours, and the EMF meter is just like the equipment professional ghost hunters use. Children age seven and younger may tour for free.

Farnsworth House Candlelight
Ghost Walks and Civil War
Mourning Theatre $$
401 Baltimore Street
(717) 334-8838
www.farnsworthhouseinn.com
The Farnsworth House gives you options on how you want to connect with the supernatural. You can go on one of their candlelight ghost walks or descend the house's staircase to the "viewing parlor," where you hear stories told by candlelight of ghosts still believed to haunt the town and battlefield. The theater presentation lasts an hour, and the Civil War Mourning Theatre has been featured on A&E's *Unexplained Sightings* and *Unsolved Mysteries* series. It's held nightly in season, as are the candlelight walking tours. Walking tours are led by guides dressed in period clothing, and many of the tales told are firsthand experiences of the guides. Candlelight walks that address the Union side

of the conflict last about 90 minutes, and they begin at 8:00 and 9:30 P.M. The Confederate side is represented on walks that depart at 8:15 and 10:30 P.M., and they last an hour. The cost is the same to take a ghost walk or to attend the mourning theater, and children age seven and younger are admitted to either for free. Tickets can be bought at the bookstore on the premises until 5:00 P.M., or you can buy tickets at the end of the walk in front of the house up to 15 minutes prior to the beginning of the show or walking tour. You can't miss the people selling the tickets—they're in period dress.

Gettysburg Ghost Tours $$
47 Steinwehr Avenue
(717) 338-1818
www.gettysburgghosttours.com
www.hauntedgettysburg.com

Gettysburg Ghost Tours offers a couple of ghost tours. Originally called the Haunted Gettysburg Tour, the renamed Black Cat Tour starts at the tour office and explores the first block of Steinwehr Avenue. Most stories on this tour focus on the first day of the Battle of Gettysburg. The Patriot Tour leaves from 241 Steinwehr Avenue and travels down the second block of Steinwehr Avenue toward Emmitsburg, Maryland. It lasts about an hour and concentrates mainly on the events of the third day of the Battle of Gettysburg. The Black Cat Tour is the scarier of the two tours, but both are appropriate for the entire family. Tours are held rain or shine seven nights a week in season, and children age seven and younger tour for free.

Ghostly Images of Gettysburg $$-$$$$
Gettysburg Tour Center
778 Baltimore Street
(717) 334-6296
www.gettysburgbattlefieldtours.com

A plethora of ghost tours are offered here in season, including walking tours, bus tours, and a tour that includes ghost stories told during dinner. Walking tours are led by guides in period dress, and they last 90 minutes. The Jennie Wade Fright

Before venturing out to hunt ghosts, you might want to pick up a bottle of "Ghost Away" at the Gettysburg Ghost Tours office at 47 Steinwehr Avenue. Kids like this sprayed on their hands to keep ghosts from getting too close.

Seeing Tour is offered nightly, and it ends with a walk through the Jennie Wade House, which many believe to be haunted. On Friday and Saturday nights from April to mid-June, and nightly from mid-June through Labor Day weekend, you can take the Soldiers Orphanage Tour, which covers Steinwehr Avenue and the National Cemetery Annex. This tour ends at the site of the Soldiers Orphanage, a place some psychics won't enter because of the ghosts they feel reside in the cellar.

If you want your destination to be a surprise, the Mystical Mystery Tour takes you on a walk off the beaten path to undisclosed sites, and it's offered on Friday nights. On Friday nights beginning in June and Saturday nights all season, you can take the Midnight in a Haunted House Tour, where psychics or ghost investigators discuss hauntings in the Jennie Wade House. The tour begins at 10:45 P.M., and you're in the house at the witching hour—midnight. The midnight tour is not appropriate for children younger than age 10.

Two bus tours are available. Spirits of the Tavern Tour is held the last Saturday of the month, and it lasts about 2.5 hours. During the tour you have the option of leaving the bus to visit three taverns for about 20 minutes at each stop. The Ghost Bus Tour, which is scheduled according to demand, is about two hours long, and guides relay ghost stories about the area countryside. Supernatural Supper is held the first and third Saturday of the month at O'Rorke's restaurant at 44 Steinwehr Avenue. As you dine, you're regaled for 75 minutes with ghost stories, and after dinner you're escorted to the Jennie Wade House for a tour. Reservations are highly recommended for all tours, and tickets for any of the tours can be picked up at the Gettysburg Tour Center or the Jennie Wade Gift Shop.

Ghosts of Gettysburg Candlelight Walking Tours $$
271 Baltimore Street
(717) 337-0445
www.ghostsofgettysburg.com

This is the original ghost tour in Gettysburg. You'll be treated to strange but true ghost tales from the bestselling *Ghosts of Gettysburg* book series by Mark Nesbitt, author of 13 books, historian, former National Park Service Ranger, and resident of Gettysburg. Mark collected his ghost stories while living in historic houses on the battlefield and in town, and they have been featured on *Unsolved Mysteries* and on A&E. The house that serves as tour headquarters dates from 1834; during the battle it was occupied by Confederate sharpshooters, and there were reports of paranormal events during the house's historical restoration. Ghosts of Gettysburg offers seasonal walking tours that cover different areas of town: the Carlisle Street/College Campus Tour, the Baltimore Street Tour, the Seminary Ridge Tour, and, new in 2005, the Steinwehr Avenue Tour. There's also a bus tour that began in 2005 and runs on Saturday evenings during the summer. Not all tours start from tour headquarters—ask where your tour begins. Tours are conducted rain or shine. The tour headquarters also houses a gift shop, a ghost bookstore, and a ghost photo gallery of spirits captured on the battlefield and in houses in town. Children age seven and younger are admitted for free on the walking tour, but children age five and younger are not permitted on the bus tours. Ghosts of Gettysburg has also partnered with Pioneer Lines to host a ghost train. See the entry for the railway in the General Attractions section of this chapter.

Haunted Battlefield at Gettysburg $$
531 Baltimore Street (in tent at rear)
(717) 337-9216, (877) 980-1313

This is the only attraction in town that guarantees you'll see a ghost during the show. That's because Haunted Battlefield puts its story about eerie sightings at the Gettysburg battlefield on a CD. An 1857 Civil War projector is used for the presentation, which also employs stereo music and sound effects. Haunted Battlefield is not a walking tour—it's held in a tent set up during the seaon behind the Blue and Grey Gift Shop. The CD features Joe Kerrigan, a local Civil War–era magician, actor, and storyteller, as the narrator. Joe also runs the Haunted Gettysburg ghost walks (see separate listing below) and performs at the dinner theater at the Fairfield Inn (see The Arts chapter). Haunted Battlefield at Gettysburg is presented nightly at 8:30 and 9:30 P.M.

Haunted Gettysburg Ghost Tours $$
27 Steinwehr Avenue
(717) 337-9216, (888) 246-4432

These seasonal walking tours are based on the books in the *Haunted Gettysburg* series, which feature eyewitness accounts of paranormal events that occurred in Gettysburg. On the tours, you actually walk through the areas and see the locations where these events are reported to have happened. Joe Kerrigan, who also narrates the Haunted Battlefield tent show behind the Blue and Grey Gift Shop (see separate listing above) and performs at the dinner theater at the Fairfield Inn (see The Arts chapter), is the driving force behind the tours. In 2005 Joe began offering a "Backstreet Tour," which takes you away from the noise of town into the backstreets of Gettysburg. Candlelight tours led by experienced guides are offered daily at 9:00 and 10:15 P.M., with an additional twilight show at 7:30 P.M. on Friday and Saturday nights. Children age six and younger tour for free.

Sleepy Hollow
Candlelight Ghost Tours $$
65 Steinwehr Avenue Rear, at The Great
T-Shirt Company
(717) 337-9322
www.sleepyhollowofgettysburg.com

Guides from Sleepy Hollow Candlelight Ghost Tours have been roaming the streets of Gettysburg in search of ghosts since 1997, making this the second-oldest ghost walk in Gettysburg. The operation is owned and operated by Cindy Codori Shultz, a sixth-generation granddaughter of Nicholas Codori of Historic Codori Farm (the site of Pickett's Charge).

Period-dressed guides lead you on an adventure that encompasses a 3-to 5-block radius within the historic district, and tours are held rain or shine during the season. Ten different storytellers are employed, each telling different stories and following different routes. Tours leave nightly from the Great T-Shirt Company, where you can buy your ticket. Tickets are also sold at the Cannonball Old Tyme Malt Shop on York Street. Or you can call the number above to reserve your place on the tour. Children age seven and younger and people requiring the use of a wheel-chair tour for free.

SHOPPING ⊕

Gettysburg is a shopper's haven, and browsing is almost an art form in this area. The main four streets in town (Baltimore, Chambersburg, York, and Carlisle Streets) have shop after shop along the way, and many people stroll along and browse in each shop. If you prefer a little structure to your shopping expeditions, this chapter is divided into different categories, such as Antiques, Gift Shops/Collectibles, and Specialty Shops. Shopping categories that have many listings (usually 10 or more) are arranged alphabetically according to the business's geographic location in relation to the square. If there aren't too many listings, shops will be listed only alphabetically. Many stores carry lots of different items, so I've done my best to list a place under the category that I feel represents the majority of its stock and the overall feel and appearance of the store. If you're looking for shops that carry mainly military memorabilia and Civil War clothing, these businesses are treated separately within the Gettysburg National Military Park (GNMP) chapter.

ANTIQUES

Abe's Antiques
22 Baltimore Street
(717) 337-2122
If you collect Lincoln memorabilia, you'll want to stop by this store. The owner even looks like Lincoln, and on some weekends he dresses the part. Abe's Antiques has been on Baltimore Street since 1994, and the antiques and collectibles offered here are reasonably priced, with many items less than $20. Lincoln-related items fill most of the back of the store, but take time to look at the stuff in the front, too. The Victrola phonograph and antique musical instruments

right inside the door are worth a long look, and it's also fun to check out the tintype photos, antique kitchen gadgets, and other collectibles at the front of the store. Be sure to take notice of the turn-of-the-20th-century cash register, too. Abe's Antiques is open seven days a week.

Antique Center of Gettysburg
30 Baltimore Street
(717) 337-3669
www.antiquecenter-getty.com
With 100 showcases of antiques and collectibles, the Antique Center of Gettysburg is bound to have something that will intrigue you. As you wander the aisles, you'll find military antiques from many different wars, toy soldiers, military-related books, antique tools, and Lincoln memorabilia. There's also jewelry, glass and pottery, and china. Upstairs you'll find more books, prints, and framed artwork. The Antique Center is closed on Tuesday.

GettysburgAntiques.com
15 Baltimore Street
(717) 338-0413
www.gettysburgantiques.com
Almost all of the dealers who display their goods here have been with owner DiAnne Smith for many years, and they have filled her store at this location with quality merchandise. Smith is a knowledgeable antiques dealer who has run shops in the area for many years. At this location, more than 22 dealers display fine china and silverware, jewelry, clocks, and Civil War art, relics, and memorabilia. Regional residents and many Trinity High School alumni will recognize the "Aunt Nellie's" sign on the wall. (Aunt Nellie's was a local store on Old Gettysburg Pike in Camp Hill where lots of kids from Trinity, including myself, used to go to buy snacks and hang out in the 1970s.) Armchair Books (see separate entry within this chapter) has a cozy

space within the store, and you can also pick up flower arrangements and sweet confections within Gettysburg Antiques.com, which is open daily.

Rx Antiques
28 Chambersburg Street
(717) 338-9092

If you're wondering about the unusual name, the owner used to be a podiatrist before he retired and opened this shop in 1998. This long, narrow shop has antique pottery and glassware, fabulous beer steins, and unusual and one-of-a-kind items. Rx Antiques is closed on Tuesday.

17 on the Square
17 Lincoln Square
(717) 339-0017
www.17onthesquare.com

With a history that dates from 1785 when James Gettys laid out the town of Gettysburg, Lot #81 (as it was originally deeded) has operated as a private residence, as varied retail stores, and as office space over the decades. In 2001 the building was sold to three sisters, Melinda, Jane, and Hannah, who spent 14 months renovating the space, which had been vacant for many years. Their logo is Antiques, Apples and Art—antiques on two floors, specialty foods such as homemade jams and unusual candy and good old-fashioned apples (in season) for sale, and lots of art in many different forms. The building houses many tenants. As you enter the building, you have your choice of turning left into the Hard Bean Cafe (see the Restaurants chapter), heading up the steps to The House of Time (see the Fine Gifts and Home Accents section within this chapter), or turning right, which takes you into a large space with lots of diverse offerings. Don't get swept into the main area just yet. You'll want to visit around the front of the store, where you'll find a fur dealer and the Seven Valleys Wine Shop (see the Specialty Shops section of this chapter). The heart of the store begins with rows of glass display cases that hold all assortments of antiques from

When shopping for antiques, be sure you and the seller are talking the same language. A true antique is at least 100 years old, a near antique is 75 to 99 years old, and anything called vintage is 25 to 74 years old.

a variety of dealers. After you've admired the fine goods, walk around to discover furniture, books, art, jewelry, local photography, military collectibles, and much, much more. New in 2005 is the Civil War Center, where you can buy period clothing that is made on the premises. As you're heading back to the entrance, don't miss Mr. Ed's candy, which is reasonably priced and delicious (see the Attractions chapter for more on Mr. Ed's Elephant Museum).

Wogan's York Street Antiques & Treats
26 York Street
(717) 337-3378

Wogan's York Street Antiques & Treats opened in 2005, and it holds a lot of the items that used to be at Mel's Antiques Mall, which closed in 2005. It's a great area for browsing, with glassware, jewelry, china, Civil War–era memorabilia, furniture, and lots more among the offerings.

APPAREL

Gracie's
9 Chambersburg Street
(717) 334-2670

Gracie's opened in the summer of 2005, and it shows off upscale practical clothing for women. Much of its stock consisted of pants suits that would be perfect for work or an evening out when I visited just after its debut. There's also a jewelry case with a nice array of selections to complete your outfit. Although the shop is small, Gracie's makes good use of its space, with clothing racks placed far enough apart to allow ample browsing. Gracie's is open every day but Sunday, with extended hours on Monday and Friday.

**Gettysburg Hospital
Auxiliary Thrift Shop
10 Lincoln Square
(717) 334-5264**

This delightful shop is filled with clothing for everyone in the family, and the clothing is priced to sell. Used as well as new clothing are intermingled, and everything is nicely arranged on hangers. There's plenty of room to look at what's on the racks, and there's a separate room full of kids' clothes. The bridal suite in the back has gorgeous gowns, most of which are new, and items to complete your wedding-day look. The thrift shop is open Monday through Saturday, and proceeds from sales at the store benefit Gettysburg Hospital.

Many shops in Gettysburg appear small from outside. Don't be deceived— there's often additional space either in back or upstairs. Sometimes it's fun just to explore how large that tiny-looking space really is!

**Moulon Rougue Boutique
52 Chambersburg Street
(717) 337-1900**

Owned and operated by Bridget Gebhart, Moulon Rougue is a charming boutique that opened its doors in April 2005. Bridget has stocked her space with an eclectic mix of clothes and accessories for women. Silky lingerie in vibrant colors and beautiful jewelry are showcased in the front room, and the room in back holds chic outfits, shoes, and accessories. Moulon Rougue is closed Monday and Tuesday.

**T&S Menswear, Inc.
1 Chambersburg Street
(717) 334-7575**

T&S has been around since the 1960s, and they've had their spot right off the square since 1991. The small shop is filled with men's fine clothing, casual clothing, and formal wear. Men can find dress shirts, sweaters, pants, and suits as well as plush robes and loungewear. The store is laid out nicely with room to browse, and it's always fun to see what's in the display window at this upscale shop. T&S Menswear is open every day of the week but Sunday.

BOOKS AND MUSIC
North of Lincoln Square

**Gettysburg Book Cellar
22 Carlisle Street
(717) 337-0557
www.gettysburgbookcellar.com**

If you love losing yourself among books, this is the place for you. Bookshelf after bookshelf is filled to overflowing with used, out-of-print, and antiquarian books. You enter by going down a few steps (hence the cellar in the name), and you're immediately surrounded by books. As you browse, each corner you turn offers the opportunity to find new treasure.

Bookcases are labeled by subject for easy hunting, and first editions are among the offerings. There are also comic books and more recent titles on display. The Gettysburg Book Cellar is closed on Monday and Tuesday.

South of Lincoln Square

**Armchair Books
(within GettysburgAntiques.com)
15 Baltimore Street
(717) 677-6964**

Armchair Books is the only book dealer among the many dealers that offer their goods at GettysburgAntiques.com (see separate entry within this chapter). Arrayed on a few bookshelves at the back of the store are books covering a lot of subjects—everything from history, nature, and drama to philosophy, religion, and travel. Some children's books are also available.

Bible Factory Outlet
Gettysburg Village Factory Stores
Junction of U.S. Route 15 and Route 97
(Baltimore Street)
(717) 334-5004
www.gettysburgvillage.com
The Bible Factory Outlet is located within Gettysburg Village, a mall outside of town that features lots of outlet shopping every day of the week (see the Outlet Shopping section of this chapter). Bibles line one wall from top to bottom in this good-size bookstore, and you'll also discover artwork, music, T-shirts, cards, picture frames, bookmarks, and more, with most items having a religious theme. There's a back shelf filled with kid-appealing books and items, and teens also get a shelf devoted to their tastes. Books vary from bibles to current fiction that has a moral message or religious theme. Bibles are available in a variety of languages and types, and there's a great selection of bible software and book covers. The store's atmosphere invites you to relax and browse a while, and I especially enjoy looking at all the plaques with inspirational messages located near the front of the store.

Book Warehouse
Gettysburg Village Factory Stores
Junction of U.S. Route 15 and Route 97
(Baltimore Street)
(717) 334-8047
www.gettysburgvillage.com
Here you can find great books at greatly reduced prices—up to 80 percent off retail. Book Warehouse stocks hardcovers and paperbacks, and you'll find books on a wide variety of subjects, including biography, how-to, science, and more. The children's section is large and bright, and special kids programs are held regularly (see the Kidstuff chapter). You'll find Book Warehouse on the end of the mall closest to the Country Inn & Suites hotel (see the

Hotels, Motels, and Resorts chapter). If you decide to check out Gettysburg Village, which I highly recommend, don't miss this gem.

Farnsworth House Military Impressions
Farnsworth House
401 Baltimore Street
(717) 334-8838
www.farnsworthhouseinn.com
This place reminds me of a scholarly library. The rich wood of the shelves holding the rows of tomes and the art prints that are displayed set the mood in this orderly and well-laid-out bookshop. You'll find extensive collections of new and out-of-print books on the Civil War and WWII, as well as books on other military history. If you've enjoyed a dining adventure at the Farnsworth House (see the Restaurants chapter), you may want to pick up a copy of *The Farnsworth House Recipe Book*; it is carried here exclusively. The bookshop, which is open daily, also carries a line of Civil War bronze sculptures, Civil War music, and art prints by Don Troiani and other well-known Civil War artists.

East of Lincoln Square

Gallery 30
30 York Street
(717) 334-0335
www.Gallery30.com
A nice selection of fiction and nonfiction books is on display at Gallery 30, which is open daily. Current releases are along the store's left wall, where you'll find one copy on display with its cover facing you. Owners Lois Starkey and William Gilmartin are extremely knowledgeable about the books they carry, so this is a great place to discuss the latest book that everyone's reading. The book section also has nooks that house different sections of books—one for Civil War and history books, one for spiritual and relaxation topics, and one for books for children. In business since 1978, Gallery 30 also sells educational

(and fun) games and toys, handmade jewelry, calendars and cards, and fine art by regional artists; see The Arts chapter for more on the art offerings.

Noteworthy Music
52 York Street
(717) 334-3522

In business since 1978, Noteworthy Music is a bit of a Gettysburg institution. It's even one of the buildings portrayed in miniature for sale in the gift shops around town. Owner Bob Ranalli, who does repairs on instruments, can often be found tinkering with something or other at his table in the back of the store. Bob also sells and rents guitars, drums, amps, music, and accessories, as well as doing sound engineering and rentals.

West of Lincoln Square

Arrow Horse
49 Chambersburg Street
(717) 337-2899

This shop is all about bluegrass music. You'll find lots of banjos for sale, and a bluegrass jam that is free and open to the public is held here every Friday night (see the Nightlife chapter). There's also bluegrass sheet music for sale, bluegrass CDs, and bluegrass-related collectibles.

Gettysburg Christian Bookstore
24 Chambersburg Street
(717) 334-8634

Since 1972, Gettysburg Christian Bookstore has been offering a wide array of items with something to please just about everyone. Of course you'll find lots of books, some on religious topics and some on the Civil War. But the bookstore also stocks plaques, cards, artwork, and knickknacks. The children's section carries a nice selection of books for various ages. (See the Kidstuff chapter for more details.) Gettysburg Christian Bookstore shares its address with Gettysburg Electronics, a small but fascinating shop at the

back of the store where you can buy metal detectors. (See the Specialty Shops section of this chapter for more on Gettysburg Electronics.)

Seminary Bookstore
Lutheran Theological Seminary
at Gettysburg
61 Seminary Ridge
(Milton Valentine Hall)
(717) 338-3005
www.ltsg.edu

This is the bookstore for students of the seminary, but it also has much to offer the public. One aisle is devoted to textbooks while the rest of the space has religious books, devotional resources, greeting cards, gifts, jewelry, and more. Maybe you'd like a toe ring with an inspirational message on it, or a beautiful silver cross. Most of the books deal with the Lutheran faith, but other Christian religions are also represented. The bookstore is open Monday through Friday; it's closed for lunchtime from noon to 1:30 P.M. Parking is available behind Valentine Hall, and the bookstore is on the right as you enter the building from the rear. Since there's very little if any signage on the seminary grounds, finding what you're looking for can be tricky. Valentine Hall is on Seminary Ridge (also called Confederate Avenue) beside the Adams County Historical Society, which is located in Schmucker Hall and which does have a sign out front. (For information on the historical society, which offers tours, see the Attractions chapter.)

FINE GIFTS AND HOME ACCENTS

Lincoln Square

The House of Time
17 Lincoln Square
(717) 334-9883
www.thehouseoftime.com
www.17onthesquare.com

Located on the second floor at 17 on the

Square, the House of Time has all kinds of timepieces available for sale, including wall clocks, cuckoo clocks, tabletop clocks, and grandfather clocks. Some of the clocks are new and some are from the early 1800s. You'll also find a large selection of vintage watches from the 1920s through the 1960s and parts, tools, and books on watch and clock making. But there is more than just buying and selling going on here. This is also the workshop of Jim Michaels, the proprietor, who has been crafting and repairing watches since 1974. Jim loves his work and spends Mondays making house calls on sick clocks. If you have an old watch or clock that holds sentimental value but no longer holds time, bring it in to Jim for an overhaul.

South of Lincoln Square

American Crafters Craft Mall
1919B Emmitsburg Road
(717) 337-9186
www.american-crafters.com
About 100 crafters are represented at American Crafters, located a mile out of town. As you pull in the parking lot, you'll see Americana-style signs and garden-related items, and inside you'll find handmade crafts, wood crafts, dried flowers, handpainted items, needlepoint, and much more. There are also some Gettysburg-related souvenirs, and Carolyn's Country Store (see listing within this section) is next door. American Crafters is closed on Wednesday.

Battlefield Baskets & Gifts
100 Baltimore Street
(717) 338-1565
www.acivilaffair.com
This charming shop that's open daily has a nice selection of Victorian gifts, including baskets, bells, teapots, tins, and porcelain dolls. The Victorian gifts occupy a small portion of the larger space that is filled with the Civil War clothing offered

by A Civil Affair. (For more on A Civil Affair, see the Civil War Clothing and Accessories section of the GNMP chapter.) If you want to surround yourself with period knickknacks while being properly dressed, be sure to visit this charming shop. Battlefield Baskets & Gifts is open daily.

Carolyn's Country Store
1919C Emmitsburg Road
(717) 338-9199
You can fill your home with handmade accents by checking out Carolyn's Country Store. Choices include wreaths, gift baskets, handpainted furniture and crafts, dolls, candles, hand-stitched pillows, and more. The store also sells fresh baked goods, gourmet coffees, and homemade soups and sandwiches.

If you notice a golden broom on display while shopping, the store you're in has won an award for its outside appearance. The golden broom is awarded quarterly by the Main Street Gettysburg organization, and all shops located in the borough are eligible. Stores are judged on outside cleanliness, exterior design and looks, and overall beautification efforts.

Habitat
1 Steinwehr Avenue
(717) 334-1218
www.tbhabitat.com
Tiffany lamps, pottery, candles, country dolls, bears, framed art, and gourmet foods and coffees are displayed in this charming clapboard Victorian house, circa 1860. Among the displays downstairs are miniature handpainted historic houses of Gettysburg by artist L. A. Fox and lots of Christmas-related gifts. Upstairs you'll find a room filled with delightful cat-related knickknacks, a room filled with country dolls and wooden novelties, and another room with all kinds and shapes of candles.

Downstairs in the back of the store you can pick out a sack of coffee and grind the beans right there. Habitat also has its own line of preserves, jams, jellies, and honey for you to take along home. The owners of Habitat also own the next two shops down Steinwehr Avenue, Camelot Gift Shop (see the Gift Shops/Collectibles section of this chapter) and Stoneham's Armory (see the Military Memorabilia Shops section of the GNMP chapter).

Little Orient
40 Baltimore Street
(717) 337-1997

This shop is located next to Ping's Cafe (see the Restaurants chapter), and it carries on the Oriental ambience you enjoy while dining at Ping's. Oriental vases, some up to 6½ feet tall, are on display throughout the space, and you'll also find Oriental artwork, jade jewelry, and silk scarves. Oriental teas and teapots, sake sets, beautifully painted sets of dishes and wooden bowls, and everything else needed to set the stage for a great Oriental dinner at home are also available. Little Orient opened in spring 2005 and is open daily.

East of Lincoln Square

Cathy's Country Home
2891 York Road
(717) 337-2883

Cathy's Country Home is a country-style house 5 miles east of Lincoln Square in which fine home furnishings for every room of your house are displayed on three floors. Each room setting is completely decorated with all the details that complete a room, not just the main furniture. There are lots of nooks and crannies in the house, especially on the third floor, so be sure not to miss any rooms. Cathy's Country Home opened in 1991, and although it's a bit out of town, most tourists who visit the store end up returning on subsequent trips to Gettysburg. Closed Tuesday.

Codori's Fine Art and Gifts
2 York Street
(717) 334-6371

This charming shop located on the square beside the Gettysburg Hotel displays beautiful examples of European fine gifts every day of the week. Among the many choices are German nutcrackers, teddy bears, dolls, handcrafted Santas, glass ornaments, chess sets, jewelry, Swiss music boxes, Russian lacquer boxes, and lots of different styles and types of nesting dolls.

McDannell Unique Gifts & Crafts
2031 York Road
(717) 334-9915

The name of this shop certainly is right on the money. Porcelain dolls and Native American art and crafts take up a good amount of the space, and you'll also find a large selection of Keystone candles, Americana crafts, display plates, garden knickknacks, gnomes, and a wealth of other unique goods. And that's just on the porch and first room you enter. In a second room is an area that contains living- and dining-room sets and the "Back Room," where you can pick up some great bargains. McDannell's, which is closed on Wednesday, is located just east of the U.S. Route 15 interchange with U.S. Route 30 (York Road).

West of Lincoln Square

Desert Flower
2747 Chambersburg Road
(717) 338-3456

If you're an aficionado of contemporary art, be sure to stop by this place, which is located about 5 miles west of the square. The outside of the property is decorated with traditional lawn and garden ornaments, and inside the store you'll find modern art and pottery, much of it in a Southwestern or Egyptian decor. The pottery runs the gamut from large, tall vases that look like Egyptian water pitchers to smaller eclectic works. You'll also find states of cactus, tin men, wooden Indians, and cowboys. Once you visit, you'll probably want to stop by frequently, since new stock is always arriving at this fun store that's open daily.

Fiddle Faddles and Crying Necessities
54 Chambersburg Street
(717) 334-8270
Although not a large store, Fiddle Faddles has beautiful handcrafted folk art and primitives. Owners Dick and Carol Cole have run Fiddle Faddles since its opening in 1997, and many of the items in the store are handcrafted by one of them. Fiddle Faddles is closed on Tuesday.

Jill's House Inc.
53 Chambersburg Street
(717) 338-0200
www.jills-house.com
Jill's House has two sides to it, so be sure to see all the cool stuff here. There are Primitive and Americana gifts, lots of examples of folk art on the walls and as knickknacks, Boyds Bears, VanMark Civil War figurines, Maple City Pottery adorned with Gettysburg farm scenes, Williraye collectibles, and Longaberger baskets and accessories, including those that are hard to find since they've been "retired." Take time to notice the thickness of the Civil War-era walls as you walk from one side of the house to the other. Owners Sandy and Irv Tarner opened Jill's House in November 2002, and the store is usually closed on either Monday or Tuesday.

GIFT SHOPS/ COLLECTIBLES

Lincoln Square

T&S Gifts and Mementos
19 Lincoln Square
(717) 334-3929
www.gettysburgstuff.com
Here you'll find lots of Americana items. There are T-shirts, sweatshirts, collectibles, Civil War memorabilia, coffee mugs bearing Gettysburg sites, and knickknacks sure to appeal to everyone. T&S Gifts and Mementos is open daily, and it's owned by Strickland Enterprises, a family-owned and -operated business that has served Gettysburg shoppers since 1970.

South of Lincoln Square

Blue & Grey Gift Shop
531 Baltimore Street
(717) 334-2472
www.gettysburgstuff.com
The Blue & Grey is owned by Strickland Enterprises, a family-owned and -operated Gettysburg-based business that does the custom screen printing and embroidery found on many of the T-shirts sold here and in their other shops in town. Besides the huge assortment of T-shirts that covers the shelves along the entire perimeter of Blue & Grey, you'll also find lots of hats, flags, and other Gettysburg memorabilia. There's even a room dedicated to children's clothes and appropriate memorabilia.

Camelot Gift Shop
3 Steinwehr Avenue
(717) 338-9516
www.tbhabitat.com
Camelot Gift Shop sits in a late-19th-century brick building between its two sister stores, Stoneham's Armory (see the Military Memorabilia Shops section of the GNMP chapter) and Habitat (see this chapter's Fine Gifts and Home Accents section). T-shirts, baseball caps, toy soldiers, and other Gettysburg memorabilia join educational games, puzzles, and cards to create a huge selection of souvenirs for kids and adults to enjoy poring over. I especially like to stop and read the many plaques that line both sides of the walls as I climb the stairs. Upstairs you'll find country crafts and dolls and a cute collection of dog-related items. (If you are a cat person,

the Habitat shop has a room full of cat-related items.)

Country Curiosity Store
89 Steinwehr Avenue
(717) 334-2100
www.dobbinhouse.com

If you like Crabtree & Evelyn products, be sure to stop by Country Curiosity—the area's exclusive Crabtree & Evelyn dealer. The shop is located at the Dobbin House, the oldest house in Gettysburg, and it's set up to remind you of a general store. Here you'll also discover souvenirs, tinware, jams, jellies, foodstuffs, dolls, and much more. It's easy to while away some time here before or after enjoying the great food served at the Dobbin House's tavern or fine-dining restaurant. (See the Restaurants chapter for more on the Dobbin House.)

Flex & Flannigan's 1863 Sutler Shop
240 Steinwehr Avenue
(717) 338-0451

In business since 1999, Flex & Flannigan's has souvenirs in the front of the shop, and then it's all clothes, clothes, and more clothes in the next three rooms up the stairs. There are lots of T-shirts with all kinds of messages on them and lots of sweatshirts in all kinds of styles and sizes. Although packed with merchandise, the store has a tiered effect that makes the area seem large, with plenty of room to browse the racks. Open late into the evening in summer.

---

i

Gettysburg stores that use "sutler" in their names do so to signal that they have the goods to fulfill the needs of Civil War reenactors. During the Civil War, a regiment usually had one sutler—a civilian camp follower who traveled with the troops and sold them "luxury" items, which could range from food and liquors to pens and paper and military goods.

Gettysburg Souvenirs and Gifts
27 Steinwehr Avenue
(717) 334-1200

213 Steinwehr Avenue
(717) 337-0020

These two stores are owned and operated by brothers, and each location is chock-full. The store at 213 Steinwehr used to house the Conflict Museum, and the store at 27 Steinwehr was formerly called Bases Loaded. The brothers changed the name to reflect that there's lots more here than baseball-card collections. Most noticeable are the abundance of T-shirts for sale. More than 350 styles are available, and they are displayed everywhere, even as you go up the staircase to the rooms above. The store at 213 Steinwehr has a more orderly layout, with lots of souvenirs on display as well as T-shirts and leather vests and jackets. Both locations have excellent selections of Beanie Babies.

Grannie's II
13 Steinwehr Avenue
(717) 334-8704, (800) 827-5127
www.grannies.com

Grannie's II offers apparel with custom screen printing and embroidery as well as Gettysburg-related souvenirs, flags, and books. VanMark military figures and soy candles from Old Virginia are also featured in the shop. Most of the shirts sold here are made by the staff at Grannie's North Fifth Street manufacturing location. Grannie's II opened in Gettysburg in 1995; the original Grannie's has been around since 1987 and is located about 20 minutes away in Emmitsburg, Maryland. Grannie's is proud to have been the first company to offer the National Fire Academy, located in Emmitsburg, embroidered class shirts, an operation they continue to this day. If you're interested, Grannie's can also custom make apparel that features your company or organization.

Great T-Shirt Company
65 Steinwehr Avenue
(717) 334-8611

This spacious store features lots of T-shirts

and sweatshirts as well as other apparel and Gettysburg-related souvenirs on its first floor. When you climb the wide stairs to the second floor, you'll discover fine dolls and Civil War–period memorabilia. Tickets for the Sleepy Hollow Candlelight Ghost Tours (see the Attractions chapter) are also sold here.

House of Bender
1 Baltimore Street
(717) 334-4315
The building the House of Bender gift shop occupies has quite a history. Built in 1817, it was a general store and a professor's home at the time of the Battle of Gettysburg. During the battle, it served as a Union hospital, and the third floor was used by Union sharpshooters. Today, the House of Bender resides in the building's first floor, offering colonial and Old Virginia soy candles, pewter, picture frames, and jewelry. Civil War books, T-shirts and sweatshirts, Pennsylvania Dutch hex signs, Civil War art, Civil War chess sets, and a myriad of souvenirs are for sale as well. House of Bender has an engraving service for plaques and awards. The store is open daily.

Spin Wheel Fashions
42 Baltimore Street
(717) 337-2214
After residing at 46 Chambersburg Street for 17 years, Spin Wheel Fashions relocated to this new location in spring 2005. Here you'll find lots and lots of T-shirts, all on hangers for easy inspection. Sweatshirts, sweatpants, and baseball caps round out the apparel selections, and some books on the Civil War and Gettysburg-related souvenirs are also available. Ask about their custom silk screening and embroidery. Spin Wheel Fashions is open daily.

The Turning Point
244 Steinwehr Avenue
(717) 334-5993
www.gettysburgstuff.com
The Turning Point is owned by Strickland Enterprises, a Gettysburg family-owned

and -operated business that runs numerous shops in town. This shop has lots of Gettysburg-related souvenirs and apparel, and one section of the store is reserved for Christmas collectibles. You'll find Department 56, Dickens Village, Snowbabies, and other series on display.

East of Lincoln Square

Crabtree General Store
38 York Street
(717) 337-9017
This delightful store is owned by Yvonne Nitz. Yvonne's husband was one of President Eisenhower's Secret Service agents, and he and Yvonne visited Gettysburg with Ike. Although her husband has passed away, Yvonne has made Gettysburg her home. She ran an ice-cream shop on Lincoln Square during the 1990s before opening Crabtree General Store in 2005. The store consists of two rooms that hold fine gifts, everyday staples, snacks, souvenirs, 80 varieties of hot sauces, books, and many other items. A back room is all about kids—here you'll find toys, dolls, school supplies, and much more. If you forgot something at home, you can probably find a replacement here.

West of Lincoln Square

The Front Porch on Buford
114 Buford Avenue
(717) 334-0808, (717) 495-4510
www.thefrontporchonbuford.com
One-of-a-kind items for the garden and house decorate this beautiful two-story Victorian house that sits across from the post office. The Front Porch on Buford fills its two floors with furniture, fine linens, designer jewelry, gourmet food, home and garden accents, antiques and reproductions, prints and frames, and more. Goods are creatively grouped together in galleries throughout the house, and unique treasures await around each corner. Find-

ing that perfect gift for someone special is easy here, and a gift registry is available for weddings and anniversaries. Baby gifts are also on display, and gift baskets can be custom-made. The Victorian's front porch has comfy chairs where nonshoppers can rest a bit, and during nice weather they can treat themselves to cookies and lemonade and read a magazine (*Fortune, Field & Stream,* and *Popular Science* are usually available) while they wait for the shoppers of their group. Inside, there's a children's nook, a tiny portion of the store that has a table with chairs where kids can draw or play while you shop. The Front Porch on Buford is open Tuesday through Saturday and by appointment on Sunday and Monday.

JEWELRY

Coffman Jewelers
28 Baltimore Street
(717) 334-1510

Talk about staying power—Coffman Jewelers was established in 1948. Today the third generation of this family of jewelers will serve you in this elegant shop. You'll find exquisite diamonds and gemstone jewelry within the glass cases on each side of the store. Prices are reasonable—and browsing is always free!

The Jeweler's Daughter
49 Steinwehr Avenue
(717) 338-0770
www.jewelersdaughter.com

The Jeweler's Daughter is a line of jewelry that focuses on the period from 1840 to 1870. The jewelry fills two cases, and the reenactment clothes of the Regimental Quartermaster (see the Military Memorabilia Shops section of the GNMP chapter) surround the cases. The stones and styling of the jewelry have been researched to ensure that the pieces truly represent the era. The Jeweler's Daughter also repairs antique jewelry and watches, many times right on the premises.

Mine Run Gems
53 Steinwehr Avenue
(717) 334-9398

Mine Run Gems owner C. S. Hammer announced in spring 2005 that he is retiring once he sells his merchandise. If the shop is still around when you visit, this is an excellent opportunity to acquire fine jewelry at a good price. Be sure to look for the custom jewelry made by C. S. himself.

MARKETS

If your kids like to eat fresh-from-the-field fruit, see the Kidstuff chapter for farms and orchards that allow you to pick your own vitamin-filled treat.

Gettysburg Farmers' Market
Lincoln Square
(717) 334-8151 (chamber of commerce)

Since 1992 the Gettysburg Farmers' Market on Lincoln Square has been held on Saturday mornings beginning at 7:00 A.M. from spring to early fall. This is a "producer only" market, meaning that vendors must grow, produce, bake, or otherwise create their wares. You'll find fresh produce, baked goods, herbal products, and more. Ask a vendor for tokens for on-street parking near the market or park in the Racehorse Alley parking garage behind the Gettysburg Hotel.

Round Barn and Farm Market
298 Cashtown Road, Biglerville
(717) 334-1984
www.roundbarngettysburg.com

The historic Round Barn, located 8 miles west of Gettysburg, was built in 1914. It's one of only three round barns, also called barrel barns, left in Pennsylvania, and it's owned by Knouse Fruitlands, Inc., which is owned and operated by the Knouse family. The family bought the barn in 1985 and opened the market in 1993 for two weeks during the National Apple Harvest Festival (see the Annual Events and Festivals chapter). Those two weeks were so suc-

Apple Country

When in Gettysburg, you're never far from a fruit farm, and Adams County is especially known for its apples. There are even two festivals held in honor of apples—the Apple Blossom Festival in May and the National Apple Harvest Festival in October (see the Annual Events and Festivals chapter for more on these festivals). Apples are low in calories, fat free, sodium free, cholesterol free, and an excellent source of fiber. Here's a short list of the more than 100 varieties of apples that are grown in the United States.

Empire: Color is red or green; sweet-tart taste

Fuji: Color is a red blush with green and yellow stripes; sweet taste

Gala: Color is red-orange with yellow stripes; sweet taste

Golden Delicious: Color is yellow-green with a pink blush; sweet taste

Granny Smith: Color is green, sometimes with a pink blush; tart taste

Jonagold: Color is bright red and gold; sweet or slightly tart taste

Jonathan: Color is light red stripes over yellow or deep red; moderately tart taste

McIntosh: Color is red or green; sweet-tart taste

Newtown Pippin: Color is green; slightly tart taste

Red Delicious: Color is striped to solid red; sweet taste

Rome: Color is deep solid red; slightly sweet taste

cessful they decided to open the barn for the next year's season, and it's been operating every year since on a daily basis from May through October. The Round Barn offers one of the largest selections of varieties of apples throughout the season, and whatever produce is in season is sure to be on sale here, as well as crafts, clothing with Red Barn logos, jams, jellies, preserves, candy, fudge, and lots more. The barn itself is an attraction; its circumference is 282 feet, with a diameter of more than 87 feet. It was constructed around a central silo measuring 60 feet high and 12 feet wide, with a storage capacity of 145 tons of silage. The silo is the hub, with 38 spokes that form the interior structure and support for the second floor. All but one of the spokes are single lengths of wood—each nearly 37 feet long. As originally constructed, the barn could house 50 head of cattle and about 16 horses or mules. After you check out the wide selection of goods on the first floor, climb the narrow steps to the second floor. When you enter, go ahead and look up, and up, in awe at the magnificent construction—everyone does. To reach the Round Barn, head out of town on Chambersburg Road (US 30 West), make a right onto Cashtown Road, and follow the signs for Round Barn. The barn is less than 0.5 mile from the turn onto Cashtown Road.

MINIMALLS

The shops below offer you downtown shopping in quaint settings, but there are also a few shopping centers around town that offer more everyday shopping experiences. At the east end of town along York Street you'll find a Wal-Mart on one side of the road and the Peebles Shopping Center on the other. The main store in the shopping center is the Peebles department store. There's also a Giant food store along this stretch of road. At the western end of town there's a Kennie's food market along West Street and the Gettysburg Shopping Center on Springs Avenue, which has eateries and a Dollar General store. The North Mall, north of town along U.S. Business Route 15, is the home of the Gettysburg campus of the Harrisburg Area Community College (see the Education and Child Care chapter). It also houses among its tenants a Weis grocery store as well as the area's Curves for Women (see the Recreation chapter).

Old Gettysburg Village
777 Baltimore Street

This charming area has the ambience of a small village, with its shops connected by wooden walkways and lots of places to sit and relax. There's a separate parking lot for the village behind the Gettysburg Travelodge, which can be accessed from Baltimore or Steinwehr Street. The biggest store in the village is the Horse Soldier (see the Military Memorabilia Shops section of the GNMP chapter), which expanded as space became available. The Horse Soldier has a separate gift shop, called Hallowed Ground, which offers mainly T-shirts and a small selection of books, souvenirs, and gifts. Other shops within the village include Highland Rose

Civil War Sutlery (see the Civil War Clothing and Accessories section of the GNMP chapter), Caldwell's Originals (see The Arts chapter), and the Moccasin Shop, where you can find Minnetonka Moccasins in all styles and sizes.

Patriot Point
241 Steinwehr Avenue
(717) 337-0080
www.patriotpoint.us

Although it appears to be one shop from the outside, Patriot Point actually consists of a number of businesses under one roof. Many people wonder about the wooden beams on the outside of the building that resemble an upside-down V. These are actually the remains of a steeple that used to hold a cross when the building was the Prince of Peace Museum during the 1970s.

Knowing which business you're in while browsing Patriot Point isn't always easy, especially since the goods in the stores often complement one another. Just find what you want and someone will point you toward the correct cash register. Among the stores are The General's Store, where you can stop for some refreshments before perusing the gifts, T-shirts, and Civil War souvenirs stocked here, and Supply Wagon Sutlers, which offers supplies for the reenactor. Also located here are Patriot Point Theatre and the U.S. Christian Commission Museum. (See The Arts chapter for more on the theater and the Attractions chapter for more on the museum.)

OUTLET SHOPPING

Gettysburg Village Factory Stores
Junction of U.S. Route 15 and Route 97
(Baltimore Street)
(717) 337-9705, (800) 868-7553
www.gettysburgvillage.com

Gettysburg Village is reminiscent of a quaint Main Street in 1860s America. Brand-name outlets line each side of a wide boulevard, and there's parking right in front of the stores. Among the 70 stores at this 260,000-square-foot shop-

Patriot Point minimall pays homage to our troops with its Wall of Honor, where photos of military personnel are displayed. You can bring in a framed photo (no larger than 4 inches by 6 inches) or send in a photo by mail. Patriot Point also collects and disperses items requested by the troops in Iraq. Call (717) 737-0080 for a list.

ping center are such brand-name factory outlets as Old Navy, Liz Claiborne, Van Heusen, Casual Corner, Bass, Etienne Aigner, OshKosh B'Gosh, Pfaltzgraff, Eddie Bauer, GAP, Dress Barn, and Zales the Diamond Store. There's a bible outlet and a book outlet (see the Books and Music section in this chapter) and other specialty stores, such as Kulpsville Antiques and the Civil War Store, where you can find lots of Gettysburg and Civil War clothing and memorabilia. A food court, with choices from barbecue, sandwiches, and pizza to Chinese, and an entertainment area are located at the one end of the mall. And there are plenty of places to find snacks along the way, including Harry and David and Pepperidge Farms outlets, an Auntie Anne's pretzel store, and the Fuzziwigs Candy Factory. Fuzziwigs is a fun store that stocks delicious candy and nostalgic items such as lots of different Pez candy and dispensers. The Elan Tea Room also calls Gettysburg Village home. Not attached to but on the mall grounds in separate buildings are Country Inn & Suites (see the Hotels, Motels, and Resorts chapter), a TGI Friday's restaurant, and a nine-screen movie theater (see the Recreation chapter). Gettysburg Village is located just a few miles south of town off Baltimore Street.

SPECIALTY SHOPS

Lincoln Square

Seven Valleys Wine Shop
17 Lincoln Square
(717) 339-0017
www.17onthesquare.com
This store is tucked into a corner of 17 on the Square, but it makes good use of its small space. The winery, located outside Shrewsbury, Pennsylvania, produces 3,000 bottles a year, and this shop showcases the winery's full range of wines. There's an experienced wine steward who will be more than willing to help you select just

During September, many of the stores at Gettysburg Village collect nonperishable goods to send to the troops overseas and sell stars you can use to send messages. The stars come in three colors: $10.00 for a red star, $5.00 for a blue star, and $1.00 for a white star. Each star has plenty of space to write a greeting, your name, and your hometown.

the right wine for your occasion, and free tastings are available. The wine shop is open daily.

North of Lincoln Square

An Early Elegance
113 Carlisle Street
(717) 338-9311
(800) 750-6130 (orders only)
www.anearlyelegance.com
Owner Mary Myers established An Early Elegance in 1988, and she's had a shop in Gettysburg since 1995. She started out on Steinwehr Avenue, resided for a while in Old Gettysburg Village, and moved in fall of 2005 to this location right up the street from the Majestic Theater (see The Arts chapter) and the Lincoln Diner (see the Restaurants chapter). Mary's new space is bright and welcoming, and there's lots of room for her to display her goods, which include more than 300 loose or bagged teas, tea accessories, books, and ladies' hats and accoutrements. An Early Elegance is the largest tea merchant in the area. The store is open seven days a week year-round.

Tommy Gilbert's Hobby Shop
346 East Water Street
(717) 337-1992
www.gilbertshobbies.com
Although it's not in an area with a lot of

other businesses, this hobby shop is definitely worth a separate stop. You'll find art supplies, kits to build models from scratch, and lots of stuff for the railroad builder. Tommy's main claim to fame is his Gettysburg souvenir rail cars, which he designs himself and has produced by Co. K. The two box cars that are currently available come in HO, O, and N gauge, and other cars are in development. There are also lots of brass engines and other cars to pick from here, as well as all the accoutrements a great railroad layout needs.

Tommy's store is open daily year-round except on New Year's Day, Easter Sunday, Thanksgiving, and Christmas. Tommy's uncle started the business, which was then located along Steinwehr Avenue, in 1944, and Tommy's been at this location since 1987. To get to the shop from Lincoln Square, travel 1 block up Carlisle Street and turn right onto East Water Street. After you cross North Stratton Street, the store is located near the end of the street on the left.

South of Lincoln Square

Boyds Bear Country
75 Cunningham Road
(717) 630-2600, (866) 367-8338
www.BoydsBearCountry.com
This 120,000-square-foot store, which bills itself as the World's Most Humongous Teddy Bear Store, houses 70,000 Boyds bears, hares, and other friends about 5.5 miles south of Lincoln Square off Steinwehr Avenue. The stuffed animals come in all sizes, and the displays throughout the store are stunning. The animals are clothed in different costumes and placed in settings such as a Civil War encampment, a farm, Noah's Ark, and many, many more creative ways. Boyds Bears and collectibles have become collectors' items, and certain bears are retired each year, which increases the bears' worth. Benches

are placed by the store's second- and third-floor windows so you can sit and enjoy fantastic views of the countryside. The store also has a beautiful two-story stone fireplace, and live entertainment is often featured in the first-floor atrium. The first floor also houses the Boyds History Hall Free Museum, which chronicles the inspirational story of Boyds Bear Country. You can make your own teddy bear at Digby's Super Duper Bear Factory™ or adopt a baby bear cub at Boyds Teddy Bear Nursery™ on the third floor. This floor also contains lots of outfits for clothing the new member of your family. The downstairs is devoted to satisfying your hunger, offering dining areas that serve full meals and sandwiches, a bakery, an ice-cream store, and a candy store. Boyds Bear Country is open to 6:00 P.M. daily.

Gettysburg Cigar Co.
523 Baltimore Street
(717) 339-0400
www.gettysburgcigarco.net
Owner Gary Mohan first came to Gettysburg on a trip to research an ancestor who had been in the Battle of Gettysburg. Gary and his wife liked the town so much they decided to make it their own. Some of the fine cigars available here are Arturo Fuente (including opus x), Drew Estate, Cusano, and Padron (1964 series). Gary also has a beautiful selection of pipes, many in custom-designed cases. Be sure to check out his Church Warden pipes when you stop by. If you're not really a smoker but you'd love to walk the battlefield with a cigar, Gary can also steer you to a mild blend that won't have you regretting your indulgence. Also available are tobacco melds, snuff and chew, period-appropriate pipes, and logo shirts and hats. Gettysburg Cigar Co. is closed on Tuesday.

Holiday Spirits
302 Baltimore Street
(717) 873-9379
This shop is all about Christmas, no matter what time of year it is. Beautifully deco-

rated trees are throughout the store, and yuletide offerings beckon from all corners. The ornaments and decorations are reasonably priced, and the entire store is just a delight to browse in. The downstairs has a myriad of items while the upstairs rooms are decorated by theme. There's the Americana Room, with lots of patriotic Christmas items, the Victorian room, the Lodge, with all kinds of wooden treasures, and the Kids Room.

Irish Brigade Shop
504 Baltimore Street
(717) 337-2519
www.irishbrigadegiftshop.com
This elegant, air-conditioned shop celebrates the Fighting Irish brigade of the Union Army and all things Irish on T-shirts, hats, and sweatshirts, through music and videos, and with beautiful Irish fine gifts. Claddagh rings are among the jewelry offerings, and Irish cut glass and china are on display. Irish sayings adorn lots of the merchandise, often making your visit quite amusing. Open daily, the Irish Brigade also has clothes for the little ones that are sure to make anyone say, "Ahh, isn't that cute." The Web site mainly concentrates on the Irish Brigade, while the store has a much broader selection of Irish goods.

Just Friends Gift Emporium
312 Baltimore Street
(717) 334-9995
Just Friends was opened in April 2004 by four friends who wanted a place to showcase their homemade candies, silk and dried flower arrangements, and other crafts. This place certainly fits the bill, with enough space available to offer wicker furniture, candles, Christmas collectibles, Victorian tea sets, art prints, Victorian handmade jewelry, all-natural lotions, and much more. Be sure to take a walk up the stairs so you don't miss any of the unique gifts on display. Just Friends is closed on Monday and Tuesday.

Servant's Old Tyme Photos
237 Steinwehr Avenue
(717) 334-7256
You can dress in period clothing and have your picture taken in the building where General Reynolds was taken after he was shot and killed on the battlefield during the first day of the Battle of Gettysburg. Pictures are taken with a digital camera, and prices are based on the number of people in the photo. The cost for two people is $20, and the wardrobe and accessories are included in the price. After you've sat for your portrait, you choose which picture you want printed out. You receive either two 5- by 7-inch or one 8- by 10-inch portrait with one standard heirloom-look mat. In 2005 Servant's began offering photos that look like paintings on canvas, and you can either have your photo taken there or bring in a photo for this service. Servant's Old Tyme Photos is open daily within the stone building known as the Historic General Reynolds House.

Wilderness Lodge Leather & Hat Shop
11 Steinwehr Avenue
(717) 334-8866
Here you'll find a fine selection of leather goods, including hats, handbags, wallets, belts, vests, chaps, gloves, and jackets. The case in the front of the store contains jewelry also. You're likely to find Jake the Black Cat among all the great-smelling leather, probably in the back of the shop sleeping. Give him a pet as you browse the shop, which also has jars of hot sauces for sale.

The staff of Wilderness Lodge Leather & Hat Shop are fun people. If you want to have a little fun too, have someone you're with ask for one of their business cards. When the clerk gives out the card, it looks like a folded $20 bill.

East of Lincoln Square

Battlefield Harley Davidson/Buell
21 Calvary Field Road
(717) 337-9005
www.battlefieldharley-davidson.com
Open since July 2000, this large Harley Davidson store is located about a mile east of the US 30 and US 15 interchange. Open daily, you'll find everything here you need to ride your hog in style. You can also buy a bike here, rent a bike, or have your bike repaired. Battlefield also participates in many area events, such as History Meets the Arts in April (see the Annual Events and Festivals chapter), when they host artists who create hog art.

Chrome Gardens
147 York Street
(717) 337-3725
www.chromegardens.com
This is Gettysburg's tattoo and body-piercing shop, open since 1994. Owner Stacy McCleaf has won numerous awards for her tattoo and flash designs and considers herself an artist, which is why you won't find any temporary tattoos in this shop. Most tattoos done here are custom designed, and strict sterilization techniques are employed. You must be 18 years old to enter the shop, and there is no smoking or alcohol allowed.

The Homefront
25 York Street
(717) 337-3741
www.thehomefront1940s.com
The motto of this fun store is "Swing into the 40s," and you will be immersed in the decade as soon as you walk through the door. You can grab an old-fashioned bottle of Coke out of the icebox (Cokes are free to servicemen), check out the milk box complete with milk bottles, and marvel at all the memories that the items of the store evoke. Among the treasures are vintage furniture, collectibles, fashions, and lots of 1940s art on the walls. Be sure to check out the reproductions of Crosley radios, record players, and phones, and the old cameras that are tucked into one corner of the store. Though this shop is just one room, it's crammed with lots of nostalgia, and it's a fun place to reminisce about the way things used to be.

West of Lincoln Square

Carver's Toyland
305 Buford Avenue
(717) 334-6937
This place is easy to find—its sign is in the shape of a train engine. Carver's Toyland stocks trains—Lionel, American Flyer, Thomas the Tank, HOs of all gauges—and all the accessories to complete your railroad layout. The owner compares the place to Madison Hardware of New York City in the 1950s, where you could pick up any and all types of toy trains and accessories. Though it looks really small from the outside, the shop just keeps unfolding into additional rooms once you're inside, with each room holding more train-related treasure. One of the rooms even has a working train layout that you can run. You can bring your trains here for repair, and Mr. Carver also repairs clocks. The store has cuckoo clocks, grandfather clocks, and unique clocks for sale. Christmas collectibles are Mrs. Carver's passion, and one room is filled with cases of whimsical offerings for sale. Although it's not for sale, be sure to check out Mrs. Carver's personal collection of Christmas memorabilia that's on display. The Carvers have been at this location since before 1975, and they buy and sell their trains and collectibles seven days a week.

Gettysburg Electronics
24 Chambersburg Street
(717) 334-8634, (717) 334-1282
Gettysburg Electronics has a wide range of metal detectors in a few aisles at the back of the Gettysburg Christian Bookstore, also at this address. (See the Books and Music section of this chapter for more

on the Gettysburg Christian Bookstore.) An avid detectorist himself since the late 1960s, owner Don Hicks opened the place in 1972. Don supplies lots of accessories for treasure hunting, and he's also a wealth of knowledge on the subject. Don't be shy about bartering if you have some Civil War relics or other cool stuff you've found with your detector; Don will sometimes accept these as partial payment on your purchase. If you're considering hunting for relics on the battlefield—*don't*. Metal detectors or any relic hunting is prohibited in the park (and all national parks), and heavy fines and confiscation of your equipment and even your car await you if you disobey the rules.

Hacienda Shiloh—International Garlic, Teas & Herbs
327 Knox Road
(717) 642-9161
www.haciendashiloh.com

Hacienda Shiloh means House of Tranquillity, and this small organic herb farm tucked away in the backroads of Gettysburg certainly lives up to its name. You wind along country lanes to a home that sits on a hill about 8 miles west of town, surrounded by trees and nature. Follow the path to the garden and garlic shed, where more than 20 varieties of garlic from Russia, Italy, France, the Czech Republic, Germany, Poland, and Israel are hanging. After you admire the plants and garlic, head back to the small shop that's attached to the house to discover a grand selection of culinary and medicinal herbs; more than 120 custom-blended teas; handmade herbal soaps, salts, and lotions; dehydrated rice, soup, and stew blends that are ideal for camping meals; beeswax candles; herbal blends, rubs, and salt substitutes; and much more. Hacienda Shiloh has one of the largest collections of medicinal herbs in the Mid-Atlantic region, and the owners supply herbs to the practitioners at the nearby Gettysburg Holistic Health Center (see the Health Care and Wellness chapter). Gift baskets are available, and one corner of the store has

leather goods, medicinal head wraps, bead jewelry, and a wealth of other eclectic items. To reach Hacienda Shiloh, head west from town on Route 116 (Middle Street), and turn right when you reach the Needle & Thread Fabrics shop (see the Civil War Clothing and Accessories section of the GNMP chapter). Follow the country road for about 3 miles and veer left onto Knox Road at the KOA Kampground (see the Campgrounds and RV Parks chapter). Hacienda Shiloh is about a mile farther on the right.

Petite Puppy Boutique
51 Chambersburg Street
(717) 337-2456

The Petite Puppy Boutique opened in July 2005, and it's run by a mother-and-daughter team who loves animals. When they were operating as Noah's Ark in Fairfield, they used to have all kinds of animals, but they now specialize in teacup and toy breeds of dogs and purebred cats. They also carry just about every pet accessory you can imagine. Four seamstresses create the clothes by hand, and there's a wide selection of designer leashes and collars. Puppy handbags, handcrafted pet beds, and designer feeding bowls are also available for the discerning pet. The pets for sale are at the back of the store, and there's a bench available so you can sit and watch the animals' antics. One side of the store is dedicated to a grooming salon and a gourmet bakery for dogs and cats, so you can take a treat home to your pampered pet. The Petite Puppy Boutique is closed on Wednesday.

Rose Garden Natural Food
39 West Street
(717) 338-0835

A large selection of natural and unprocessed food, organic produce, bulk products, and vitamin supplements can be found at this store located in the Gettysburg Shopping Center, which is next to the Dollar General that's along Chambersburg Street. Owners Jacky and Kitty Rose began the store in 1997, and it's open every day but Sunday. Three-quarters of the store is dedicated to natural food selections, while the rest of the area holds health-related items. Also stocked are environmentally safe cleaning supplies and laundry detergent, organic personal-hygiene items, books on categories from cooking to healthy healing, and natural pet foods. When buying bulk products, shoppers can bag just the amount they want.

Yellow Canary Market
45 Chambersburg Street
(717) 334-9390

This gourmet market reminds me of shops found in New York City—it's narrow and small, and two people browsing at the same time can easily bump into each other. Fresh breads, aged cheese, gourmet groceries, and items from the menu of the Blue Parrot Bistro next door (see the Restaurants chapter) beckon you toward the display cases, while interesting cookware and glassware beg to be filled with the delicacies found there. The market is closed on Monday and Tuesday.

SWEETS & TREATS

Cannonball Olde Tyme Malt Shoppe
11 York Street
(717) 334-9695

This small shop has only five tables, but it carries 49 flavors of milk shakes and malts. Cones, sundaes, ice-cream sodas, and banana splits round out the ice-cream treats, while soups, sandwiches, salads, wraps, and quesadillas are available for those who like to eat before they snack.

Look up and a little to the left of the entrance to Cannonball Old Tyme Malt Shoppe and you'll see how the shop got its name. Yep, that's a projectile from the Battle of Gettysburg embedded in the wall.

Cannonball is a family-run business that's open seasonally; during the season it's closed on Tuesday. If you've never had a phosphate or a malt, this is a great place to treat your taste buds.

Garrahy's Fudge Kitchen
625 Baltimore Street
(717) 334-7342

This small shop is across from the Gettysburg Tour Center at the entrance to Old Gettysburg Village. All that's sold here is great-tasting fudge, and the no-frills store consists of a glass case where the fudge is displayed and an area where the fudge is made, which is in plain view. Since there's only one thing to buy here, and the fudge comes in only six flavors, you can get your fudge quickly and be on your way, happily satisfied and avoiding long lines elsewhere. Garrahy's Fudge Kitchen is open daily.

Gettysburg Pretzel Co., Inc.
1875 York Road
(717) 338-9081

The pretzels here are hand-rolled and baked in a brick oven, giving them a just-baked taste. The store consists of a counter and some shelves that hold boxes of hard pretzels. Soft pretzels are sold out of a large cardboard box on the counter. The whole operation occurs at this building, from the making of the dough to the rolling and the baking of the pretzels. If you're curious how it's done, tours are cheerfully given. Pretzels can be shipped throughout the country, and once you taste these goodies, you'll be placing your order.

Kilwin's of Gettysburg
37 Steinwehr Avenue
(717) 337-2252
www.kilwins.com

The first Kilwin's was opened by Don and Katy Kilwin in 1947 in Petoskey, Michigan. Today there are franchises in 10 states. Sisters and co-owners Paige Levan and Polly Parone opened the Gettysburg Kilwin's, the only one in Pennsylvania, in

1993. Since then they have been treating the people in Gettysburg to homemade chocolates, fudge, and ice cream daily from the ground floor of a 100-year-old frame house. If you're lucky, you can watch the chocolate being made in the shop; the heavenly smells alone make the trip worthwhile.

Kool Scoops
531 Baltimore Street
(917) 613-8046
This seasonal shop is a walk-up window at a small building that looks like it used to be a garage. Italian ice and ice cream are available in cones or dishes for walkaway orders; there are no seats here. Because you simply look over the ice-cream flavors and make your selection, the line here

moves quickly—a welcome relief on a hot day.

Sunset Ice Cream Parlor
33 Steinwehr Avenue
(717) 337-3125
With its bright orange, red, and yellow exterior, you can't miss the Sunset Ice Cream Parlor. This old-fashioned ice-cream shop sells Sunset brand ice cream, which is made in Williamsport, Pennsylvania. The bright colors outside are carried inside, where there are about five small tables that give you a place to enjoy your ice cream while cooling off in the store's air-conditioning. Outside there are picnic tables for those who prefer to people watch as they enjoy their treats. Sunset accepts cash only and is open daily.

THE ARTS

The Arts are an integral part of the Gettysburg community, and many shops feature the works of local artists on their walls and shelves. You'll find galleries boasting the art of well-known Civil War artists alongside the works of regional artists, and this delightful mix guarantees a new experience on every visit. The biggest event for those who admire fine art is the annual History Meets the Arts, held every April, when the town galleries show off their collections and host artists and events throughout the weekend. (See the Annual Events and Festivals chapter for more on History Meets the Arts.) But you can be sure there are plenty of places in town to discover interesting art anytime you visit. Although a great many of the galleries offer art representing the Civil War genre, you'll also discover contemporary and unique shops along the way. Entries for Gettysburg galleries and studios are listed alphabetically within geographic direction from Lincoln Square.

The performing arts are also well represented here, as they have been for decades. The Totem Pole Playhouse has been entertaining theatergoers since the 1950s, and the Majestic theatre hosted the Eisenhowers during the fifties when Ike was president. Today both theaters are still integral parts of the local entertainment scene, which has grown to include dinner and regional theater. Of course, arts flourish best when they are locally supported, and Gettysburg has numerous organizations that promote art throughout the region.

GALLERIES AND STUDIOS

Lincoln Square

Hard Bean Cafe
17 Lincoln Square
(717) 338-0929
www.17onthesquare.com
The Hard Bean Cafe has provided exhibition space for local artists since 2002. Exhibits run for two months, with each new exhibit opening on the first Friday of the scheduled month. An artists' reception with snacks and beverages is held on opening night. For a rundown of the delicious treats available here, see the write-up in the Restaurants chapter.

North of Lincoln Square

Schmucker Art Gallery
Gettysburg College
North Washington and Water Streets
(717) 337-6125
www.gettysburg.edu
This 1,600-square-foot gallery space is located on the main floor of Schmucker Hall on the Gettysburg College campus. Seven to eight different exhibitions are displayed at the gallery each year, and everyone from the campus and the community is welcome to attend the opening receptions that are held for each event. Every year includes shows by local, national, and international contemporary

---

Many galleries host artists on the first Friday of every month during the summer season, usually from 6:00 to 8:00 P.M. You can meet the artists and enjoy wine and cheese as you admire the art. It's part of the town's First Friday program, where some businesses hold special events or stay open longer. Look for colorful First Friday flags outside participating shops.

artists, a faculty exhibition, a student exhibition, the annual senior art major show, and traveling exhibits.

During the summer, the gallery is open every day but Monday and is closed on college holidays. You can park for free in one of the visitor parking lots on campus, and some free two-hour parking can be found on North Washington and Water Streets. The main entrance is through the quadrangle side of the building.

South of Lincoln Square

Aces High Gallery
433 Baltimore Street
(717) 337-0779
www.aceshighgallery.com

Aces High is owned by Steve and Barbara Shultz, who were raised in Gettysburg. Steve left his position as chef at the historic Farnsworth House and Barbara left a career in real estate in January 1992 to open an art/picture framing studio, which they named Lasting Impressions. Steve decided to sell some of his collection of WWII aviation art at the studio, and in 1995 the couple renamed the business to reflect this, giving it its current name. Aces High is open daily and offers diecasts, model kits, prints, posters, frames, and autographed books and photos. Many veteran gatherings, book signings, and symposiums are also held at the gallery. Aces High Gallery is located within A Sentimental Journey Bed & Breakfast, which the Shultzes also own and which consists of five rooms decorated in WWI- and WWII-era decor. (See the Bed-and-Breakfasts and Guesthouses chapter for more details.)

Caldwell's Originals
Old Gettysburg Village
777 Baltimore Street
(717) 334-6737

This unique shop showcases the sculptured sports and historical miniatures and dioramas of Chuck Caldwell, who opened Caldwell's Originals in 1981. Chuck began sculpting at the age of three, when his mother gave him clay to quiet him in church. Today he has sculpted almost 14,000 miniatures. His work appears in many museums, including the Franklin Mint, and within the Hall of Presidents in Gettysburg. Chuck also created the model for the Korean War Veterans Memorial in Washington, D.C. His work has been sold to people in every state and in 14 foreign countries.

Chuck's shop is beside the Horse Soldier (see the Military Memorabilia Shops section of the GNMP chapter) in Old Gettysburg Village. Since he deals mainly in work that is commissioned, his store hours are a bit erratic, but generally he's around from noon to 4:00 P.M. except on Wednesday, when the shop is closed.

Civil War Fine Art
333 Baltimore Street
(717) 338-3463
www.civilwarfineart.com

Artist and owner A. V. Lindenberger's work is featured at Civil War Fine Art, a cozy space that opened in 2004. Amy works in colored pencil, and you can often watch her drawing as she sits by the window along Baltimore Street. Originals and prints are offered at the gallery, and there's something to fit everyone's price range. In 2004 Amy completed the 15th image in her series "Beyond the Battlefield," which focuses on the Civil War soldier and those who loved him. Because Amy has another studio in Ohio, where she also teaches art, the studio in Gettysburg is open only for limited hours, usually Friday from 4:00 to 8:00 P.M., Saturday from 11:00 A.M. to 8:00 P.M., and Sunday from 11:00 A.M. to 2:00 P.M.

Gallon Historical Art, Inc.
9 Steinwehr Avenue
(717) 334-0430
www.gallon.com

Here you can enjoy historical art created by Dale Gallon, a well-known artist in the

Civil War market for more than 25 years. Dale has more than 100 images in his complete works, which include paintings and limited-edition prints. He has published four limited-edition prints each year since 1980, and his work is displayed in many prominent places, including the Pentagon and the U.S. Army War College. Known for his historical accuracy and attention to detail, Dale identifies important people and landmarks on the upper and lower borders of his prints. He also employs a staff historian, who is responsible for researching every detail of the scene depicted and writing a historical essay that accompanies each print.

Although Civil War painter Dale Gallon is closely associated with Gettysburg, he is not a native of the area. Born in California, Dale moved to Gettysburg in 1988. He released his first limited-edition Civil War print in 1980 and has published a new image every three months since.

Gettysburg Historical Prints, Inc.
219 Steinwehr Avenue
(717) 334-3800, (888) 447-2515
www.fhphistoricalprints.com
This spacious shop has the feel of an art museum with its open layout and recessed lighting above the artworks. The framed work of John Paul Strain, Tom Freeman, Keith Rocco, Ron Tunison, Mort Künstler, and other notable artists hangs throughout the gallery, and unframed prints are available as well. Framing services are also available in the shop, which is open daily. The gallery offers a 60-day layaway program—your purchase is divided into three equal payments on your credit card and your art ships when you've made your last payment.

The Inkwell Autograph Gallery
529 Baltimore Street
(717) 337-2220
www.inkwellgallery.com
Opened in 1995, this treasure is tucked away in a small space across from the Jennie Wade House. Although the gallery isn't huge, it holds the largest selection of authentic Civil War autographs to be found in one place in Gettysburg. The offerings are varied, running the gamut from lower-priced autographs for the beginning collector to utmost rarities worthy of the finest collections. Autographs are guaranteed authentic, and many are museum-quality framed. For those who collect all things Lincoln, you will definitely want to visit here. The gallery also displays autographs of athletes, politicians, and celebrities; browsing at this place is a must. Many of the signed books for sale were obtained personally by the owner, who travels to meet the famous signatories and witness the signing. The gallery is closed on Wednesday.

Kreations Gallery
15 Baltimore Street
(717) 334-8333
Owner Ken Knoll opened this gallery in May 2004, and he has plans to expand the already large area and add a coffee shop. Currently this spacious gallery shows off the talents of area artists, with 80 percent of the work displayed created by local artists and 20 percent by regional artists. There's a lot of work in wood here, and you'll find all kinds of styles, including contemporary and abstract. The art being showcased is rotated often, and there always seems to be another interesting piece to discover here.

R.J. Gibson & Co. Historic Photographers
Arbor House
76 Steinwehr Avenue
(717) 337-9393
www.civilwarphotography.com
Photographs are taken the way they were in 1860 at this studio. A camera from the

time of the Civil War is used to take your picture, and the photograph is developed using the wet-plate process that was utilized in those days. This is a painstaking and exact process where the photo is taken on glass. Owner Rob Gibson left his job as an engineer at General Motors to open a Civil War-era photo studio in Gettysburg in 1999, and today he is considered the world's foremost wet-plate photographer. His movie credits include *Gods and Generals* and *Cold Mountain*, and his latest work is from Steven Spielberg's miniseries *Into the West*. He has also given demonstrations and lectures at the Smithsonian Institute and has appeared on and done consulting work for PBS, the History Channel, and A&E.

At this shop you'll truly experience what having your picture taken was like in the 1860s, and you'll end up with a photograph that is authentic to the times. Development of your photograph is done using 1860s laboratory equipment and techniques, and either a military or civilian wardrobe is provided for you to wear. The studio is open seven days a week, and walk-ins are welcome. Most people choose to have a 5-inch by 7-inch plate taken, which costs around $95.

East of Lincoln Square

American Historical Art Gallery & Framery
34 York Street
(717) 334-0172
www.americanhistoricalart.com
This is a friendly store where you can lose yourself while admiring the fine-art prints and originals on the walls and the bronze sculptures and other forms of historical art located throughout the gallery. If you see something you like, you can get it framed here as well. American Historical Art features the works of many well-known artists, such as John Paul Strain, Thomas Kinkade, Keith Rocco, and Jim Phelps. It also offers the complete set of Battlefield Monuments, miniatures of pop-

ular monuments, markers, and buildings of Civil War national military parks. In addition to the historical art, two glass cases near the front of the store contain Hummels and Swarovski crystal. The rear of the store is occupied by Aunt Pittypat's Tea Room (see the Restaurants chapter), and Aunt Pittypat's Bed & Breakfast is located next door (see the Bed-and-Breakfasts and Guesthouses chapter).

Artworks
42 York Street
(717) 334-4250
Opened in April 2005, Artworks features the work of local and regional artists. The front of the store contains paintings, pottery, and fine gifts. Handmade quilts are on display, and the lady who makes some of them is often sitting in the shop sewing as she minds the store on Wednesday. Owner Linda Atiyeh is enthusiastic about her new venture and about the artists whose works she displays. A room in the back has a good selection of T-shirts bearing original designs. This fun and visually stimulating gallery is open daily.

Gallery 30
30 York Street
(717) 334-0335
www.Gallery30.com
Gallery 30 has been operating since 1978, and owners Lois Starkey and William Gilmartin have run the place since 1993. Manager Meghan Riordan is extremely friendly and very knowledgeable about the art and books displayed in the shop. (See the Books and Music section of the Shopping chapter for more on the books offered at Gallery 30.) The work of local and regional artists is displayed throughout the gallery in the varied forms of paintings, fiber art, pottery, blown glass, contemporary crafts, handmade jewelry, and other mediums of fine art. Be sure to check out the children's section in the back of the store, where you'll find toys, board and card games, and educational and fun games and puzzles. Gallery 30 is open daily.

Just Jennifer Gallery and Framery
33–35 York Street
(717) 338–9099 (gallery),
(717) 338–9609 (framery)
www.JustJenniferGallery.com
Just Jennifer is actually two stores; each
store has its own entrance. The gallery
showcases Native American and silver
jewelry, fine art from more than 40 artists,
gifts, candles, housewares, pottery, glassware, spa and bath products, and gourmet foods. The walls of the staircase and
the second floor of the gallery contain the
fine art that's for sale, and no one younger
than age 16 is allowed upstairs without
adult supervision. The downstairs area of
the gallery groups the rest of the offerings
in eye-catching displays. The framery
offers custom framing and has more than
2,000 frame samples in stock. The gallery
is closed on Monday and Tuesday, and the
framery is closed on Sunday and Monday.

Wentz Stained-Glass Studio
48 York Street
(717) 334–0906
www.wentzstainedglass.com
Items made of stained glass in all shapes
and sizes shimmer in Wentz's window display, beckoning you inside, and owner
Bonnie Wentz is likely to be the one
greeting you as you enter. Bonnie opened
this working stained-glass studio in 1982,
and custom work is de rigueur here. You'll
be able to admire glass bead jewelry,
stained-glass suncatchers, candle lamps,
wind chimes, and many more unique gifts.
Custom-designed windows, lamps, and
cabinet doors show Bonnie's breadth of
experience, knowledge Bonnie imparts to
students through workshops held in the
studio. Supplies and the tools needed to
make your own stained-glass masterpiece
are available, and Bonnie also sells patterns. The studio is open every day but
Sunday, when all you can do is admire the
cool stuff in the front window.

West of Lincoln Square

Gettysburg Frame Shop and Gallery
17 Chambersburg Street
(717) 337–2796, (800) 899–9714
www.gettysburgframe.com
Here you'll find artwork concerning the ·
American Civil War, with art available for
all price ranges. You'll be able to choose
from limited-edition prints, canvas edition
prints, giclees, original paintings, and
shadow boxes. Art can be bought framed,
or you can pick out a print and a frame
that will be uniquely yours. Sculpture,
books, music, and replicas of Civil War–era
weaponry are also available. The gallery
has been in business since 1989 and features the work of such highly respected
military artists as Don Troiani, Larry Runk,
Paul Bender, and John Paul Strain. Gettysburg Frame Shop and Gallery is open
daily.

Lord Nelson's Gallery
27½ Chambersburg Street
(717) 334–7950, (800) 664–9797
www.lordnelsons.com
Located within the James Gettys Hotel
(see the Bed-and-Breakfasts and Guesthouses chapter), this two-story gallery is
the country's largest exhibitor of Eastern
American Indian/Frontier art of the
French and Indian War period. Lord Nelson's also features wildlife art, and the
Native American/Frontier and wildlife art
comprises about half the gallery. The
other half has Nostalgic/Americana art,
sculptures crafted from bronze, Native
American pottery, handcrafted gifts, deco-
rative decoys, art glass, soapstone, collectibles, and a large collection of books
and fine accoutrements dealing with the
French and Indian War period. The art
prices range from prints for $40 to
framed works by well-known artists selling
for $20,000. Business began in 1990 as an
import shop selling Guatemalan goods
and Belgian lace and chocolates, among
other things. Nelson was their 14-year-old
Black Lab, whom they named the store
for. One of the co-owners of Lord Nelson's

purchased the building that is now the James Gettys Hotel in 1995, and the space between the first floor of the hotel and gallery is fluid, with archways leading from one area to the other. Lord Nelson's Gallery is open daily.

SUPPORT ORGANIZATIONS

Adams County Arts Council (ACAC)
18 Carlisle Street, Suite 201
(717) 334-5006
www.adamscountyartscouncil.org
Started by a small group in 1993, the Adams County Arts Council has evolved into a 500-member nonprofit agency supporting artistic efforts throughout the county's schools and communities. The council partners with organizations and businesses to promote art in many forms in Adams County, and they accomplish their goal in many ways. Every Saturday during July, member artists add their work to the wide array of goods available at the farmers' market in Lincoln Square, and the council's Arts in Education program has brought musical groups, theater companies, dance troupes, and other artists into every school district in Adams County. Financial support for many arts programs and projects throughout the country are provided by the Adam County Arts Council's STAR (Supporting the Arts Regionally) grant. Dancing the night away in the Gettysburg Hotel Grande Ballroom at the council's annual Masquerade Ball is one of many fun ways this organization raises money to support regional arts.

Adams County Public Library System
140 Baltimore Street
(717) 334-5716
www.adamslibrary.org
The Adams County library system is made up of four member libraries, one federated library, and a bookmobile. The library in Gettysburg is the system's main branch, and programs for children and the community at large are offered. Children's programs include story times for pre-

schoolers and a book club for middle-school students, and all levels of computer courses are offered free to members of the community. The Gettysburg branch is open seven days a week, and the library system's bookmobile runs five days a week and visits an average of eight locations a day. A bookmobile first started operating in the county in 1946, and the current bookmobile is the system's fourth. It is being replaced after 16 years of service, and the new bookmobile should be on the road in March 2006. The 28-foot vehicle will hold around 3,000 volumes of books, and it will also bring videos, DVDs, books on tape, magazines, and, eventually, computers to county residents.

Gettysburg Community Concert Association
(717) 334-3788
www.gettysburg.com/gca/gcca.htm
This member-supported nonprofit organization has been in existence since 1939, and its purpose is to cultivate an interest in good music and dance. The association provides opportunities for its members to attend performances by outstanding professional artists that are held in the Gettysburg Area Middle School and High School auditoriums. Members may also attend for free the concerts of associations in Chambersburg and Waynesboro in Pennsylvania and Hagerstown and Westminster in Maryland. The association also conducts community outreach programs, such as in-school visits by performers.

Main Street Gettysburg
59 East High Street
(717) 337-3491
www.gettysburgpa.org/mainstreet.html
Main Street Gettysburg is a nonprofit organization committed to the preservation and revitalization of historic Gettysburg for the benefit of its citizens, businesses, and visitors. The organization arranges incentives and zero-interest loans for businesses to aid in the revitalization of storefronts, facades, and resi-

dential buildings. This group often leads the effort to restore and preserve local landmarks, and its goal is to help guide Gettysburg's future and maintain its historic integrity by forging partnerships among key preservation, community, and government groups as well as interested citizens from all over the United States. Two prominent projects that Main Street Gettysburg has undertaken are the restoration and preservation of the David Wills House on Lincoln Square and the Lincoln Train Station off Carlisle Street.

Introduced in the summer of 2005, the newest endeavor by Main Street Gettysburg is a 90-minute walking tour of the town. The tour is led by a licensed tour guide, and it highlights the civilian experience during the Battle of Gettysburg. (For more on this and other tours available, see the Attractions chapter.)

PERFORMING ARTS

Gettysburg Civil War Era Dinner Theatre
The Fairfield Inn 1757
15 Main Street, Fairfield
(717) 337–9216, (888) 246–4432
www.civilwartheater.com
The Fairfield Inn opened its dinner theater in August 2001, and entertainment is provided by Civil War illusionist and storyteller Joe Kerrigan. The one-man show lasts 2½ hours, and Joe comes to life as three different characters. He leads off as Professor Kerrigan, who performs Civil War–era magic, and then he changes to a gifted storyteller who talks about being a civilian at the time of the Battle of Gettysburg. This character also chills the audience with a few stories of ghosts haunting the area. Joe then stages a theatrical re-creation of a Civil War séance. A full-course meal accompanies all this fun, and you can catch a show Tuesday through Saturday at 7:00 P.M. and Sunday at 1:00 P.M. Reservations are required, and the dinner theater costs $39.95 for adults and $19.95 for children age 12 and younger.

Gettysburg Stage
(866) 859–5192
www.gettysburgstage.org
With the support of the Adams County Arts Council (see the earlier listing within this chapter), Gettysburg Stage was founded in the summer of 2003. A non-profit organization, it consists of professional and amateur artists from the region. Rather than having a permanent performance space, this regional theater company puts on productions at area venues, including the Civil War–era GAR (Great Army of the Republic) building on East Middle Street and the Gettysburg Dance Center off U.S. Business Route 15.

Six productions are staged each year, with shows running for two weekends. Tickets are typically $12, but the price can vary depending on location, play, or age discounts. For reservations, call the toll-free number above, which is a recording. You're given information on current and upcoming performances and asked to leave a message with your reservation request. The message is then forwarded to the volunteers at Gettysburg Stage, and someone gets in touch with you.

Majestic Theater Performing Arts
& Cultural Center
29 Carlisle Street
(717) 337–8235
www.gettysburg.edu
www.gettysburg majestic.org
Since the Majestic Theater opened its doors in November 1925, it's not surprising to find that it's listed on the National Register of Historic Places. It was constructed as an annex to the Gettysburg Hotel, and when it opened, it was the largest vaudeville and silent-movie theater in southeastern Pennsylvania. The Eisenhowers also added to the theater's history—they attended performances held at the Majestic, and part of the theater was sometimes used for press conferences with President Eisenhower. Gettysburg College purchased the theater in the early 1990s and conducted a five-year

study to determine the best use for the property. It was decided to restore the theater and operate it as a community center for the performing arts and movies. After closing in March 2004 to undergo a $16 million renovation, the theater's 80th anniversary was celebrated with its grand reopening on November 14, 2005, exactly 80 years from its original opening night. The Vienna Boys Choir was among the first performers to appear in the 850-seat theater beautifully restored to its 1925 Colonial Revival style. About 30 live performances will be held here annually. You'll want to look up while attending a performance and admire the theater's original pressed-tin ceiling, which was removed, renovated, and reinstalled. In addition to the theater, the center also has two movie theaters with stadium seating, and movies will be shown nightly. In Cinema 1, each row will have a "cuddle seat"—a seat for two that has no armrest in the middle. There's also an art gallery, well-appointed bathrooms, a cinema cafe, and a backstage production wing with a rehearsal studio. State-of-the-art theatrical systems for lighting, rigging, sound, and film projection round out the theater experience.

Patriot Point Theatre
Patriot Point
241 Steinwehr Avenue
(717) 337-0080
www.patriotpoint.us

This black box–style theater of about 1,200 square feet is equipped with full sound, lighting, and multimedia capabilities. It's a versatile performance venue that allows great flexibility in staging and audience seating. Throughout the year, the theater hosts live entertainment, musical theater, comedy shows, dance recitals, living-history presentations, film screening, weddings, and private events. During the 2005 season, groups of 10 or more were able to reserve the theater for interactive programs led by Charlie Tarbox, Gettysburg's resident military historian.

Music, Gettysburg! offers more than a dozen concerts a year at the chapel of Gettysburg Lutheran Theological Seminary, which is noted for its superb acoustics. Begun in 1980, the concert series features international, regional, and local musical artists, and music presented ranges from popular to Civil War to the classics. Call (717) 334-6286, ext. 2100, or visit www.musicgettysburg.org for information.

Totem Pole Playhouse
Caledonia State Park
40 Rocky Mountain Road, Fayetteville
(717) 352-2164, (888) 805-7056
www.totempoleplayhouse.org

Opened in the early 1950s, Totem Pole Playhouse presents professional summer theater within Caledonia State Park. The late William H. Putch was the playhouse's second artistic director, and he guided the playhouse to national prominence during his tenure from 1954 to 1984. Working closely with his wife, actress Jean Stapleton, William Putch was responsible for 270 productions at Totem Pole, in addition to directing several national tours. Totem Pole Playhouse is one of the few remaining summer theaters that maintains a resident company of actors. In fact, Wil Love has been performing on this stage since 1971 and is also associate artistic director.

Interspersed with the regular faces have been a series of well-known actors, including Keir Dullea, Sada Thompson, John Ritter, Sandy Dennis, Harry Groener and Curtis Armstrong.

Six plays are staged per season in the now air-conditioned playhouse, and a post-show discussion is scheduled for one night during each play's run. Here the audience can join the cast, staff, and directors for informal chats about the show and the playhouse. Plays are held in the evening on Tuesday through Saturday, and matinee shows are held on Wednesday, Saturday,

and Sunday afternoons. Tickets run around $30, and three subscription plans are available. Students can attend any performance for just $10. Children younger than age five are not admitted to the theater.

The current artistic director, Carl Schurr, who first appeared on the Totem Pole stage in 1975, was instrumental in establishing in 1994 the Caledonia Theatre Company (CTC), a nonprofit organization that exists to preserve, secure, and promote professional theater at Totem Pole Playhouse. CTC is responsible for the popular summer theater camps for students age 8 to 15 that are hosted by Totem Pole Playhouse. Call (717) 264–6675 for more information on the camps.

KIDSTUFF 👬

Kids love stories, and Gettysburg has some of the best. Stories of honor and bravery in wartime, stories of ghosts and eerie happenings, stories of the Underground Railroad—you can find them all and many more as you explore Gettysburg and the battlefield. The area also allows kids to get physical, whether it be by hitting a golf ball, driving go-karts, or making a teddy bear. And the richness of the orchards that surround the area gives the kids an opportunity to commune with nature, and to eat some fruit that they pick themselves.

Gettysburg has something for every member of the family. Many of the other chapters of this book have activities kids would also enjoy; be sure to especially check out the Recreation and Attractions chapters for other kid-friendly fun. Most of the activities within this chapter are either free of charge or cost between $4.00 and $6.00 per child.

PRICE CODE

Prices represent the cost for one adult admission. Most places reduce the price for children and senior citizens, but each establishment sets its age ranges differently, so be sure to ask about prices for specific ages. Many attractions allow children younger than a certain age to be admitted for free, and I'll mention this in the write-ups where it applies.

$	$2.00 to $5.50
$$	$5.51 to $7.50
$$$	$7.51 to $15.00
$$$$	More than $15

AMUSEMENT COMPLEXES

Allstar Events Complex $$
2638 Emmitsburg Road
(717) 334-6363, (888) 497-9386
www.allstarpa.com
This place is a kid's dream—two go-kart tracks, two minigolf courses, batting cages, a virtual-reality ride, virtual-reality golf, billiards, video games, and more. But since Allstar is a 50,000-square-foot expo center (with parking for 2,000-plus cars), you need to call ahead to make sure it's not already booked with large parties. And unfortunately, the paddleboats that you see on the 14-acre lake are available only to groups. Groups also rent the basketball court, volleyball court, and soccer fields (one of which is indoors). Each activity is individually priced, and activities are paid for with tickets, tokens, or cash based on half-hour or hourly rates. For instance, the minigolf and go-kart tracks are paid for with tickets, the batting cages take tokens, and billiards and virtual-reality golf are paid for in cash. Your child must be 58 inches tall to drive on the Family Track and 60 inches tall to drive on the oval track. There are also walking trails for those who want to connect with nature for free. A full-service snack bar is available when all the activity leads to hunger.

Gettysburg Family Fun Center $
861 York Road
(717) 334-4653
www.gettysburgfamilyfuncenter.com
There's plenty for the whole family to enjoy here. An 18-hole lighted miniature golf course with caves, waterfalls, and ponds sprawls through the area, and baseball and softball batting cages with varying speeds are also on the grounds.

Inside you'll find a huge arcade and a snack bar. Gettysburg Family Fun Center is open seven days a week, with hours from 2:00 to 10:00 P.M. Monday through Thursday, from 2:00 to 11:00 P.M. on Friday, from noon to 11:00 P.M. on Saturday, and from noon to 10:00 P.M. on Sunday. The last tee-off for the golf is allowed one hour before closing time. If your kids are age four or younger, their round of golf costs only $1.00 when they play with a paying adult.

ATTRACTIONS

American Civil War Museum $
297 Steinwehr Avenue
(717) 334-6245
www.e-gettysburg.cc
Kids will enjoy all this museum has to offer inside (see the Attractions chapter), and outside they will find reenactors in living-history encampments on weekends from April through November. A different unit camps in front of the museum each weekend, and some civilian reenactors are usually on hand. Reenactors have in-depth knowledge about the history they're representing, and they will answer all your questions gladly. The encampments have been held for more than two decades, and you can wander around for free. Most Saturdays from June through August the museum also runs a program where kids can make a craft representative of the Civil War era. The program lasts about 30 to 45 minutes. One week kids may make a drum, the next week it's a yarn doll, and another Saturday might find the kids making a haversack.

Boyds Bear Country
75 Cunningham Road
(717) 630-2600, (866) 367-8338
www.BoydsBearCountry.com
Kids will love this 120,000-square-foot store where 70,000 Boyds bears, hares, and other friends hang out. Located about 5.5 miles south of Lincoln Square off Steinwehr Avenue, the store has displays that

appeal to all ages. There are bears on Noah's Ark, bears in NASCAR regalia, bears in Civil War and military garb, and bears in college sweaters. Kids are especially interested in making their own bear at Digby's Super Duper Bear Factory™ on the third floor. As you enter the factory, you don a yellow construction hat and grab a time card. Then you pick out your future stuffed animal and assemble it at stations along the way. The last step is to choose the Magic Bean that makes your new friend come to life. Then you name your friend and clothe him with just the right outfit and accessories. The third floor also has a Boyds Teddy Bear Nursery for those who prefer to adopt a bear, who you then name and clothe as you would have if you'd made him yourself. When kids get rambunctious, there's a play area on the third floor where they can blow off steam. When they get hungry from all the fun, the downstairs level has dining areas that serve full meals and sandwiches, a bakery, an ice-cream store, and a candy store. All this fun is available daily to 6:00 P.M.

Civil War Camp $$$$
Gettysburg Recreation Park
545 Long Lane
(717) 334-2028
Held during five days of June from 8:00 A.M. to 4:00 P.M., Civil War Camp is open to children in fourth through seventh grade. Activities allow the kids to explore what the lives of soldiers and civilians during the Civil War era (especially 1863) were like. Opportunities to learn the roles Civil War doctors and nurses played during the war are also available. Kids can attend Civil War cooking classes, listen to guest speakers, and take field trips to local Civil War sites.

East Coast Exotic Animal Rescue $$
320 Zoo Road, Fairfield
(717) 642-5229
www.eastcoastrescue.org
Formerly known as the Gettysburg Game Park, in 2000 this area became a nonprofit wildlife sanctuary rather than a pri-

vate zoo. Besides saving unwanted exotic animals, the sanctuary also strives to educate the public about these animals' special needs, so people realize what is involved before deciding to own a wild species. Animals you're likely to see include antelope, deer, elk, goat, sheep, llama, prairie dogs, skunk, parrot, macaw, cockatoo, geese, emu, conure, ostrich, peacock, gibbon, Rhesus monkey, ringtailed lemur, tigers, lynxes, and a lion. The rescue is located 9 miles southwest of Gettysburg off Route 116 and is open only weekends. Children younger than age two are admitted free.

Eisenhower National Historic Site $
97 Taneytown Road
(717) 338-9114
www.nps.gov/eise/
Eisenhower National Historic Site preserves the house and farm where the Eisenhowers lived in the 1950s and 1960s. While exploring the grounds, the farm, and the house, kids can become Junior Secret Service Agents. Kids age 7 through 12 who visit the site receive a Secret Service Agent Training Manual, which contains assignments that must be completed to earn a Secret Service badge and certificate. These interactive tasks are fun and informative, such as reporting to a senior agent using code names and correct procedures. For more on all the activities at the Eisenhower National Historic Site, see the Attractions chapter. The site is open daily except for New Year's Day, Thanksgiving, and Christmas, and you reach it by taking a shuttle bus from the visitor center at Gettysburg National Military Park. Although the Secret Service program is free, the Eisenhower Farm has an admission fee.

Explore & More Hands-on
Children's Museum $
20 East High Street
(717) 337-9151
www.exploreandmore.com
Explore & More was created by preschool teachers, and this is a place where kids will learn as they play. Seven rooms hold activities that are especially geared toward kids age three through eight, but everyone will have fun as they participate. Popular activities include standing inside a bubble made by a giant bubble machine, learning about building and assembly lines in the construction zone, and playing in an 1860s-era house and general store in the room that's dedicated to the Battle of Gettysburg and life in the 1860s. The museum also has an educational toy store, where you can pick up something that will continue the fun of learning at home. To reach the museum, travel south 2 blocks from Lincoln Square and make a left onto High Street; the museum is on the left.

Kids seem especially drawn to the area of the battlefield known as Devil's Den, where there are huge rocks that existed long before the Battle of Gettysburg took place. Climbing around Devil's Den is fun, but you need to warn your kids to watch for snakes sunning themselves on the rocks.

Gettysburg National Military Park
97 Taneytown Road
(717) 334-1124
www.nps.gov/gett/home.htm
The park has many programs that are specifically geared toward kids. Probably the best known is the Junior Ranger Program, which is open to kids age 5 through 13. Children become junior rangers by completing an activity guide as they visit the battlefield. Details on this program and other kid-friendly programs can be obtained at the visitor center information desk, or you can check out the park's Web site. Perhaps your kids would like to join the army and see what being a soldier in the Civil War was like. If so, don't miss the program that ends with the kids reenacting Pickett's Charge. Or maybe the whole family would enjoy viewing some of the park's educational shows together.

Civil War Soldier Food

If your kids are attending one of the many programs at the military park or attending a Civil War camp, maybe you'd like to send them off on their day with some authentic Civil War food. Staples of the diets of soldiers from both sides were hardtack for the Union soldiers and johnnycake for the Confederates. Both are very easy to make. I found these recipes on the military park's Web site (www .nps.gov/gett/), which has a wealth of interesting tidbits you and your kids can browse at your leisure.

Hardtack
2 cups of flour
1/2 to 3/4 cup of water
·1 tbsp. of Crisco or vegetable fat
6 pinches of salt

Mix the ingredients together into a stiff batter, knead the dough several times, and spread it out flat to a thickness of 1/2 inch on a nongreased cookie sheet. Bake the dough for half an hour at 400 degrees. Remove the dough from the oven and cut it into 3-inch squares. Punch four rows of holes into each square, with four holes in each row. Turn the dough over, return it to the oven, and let it bake another half hour. Turn the oven off and leave the hardtack in the oven with the door closed until it's cool.

Johnnycake
2 cups cornmeal
2/3 cup milk
2 tbsp. vegetable oil
2 tsp. baking soda
1/2 tsp. salt

Mix the ingredients into a stiff batter and form eight biscuits. Place the biscuits on a lightly greased cookie sheet and bake at 350 degrees for 20 to 25 minutes or until brown.

The visitor center is open 8:00 A.M. to 5:00 (sometimes 6:00) P.M. daily. Call or stop by the visitor center or check the Web site for the full roster of programs offered at the park.

Land of Little Horses $$
125 Glenwood Drive
(717) 334-7259
www.landoflittlehorses.com
This was always a must-see attraction for my nephews from Oregon when they visited during the summer. Kids (and adults) love the arena shows, in which miniature ponies perform routines and show off their smarts. The ponies are Falabella miniature horses, and you'll see horses that are only 26 inches tall! More than 100 creatures make their home within the animal park, including llama, fallow deer, miniature donkeys, miniature cows, and sheep. There's also a nature area, hayrides, a mining sluice where you can mine for gems, and a butterfly house and garden to enjoy. The Hobby Horse Cafe is open for a snack or a complete meal when

hunger strikes, and a visit to Gift Horse gift shop will surely uncover just the right memento of your trip. During June, July, and August, Land of Little Horses is open daily until 5:00 P.M., and arena shows are at 11:00 A.M. and 2:00 P.M. (Only the 2:00 P.M. show is offered on Sunday.) From the square, head west on Chambersburg Street (U.S. Route 30) for about 3 miles, turn left onto Knoxlyn Road, and follow the signs for about another 3 miles. Admission doesn't include rides on the antique carousel, the mechanical pony cart, the hayride, or the pony ride.

Junior Naturalist Camp $
Strawberry Hill Nature Center
1537 Mount Hope Road, Fairfield
(717) 642-5840
www.strawberryhill.org
The Junior Naturalist Camp teaches kids about the natural world in a fun way through an assortment of hands-on activities, games, and crafts. It's one of the programs offered by Strawberry Hill Nature Center & Preserve, which has walking and hiking trails and offers nature programs within its 609 acres. (See the Recreation chapter for details on all there is to do at Strawberry Hill and directions to get you to the fun.) At the naturalist camp, kids from age 4 to 10 explore ponds and streams and take hikes through forests to learn how various habitats support different animals and plants. Camps are held from the end of June to the beginning of August, rain or shine. The number of days of the camp varies, but all camps are daylight hours only; these are not overnight excursions. For instance, in 2005 the first camp was held June 28 and June 29 from 9:00 A.M. to noon on each day. Different sessions are held for children age 4 to 6 and children age 7 to 10, and some of the older age group's sessions include a cookout on one of the days. The number of children involved is limited to 10 for the younger age group and 12 for the older group. Cost is based on the length of the program, with members of Strawberry Hill paying slightly less per hour than non-

members. Two staff members work with each of the camps and cookouts, ensuring that each camper receives personal attention and the chance to be an active participant in all activities.

BOOKSTORES

Book Warehouse
Gettysburg Village Factory Stores
Junction of U.S. Route 15 and Route 97
(Baltimore Street)
(717) 334-8047
www.gettysburgvillage.com
Book Warehouse is a great place to find books for children (there are books for adults, too). Prices are discounted up to 80 percent throughout the store. It's one of about 70 stores that make up the Gettysburg Village, which has many brand-name outlets. There's a large children's section within Book Warehouse, and Story Time is held every third Saturday of the month. Children receive a gift, and adults who accompany each child can register to win a $10 Gettysburg Village gift certificate.

Gallery 30
30 York Street
(717) 334-0335
www.Gallery30.com
Gallery 30 is a bookstore and a gallery, and the back of the store is devoted to kid-oriented items. Books that appeal especially to kids line the shelves, as you would expect, but Gallery 30 also has a good selection of toys, games, and puzzles. They're displayed in very kid-friendly fashion, and touching is not a no-no here. Many of the items serve an educational purpose that's accomplished in a fun way, and kids seem to really enjoy having their own space to browse. Older kids will also enjoy looking at the varied forms of art that occupy the one side of the store. They can admire the paintings, handmade jewelry, pottery, and other art created by local and regional artists. Gallery 30 is open daily.

Pick Your Own Fruit

Adams County leads the state in the amount of fruit that's produced and processed within a county, and there's no fresher fruit than the fruit you pick yourself. These three farms are all about 10 miles from town, and each is open daily. You should call ahead for specific picking hours and to find out what's being harvested at the time you want to visit.

Boyer Nurseries & Orchards, Inc.
405 Boyer Nursery Road, Biglerville
(717) 677–8558, (717) 677–9567
www.boyernurseries.com

Brent's Berry Farm
138 Brent Road, Fairfield
(717) 642–8354, (717) 642–1555

Hollabaugh Bros. Inc. Fruit Farms
& Market
481 Carlisle Road, Biglerville
(717) 677–9494, (717) 677–8412
www.hollabaughbros.com

Gettysburg Christian Bookstore
24 Chambersburg Street
(717) 334–8634
Although the children's section in Gettysburg Christian Bookstore isn't particularly large, it is very inviting. Lots of colorful book covers draw the little ones in, and a nice selection of titles awaits the older siblings. The kids will also enjoy checking out the metal detectors that are sold at Gettysburg Electronics, which shares an address with the bookstore.

MINIATURE GOLF

Both of the amusement complexes in Gettysburg have miniature golf courses among their offerings. See the Amusement Complexes section within this chapter for full details.

Granite Hill Adventure Golf $
Granite Hill Campground
3340 Fairfield Road
(717) 642–8749, (800) 642–TENT
www.granitehillcampground.com

Although Granite Hill Adventure Golf is within the Granite Hill Campground, you don't have to be staying at the campground to enjoy a round of minigolf. The 18-hole course is sculpted from a stone mountain overlooking the campground's Bass Lake, where boating and fishing are also available to the public. The golf is challenging, with realistic water hazards, sand traps, and roughs, and many players say it's the best course they've ever negotiated. Granite Hill Campground is located 6 miles west of town along Fairfield Road (Route 116), and the lake and golf course are to the left as you enter the campground. A snack bar is also nearby for when hunger hits. The entire facility is open April through October, with daily hours during June, July, and August. (See the Campgrounds and RV Parks chapter for more on Granite Hill Campground.) Minigolf hours are from 10:00 A.M. to 10:00 P.M. daily.

Mulligan MacDuffer Adventure Golf & Ice Cream Parlour $$
1360 Baltimore Pike
(717) 337–1518
www.mulliganmacduffer.com

MacDuffer has been a favorite of locals since 1989, with its great combination of minigolf and ice-cream treats. Its two 18-hole minigolf courses sit on more than four acres, and the courses feature great landscaping, waterfalls, streams, and even caves. The "clubhouse" is an ice-cream parlor that's decorated with all kinds of golf memorabilia, and it has a video game room, too. Soft pretzels, hot dogs, and nachos are available in addition to the ice cream. You can enjoy your food at tables inside or outside on the 35-foot deck, where you have a spectacular view of both golf courses and the pond. Located about a mile south of town off Baltimore Street, MacDuffer is open from April through October. During June, July, and August, it opens daily at 10:00 A.M.; closing time is 11:00 P.M. Sunday through Thursday and midnight on Friday and Saturday. MacDuffer also operates a frequent golfer club. Every day a member pays full price for a round of golf, it's recorded on his club card. Club cards never expire, and the number of visits recorded can span from season to season. Free games of golf are awarded after you reach 10 and 15 visits, and free ice cream is the prize for having played 20 rounds of golf. You can also print coupons off the Internet for savings, and if you print out, color, and bring in the picture of Mulligan MacDuffer's golf scene that's on the Web site, everyone in your group gets a dollar off the price of their golf.

ANNUAL EVENTS
AND FESTIVALS

There always seems to be something going on in Gettysburg lately. Businesses in town work hard to draw visitors throughout the year, and their efforts seem to be paying off. Summertime is still the most-visited time for Gettysburg, and there are many Civil War-related events held then, especially around the anniversary of the Battle of Gettysburg. But many popular annual events have nothing to do with Gettysburg's Civil War history; instead, they celebrate the beauty of Gettysburg's setting and the area's rich agricultural heritage. One of the largest festivals is the National Apple Harvest Festival, where everyone gathers at the fairgrounds to check out the arts and crafts and to enjoy all kinds of goodies made with apples. Most annual events here reflect the area's laid-back nature. Many involve nothing more than enjoying the day—listening to music, checking out some art or wine or apples or whatever, having something good to eat, and spending time with friends.

Most of the agriculture-related festivals are held within 15 miles or so of Gettysburg, in the middle of orchards and farms. The spring and fall bluegrass festivals, also very popular events, are held at a local campground, and some events are held at the Eisenhower National Historic Site. But there are also many events that are held right in town. By traveling only to the streets of Gettysburg, you can find art festivals, tours of historic sites, antiques shows, music festivals, and wine festivals.

Annual events are listed by month in order of occurrence. Keep in mind that dates of festivals do sometimes change, so double-check the date(s) of any event that you're particularly interested in.

APRIL

History Meets the Arts
Locations throughout town
(717) 334-8151
www.hmtarts.com/
The work of about 75 artists, sculptors, authors, and artisans is presented at this show, and all eras of American history are represented—the Colonial era, the French and Indian War, the American Revolution, the Civil War, the American West, WWI, and WWII. You can also enjoy the art of other genres—aviation art, wildlife paintings and sculpture, Native American prints—as you stroll from gallery to gallery.

History Meets the Arts was first held in April 1998 when a group of galleries in town decided to put on a cooperative show with each gallery hosting their own artist(s) on the same weekend. The show was an instant success and has continued to be so year after year. Some of the participating artists come back annually and have quite a following, with the artists often creating special works just for the show. Although attendance figures aren't available since it's a free show where people stroll from venue to venue, the event does fill the hotel rooms in town, so be sure to call early for your accommodations.

The show draws visitors from all over as well as Gettysburg residents. Since each gallery decides for itself which artist(s) they will showcase, the type of art presented varies each year. One gallery may be presenting Native American art, another Civil War prints, another wildlife sculptures . . . the possibilities are endless, and this is what keeps the locals as well as visitors returning every year.

Tom Freeman, whose artwork hangs in the White House and the Vatican, attended the 2005 show, as did John Barrett, weapons safety instructor for Mel Gibson's film *The Patriot*. John showed his hunting bags, which he makes in such a way that they seem to be from the mid-1700s. Joseph L. Galloway, coauthor of *We Were Soldiers Once . . . and Young,* signed his best-selling book, which was made into the movie of the same name starring Mel Gibson.

MAY

Doors Open Gettysburg
Various locations, beginning at the
Rupp House History Center
(717) 334-0772, (717) 334-7292
www.friendsofgettysburg.org
This relatively new event began in 2004 as a way for the Friends of the National Parks at Gettysburg (see the Gettysburg National Military Park chapter) to highlight National Historic Preservation Month. The doors to some of Gettysburg's most historic sites, some of which are usually not open to the public, are available for tours on one day in early May. Visitors tour at their own pace, and a shuttle bus transports tourists between sites. The tour begins at the Rupp House History Center (see the Attractions chapter), includes eight locations, and is free. This is a very popular event, with almost 1,000 people touring the locations during the first year it was held.

Gettysburg Bluegrass Festivals
Granite Hill Campground
3340 Fairfield Road
(717) 642-8749 (spring festival)
(717) 642-8368 (fall festival)
(800) 642-8368
www.gettysburgbluegrass.com
Gettysburg has hosted bluegrass festivals in May and August since 1979, and both festivals attract some of the top groups in bluegrass and traditional country music. During the four-day events, musicians per-

Each weekend from April through October reenactors camp at the American Civil War Museum on Steinwehr Avenue. The living-history units portray the life of soldiers and civilians of the Civil War time. For more information, contact the American Civil War Museum at (717) 334-6245.

form on the main stage, present informative workshops, and meet and greet their fans. The fall festival in 2004 featured 23 bands, and the spring 2005 festival showcased more than 50 hours of music. Past groups have included Ralph Stanley & the Clinch Mountain Boys and Riders in the Sky, both Grammy winners, and the Del McCoury Band, eight-time winners of the IBMA "Entertainer of the Year" award.

The festivals are held at the Granite Hill Campground on Route 116, 6 miles west of Gettysburg. Camping, including RV and tent sites, is available throughout the weekend, and a plain-cup rule for alcohol consumption is in effect. Tickets may be purchased for one day, two days, or four days, with fees in 2005 ranging from $25 to $115. The festivals are held in what is basically a natural amphitheater in the middle of the campground. These are rain-or-shine events, so be sure to pack rain gear as well as lawn chairs. The campground also has a pool, which is right beside the stage, so you might want to

Seeing lots of greyhounds around town? It's probably Greyhounds in Gettysburg weekend. More than 1,000 greyhounds and their owners visited during the seventh annual event in April 2005. Held to raise awareness of the greyhounds' need for adoption, there are always lots of planned activities for both dogs and owners, including a canine parade. Visit www.trianglegreyhound.org/gig to learn more.

pack a bathing suit. If you're coming for only one day, free parking is available at the campsite or in a nearby grass field.

Gettysburg Spring Outdoor Antique Show
Sidewalks around Lincoln Square
(717) 334-6274, (800) 337-5015
Antiques are a big draw in Gettysburg, and many people make this show and its sister show in September (see separate entry within this chapter) a must-attend event. More than 150 antiques dealers display their wares on tables set up on the sidewalks around Lincoln Square. With that many dealers attending, you're bound to find something that strikes your fancy. Dishes, dolls, glassware, quilts, and tinware are just a fraction of the many types of items you'll find here.

JUNE

Gettysburg Brass Band Festival
Locations throughout town
(717) 334-6274, (800) 337-5015
First held in 1997, this event features brass bands from towns in Pennsylvania and Maryland. Throughout the weekend, you'll find music being enjoyed at various town locations, with performances held at Lincoln Square, the Dobbin House, Recreation Park, the American Civil War Museum, and various other locations. The

---

Be sure to check yourself for ticks if you venture into fields or tall grass. Pennsylvania is one of the four top states for occurrences of Lyme disease, and Adams County is among the top five counties in Pennsylvania in number of Lyme disease cases. Become familiar with what a tick looks like and the symptoms of the disease before venturing out. If left untreated, Lyme disease can have serious consequences, including arthritis and cardiac and neurological disorders.

---

performances throughout town are free. A display of the bands, which does have an entrance fee, is held at the Gettysburg College stadium on Saturday. The event usually ends with a community picnic and free concert at Gettysburg Recreation Park on Sunday evening.

Lyme Jam
Gettysburg Recreation Park
545 Long Lane
(717) 334-3522
Begun in 2001, this musical festival is held to bring awareness of Lyme disease, which is transmitted by the bite of an infected tick. Bands, including local talent during the first hour, play from 11:00 a.m. to 7:00 p.m. Lyme Jam also hosts the Annual Horseshoe Tournament at the park on this day. Admission is $5.00, and children age 10 and younger are admitted free with a paying adult. The proceeds go to the nonprofit organization Ticked Off and Fed Up (TOFU), which benefits Lyme disease research, education, and awareness.

Eisenhower 50s Weekend
Eisenhower National Historic Site
(717) 338-9114
www.nps.gov/eise/
This weekend program revisits the 1950s—the clothes, the fads, the cars, and more serious topics, such as the Cold War. This look into the past is included in the admission to the site, which includes a tour of the grounds, the farm, and the house. The site has been preserved as it was when the Eisenhowers lived here during Ike's presidency and his retirement. (For more on the Eisenhower National Historic Site, see the Attractions chapter.)

During the weekend, ranger programs revisit the issues of the 1950s and the President Eisenhower era. A highlight of the 2005 weekend was an appearance by Gary Powers Jr., the son of the U-2 pilot who was shot down over the Soviet Union in 1960, who shared his views on—as well as artifacts from—the Cold War and the U-2 incident. Other topics included the Civil

Rights movement, the protection of the president, the Nike missile program, which had missiles positioned to protect major U.S. cities from nuclear attack, and the relationship between President Eisenhower and Soviet leader Khrushchev.

Civil War Institute
Gettysburg College
233 North Washington Street
(717) 337-6590
www.gettysburg.edu/academics/cwi

The Civil War Institute at Gettysburg College has been held every summer since 1983, and the program features lectures by prominent Civil War scholars. Attendees also take battlefield tours, view films, and partake in special activities, all to gain a better understanding of the intricacies of the Civil War. The program accepts 300 students each year, and a limited number of scholarships are available for students and for history teachers; check the Web site for scholarship qualifications and applications. Past Civil War scholars who have spoken during the weeklong study include James McPherson, Gary Gallagher, John Waugh, Stephen Wise, and Ed Bearss. The 2004 program centered on the navies of the war, the cavalry was the subject of the 2005 program, and the theme for the 2006 program is Civil War Medicine and Antietam. Students may sign up for the tuition-only price or the price that includes tuition and room and board for the week.

Gettysburg Civil War Heritage Days
Locations throughout town
(717) 334-6274, (800) 337-5015
www.gettysburgcvb.org

Heritage Days honors the Civil War in general and the Battle of Gettysburg (July 1–3, 1863) in particular. Events start the weekend before the anniversary of the Battle of Gettysburg and end on July 4. There are activities daily, and the program features reenactments of some of the battles that occurred during the Gettysburg battle of July 1, 2, and 3. (For more on the reenactments, see the Gettysburg

National Military Park chapter.) In addition to the reenactments, you can attend a Civil War Collectors Show and a Civil War book show (see separate listings in this chapter) and also enjoy living-history soldier encampments, period music, a Civil War lecture series, and National Park Service anniversary walks. Additional events include the Fireman's Festival (see listing within this chapter), author appearances, band concerts, and kids' programs. And each year brings new events. For instance, in a past year you could have watched a reenactment of Confederate troops taking control of the Shriver House on Baltimore Street during the day and participated in a haunted trolley tour to look for ghosts in the evening.

You can hear great music Sunday evenings in June, July, and August at the Gettysburg Recreation Park amphitheater located on Long Lane. The "Sunday in the Park" concert series is free to the public; just bring a chair or blanket to sit on. For more information, contact the Gettysburg Area Recreation Department at (717) 334-2028.

Gettysburg Civil War Collectors Show
Eisenhower Inn & Conference Center
2634 Emmitsburg Road
(717) 334-6274, (800) 337-5015

This show marked its 30th anniversary in 2004 and is considered one of the best of its kind in the United States, with hundreds of displays relating to American military history goods from 1865 and earlier. Weapons, uniforms, documents, books, photographs, accoutrements—they're all on display for both the serious collector and the interested browser. The show is held on the first weekend of the Gettysburg Civil War Heritage Days at the Eisenhower Inn & Conference Center, just 4.5 miles south of town. (See the Hotels, Motels, and Resorts chapter for more on this lodging.) For more information on future shows, contact Bill or Brendan Synnamon of The Union Drummer Boy store at (717) 334-2350. The show has an admission price of $5.00, with children age 12 and younger admitted free.

JULY

Gettysburg Fireman's Festival
Gettysburg Recreational Park
545 Long Lane
(717) 334-6274, (800) 337-5015
The Fireman's Festival features rides, midway entertainment, and a fireworks display, and it's part of the Gettysburg Civil War Heritage Days (see earlier listing). This fun annual event has been eagerly anticipated by the people of Gettysburg since 1949, and it offers something for everyone. As with many events in this area, food is a main attraction, and the soup here is one of the key reasons people attend. The chicken corn soup (a Pennsylvania Dutch staple) is always popular, and there's also a soup of the day. If you want to feel like a true Insider, bring your own container to carry out quarts and gallons of the soups. Food is served outside on the grounds as well as in the park's air-conditioned dining room. The carnival usually attracts 8,000 to 10,000 people on a weekend night.

Civil War Book and Ephemera Show
Best Western Historic Gettysburg Hotel
1 Lincoln Square
(717) 334-6274, (800) 337-5015
Let me save you a trip to the dictionary—ephemera is defined in Merriam-Webster as paper items that were originally meant to be discarded after use but have since become collectibles. This three-day event is held annually from July 1 through July 3 as part of Gettysburg Civil War Heritage Days (see entry above). The show, which was introduced in 1987, is held in the ballroom of the Best Western Gettysburg Hotel. This is the place to find just the Civil

War book you've been hunting for, since the show features new, rare, used, out-of-print, and reprinted books on the subject. More than 40 Civil War book dealers also offer photographs, diaries, letters, documents, and autographs for your perusal. For information on upcoming shows, contact Bill or Brendan Synnamon of The Union Drummer Boy store at (717) 334-2350.

Gettysburg Bike Week
P.O. Box 3333, Gettysburg, PA 17325
(800) 374-7540
www.gettysburgbikeweek.com
You'll know if you're here during Gettysburg Bike Week—there's no missing the sight or the sounds of the many motorcycles that are ridden around town during this event, which was first held in 2001. Attendance often tops more than 15,000 bikers, who participate in games and contests. There are also bands playing music and vendors selling bike-related items. Bikers also take guided motorcycle tours of the battlefield and observation rides. Many of the 2005 activities were held at the Allstar Events Complex (see the Attractions chapter) and at Battlefield Harley Davidson/Buell (see the Specialty Shops section of the Shopping chapter). Many visitors avoid town during this event (and many residents wish they could), which is usually held the second Wednesday through the second Sunday in July.

Spirit of Gettysburg 5K Run
(717) 334-9171
www.ywcagettysburg.org
Spirit of Gettysburg is one of the few races in America where participants actually traverse Civil War battlefields. Begun in 1990 and sponsored by the YWCA of Gettysburg and Adams County, this race begins along Seminary Ridge, where the Battle of Gettysburg began on July 1, 1863, and 2 of its 5 miles cover the area where the first day's battle took place. This isn't a huge event (participants usually total fewer than 1,000), but it does

draw runners from across Pennsylvania and other East Coast states. The 5K is the main race, but other competitions are also held for every age and level of ability. There's a wheelchair race, a 1-mile fun run/fitness walk, a 1-mile kids' sprint for ages 7 through 12, a ¼-mile kids' sprint, and a kids' mini-trot. Entry fees range from $10 to $25 on the day of the race, with reduced rates available with advance registration. If you preregister, you can also arrange for babysitting services for children age 10 and younger.

Adams County Irish Festival
Gettysburg Moose Park
100 Moose Road
www.adamscountyirishfestival.com
This festival celebrates all thing Irish by showcasing Irish bands and music, Irish dance, Irish food, Irish beer, and Irish crafts. Entertainment also includes Civil War reenactment groups and sword-fighting demonstrations, and Irish wolfhounds eager to be petted are usually on hand. Begun in 1999, it's held at Gettysburg Moose Park, which is off U.S. Route 30 about 1.5 miles east of its intersection with U.S. Route 15. Proceeds from the festival benefit Children's Friendship Project for Northern Ireland (www.cfpni.org), a program that promotes interaction between Catholic and Protestant teenagers of Northern Ireland. The committee also hopes to eventually open an Adams County Irish History Museum and Library to research family names and collect artifacts. Festivalgoers are encouraged to bring a blanket or chair and lots of sunscreen so they can sit back and relax for the day. Cost is $8.00, and children younger than age 12 are admitted for free. There's no charge for parking. The festival is the oldest and largest Irish festival in southcentral Pennsylvania, and more than 2,000 people attended the event in 2004.

AUGUST

Gettysburg Music Muster
Gettysburg National Military Park
(717) 334-1124, ext. 431
The Gettysburg Music Muster features Civil War bands, fife and drum musicians, and parlor music, and you can listen to all this entertainment for free. Concerts begin at 11:30 A.M. at the Cyclorama Center's outdoor stage and continue throughout the day at the stage, at the Dobbin House Courtyard on Steinwehr Avenue, and at the Gettysburg National Military Park (GNMP) Visitor Center. The final performance, which runs from 5:30 P.M. to sundown, is held at the Pennsylvania Memorial. Attendees should bring lawn chairs and blankets to spread on the ground. The music muster's 10th anniversary was in 2004, which was also the Victorian Dance Ensemble's 5th year performing at the muster. The 50-plus-member ensemble, which was formed in 1995, demonstrates dances of the mid-19th century. Be warned—audience participation is a highlight of every presentation.

SEPTEMBER

Gettysburg Wine and Music Festival
Gettysburg Recreational Park
545 Long Lane
(717) 334-8151
www.gettysburgwine.com
The first annual wine and music festival was held September 10 and 11, 2005, from noon to 6:00 P.M. Besides sampling wines from Pennsylvania and across the country, participants also enjoyed gourmet food, arts and crafts, cooking demonstrations, and live entertainment at this event sponsored by the Gettysburg Area Chamber of Commerce. The admission price ($15 for advance ticket or $20 at the door) includes all performances, cooking demonstrations, a souvenir wineglass, and wine tastings. Admission for designated drivers ($10 for advance ticket or $15 at the door) includes a souvenir wineglass

Area Events Worth the Drive

MAY

Apple Blossom Festival
South Mountain Fairgrounds
Arendtsville
(10 miles northwest of Gettysburg)
(717) 677-7444
The South Mountain Fairgrounds sit in the midst of Adams County's 20,000 acres of fruit orchards. The Apple Blossom Festival began in 1955, and today you'll find hundreds of crafters, live musical entertainment, lots of food, antique cars, and free guided orchard bus tours to see the blossoms on the trees. Admission is $5.00 for adults, with children age 12 and younger admitted for free.

JUNE

New Oxford Antique Market
& Craft Show
Downtown New Oxford
(8 miles east of Gettysburg)
(717) 624-2800, (717) 334-6274
(800) 337-5015
New Oxford is known as the antiques capital of central Pennsylvania, and this show is one of the largest and oldest one-day antiques shows on the East Coast. All permanent antiques shops in town are open, and the area around the square hosts antiques dealers, craftspeople, and artists. Crowds usually number around 20,000.

AUGUST

Littlestown Good Ole Days Festival
Littlestown Town Park, Littlestown
(10 miles southeast of Gettysburg)
(717) 334-6274, (800) 337-5015
Started in 1971, this is an old-fashioned festival offering an antiques fair and flea market, craft displays, and hometown cooking. There's also a 5K race, an antique car show, live musical entertainment, and a parade.

South Mountain Fair
South Mountain Fairgrounds
Arendtsville
(10 miles northwest of Gettysburg)
(717) 677-9663
This is a traditional country fair, where you'll find agricultural displays, musical entertainment, carnival rides, food, and more. Admission is $3.00 for adults, and children age 12 and younger are admitted for free.

SEPTEMBER

East Berlin Colonial Day
King Street, East Berlin
(19 miles northeast of Gettysburg)
(717) 259-0822
This craft festival that began in 1976 has been estimated to attract 20,000 people. It features crafts, entertainment, demonstrations, and, of course, great food,

and soft drinks, and children age 12 and younger pay no admittance fee.

Eisenhower World War II Weekend
Eisenhower National Historic Site
(717) 338-9114
www.nps.gov/eise/

Here you'll experience what Allied and German camps were like in World War II, complete with original WWII vehicles and more than 100 participants portraying military personnel from the European theater of the war. During this living-history weekend, programs are presented on medical

especially the handmade funnel cake. King Street is closed to traffic for the day as more than 100 craftspeople set up their booths along the street, selling all kinds of goods while dressed in traditional colonial wear. There are also demonstrations by colonial artisans.

Fairfield Pippinfest
Downtown Fairfield
(8 miles west of Gettysburg)
(717) 642-5640
This event has grown since 1980 to a town-wide event featuring apple products, music, crafts, and vintage cars in a street-fair setting.

Chili Cookoff
Forney Avenue ball field,
(behind KClinger's Tavern)
304 Poplar Street, Hanover
(14 miles southeast of Gettysburg)
(717) 633-9197
Admission to this fun event is $5.00 for adults (children younger than age 10 are admitted for free), and the proceeds go to different charities each year. You can partake in as much chili as you can eat, and additional food and refreshments are available, including beer for those of age. A variety of live musical entertainment is offered throughout the day. Anyone may compete in the chili cookoff; call Jeff Sherrod at the number above for details.

OCTOBER

National Apple Harvest Festival
South Mountain Fairgrounds
Arendtsville
(10 miles northwest of Gettysburg)
(717) 677-9413
www.appleharvest.com
Begun in 1964, this is one of the largest festivals in the area, attracting 18,000 to 25,000 visitors each day. Recent festivals have had more than 400 food vendors and crafts dealers and 35 to 40 groups of entertainers on six different stages. There's also lots of food, antique autos, steam engines, orchard tours, and pony rides.

Art at the Winery Fest
Adams County Winery
251 Peachtree Road, Orrtanna
(9 miles west of Gettysburg)
(717) 334-4631
www.adamscountywinery.com
Since 2000, Adams County Winery has hosted this free event that features local and regional artists, a glass-blowing and a pottery-making demonstration, live music, food, and—of course—wine.

NOVEMBER

Farm-City Day Festival
Location varies
(717) 337-5859
This free festival is held to show what it's like to live on a farm. You'll find good old-fashioned family fun, with hayrides, horsemanship shows, and lots of food, much of it free.

services, weapons and equipment, communications, transportation, and the life of the everyday soldier. World War II veterans from both sides of the conflict share their battle stories as the featured speakers. Visitors can complete their experience by having lunch in a re-created mess tent

and attending the "USO" dance held Saturday night at the U.S. Army Reserve Center, which features live 1940s Big Band music.

The weekend is held at the Eisenhower National Historic Site, which preserves the grounds, the farm, and the house where the Eisenhowers lived after Ike retired from the military, during his presidency, and after his retirement. Admission to the site is by shuttle buses that depart regularly from the GNMP visitor center. On-site parking for cars only may also be available on this weekend only, weather permitting, in a nearby farm field. For more on the activities available at the Eisenhower National Historic Site and for admission information, see the Attractions chapter.

Adams County Heritage Festival
Gettysburg Recreational Park
545 Long Lane
(717) 334-8943
Begun in 1991, this one-day event's mission is to share and appreciate the cultures of Adams County through music, food, and art. In 2004 you could be entertained by Ulali, a group of three First Nation women who sang close harmony in many styles and languages of their ancestors in the Americas; by a jazz band; by south-of-the-border music and dance; and by Appalachian fiddlers and dances. All this music is the perfect backdrop for enjoying the ethnic foods available and for attending the craft demonstrations. Admission is free.

Gettysburg Fall Outdoor Antique Show
Sidewalks around Lincoln Square
(717) 334-6274, (800) 337-5015
Antiques and Gettysburg go hand in hand, and this show lets you enjoy America of old and crisp fall weather at the same time. More than 150 antiques dealers set

up tables around Lincoln Square to display their wares, which include china, games, tinware, and myriad other items. There's also a spring antiques show held in May (see separate entry within this chapter), so you can admire antiques and enjoy the spring weather.

OCTOBER

Autumn Gettysburg Civil War Show
Various locations
(717) 642-6600 (Thomas Publications, which sponsors the show)
This show features more than 250 tables containing accoutrements, guns, swords, uniforms, documents, books, photographs, personal effects, and relics of American military history from 1865 and earlier. Serious collectors attend to buy, sell, and trade their treasures, while others come to admire the military memorabilia that's on display. Admission was $5.00 in 2005, with children age 16 and younger admitted free.

NOVEMBER–DECEMBER

Gettysburg Yuletide Festival
Various locations
(717) 334-6274, (800) 337-5015
This event celebrates the season with lots of fun happenings. The tree lighting in Lincoln Square is especially beautiful. You can see the huge tree that is decorated and lit at night as you approach the square, and the effect is just dazzling. There's also a parade and tours of decorated homes. Many bed-and-breakfast establishments open their doors so visitors can admire their Civil War–era decorations. The festival tops off the season with events downtown and fireworks on New Year's Eve.

Gettysburg hosts Memorial Day, Halloween, Remembrance Day (anniversary of Lincoln's Gettysburg Address), and Christmas parades. The Memorial Day and Remembrance Day parades are especially meaningful, with wreaths laid at the National Cemetery at their conclusions, while the Halloween and Christmas parades are just fun events.

STATE PARKS AND PUBLIC LANDS 🌳

F ive state parks, Michaux State Forest, and the Appalachian Trail are within 30 miles of Gettysburg, offering lots of opportunities to enjoy the outdoors. You'll find camping, boating, fishing, ice skating, ice fishing, horseback riding, swimming, hiking, and more.

If a park offers camping, a site can be reserved from 11 months in advance up to noon of the day of your arrival. Cabins and picnic pavilions, if offered, may be reserved from 11 months up to 2 days in advance of your arrival. Call (888) PA-PARKS between 7:00 A.M. and 5:00 P.M. Monday through Saturday to reserve your spot.

Lands that allow fishing, hunting, and/or boating have strict guidelines about these activities. For complete information on fishing and boating rules and regulations in Pennsylvania, visit the Pennsylvania Fish and Boat Commission Web site at www.fish.state.pa.us or call (717) 705-7800. Hunting rules and regulations in Pennsylvania can be found at the Pennsylvania Game Commission Web site at www.pgc.state.pa.us or by calling (717) 787-2084.

Appalachian Trail

The Appalachian Trail is a continuous, marked footpath that extends along the crest of the Appalachian Mountain range for more than 2,100 miles from Maine to Georgia, crossing 14 states along the way. It runs diagonally across eastern Pennsylvania for almost 229 miles. Forty-nine of those miles are on state forest lands, and 39 of those miles are within Michaux State Forest. The Appalachian Trail traverses Caledonia State Park, and the halfway point on the trail is located within Pine Grove Furnace State Park. Both state parks are within the boundaries of the

Michaux State Forest, which also is the site of Mont Alto State Park. The Appalachian Trail is marked by two different signs. One is a white rectangular paint blaze 2 inches wide by 6 inches high, which is usually found on trees. The other is a diamond-shaped metal marker with the trail monogram on it. About 200 people a year hike the entire length of the trail in one trip, an endeavor that usually takes four to six months to complete.

Caledonia State Park
40 Rocky Mountain Road, Fayetteville
(717) 352-2161
www.dcnr.state.pa.us
Located 15 miles west of Gettysburg, Caledonia is the closest state park to Gettysburg. It sits in Adams and Franklin Counties, 1,125 acres within Michaux State Forest in the northernmost section of the Blue Ridge Mountains known locally as South Mountain. South Mountain is mostly composed of a hard rock called quartzite, and the valleys on either side of the mountain are underlined with limestone and shale. This makes the soil ideal for fruit production, which is evidenced by the number of fruit farms in the area.

Park visitors can enjoy a range of activities, including camping, fishing, hiking, swimming, hunting, and picnicking. The park is also home to Caledonia Golf Club, an 18-hole, par 68 public course, and the Totem Pole Playhouse, a summer-stock theater that's operated here since the 1950s. (To learn more, see the Golf and The Arts chapters.)

The park is named for Thaddeus Stevens' charcoal iron furnace, which was named Caledonia (see the Close-up in this chapter for information on the charcoaling industry in Pennsylvania). Thaddeus

Stevens, originally from Caledonia County in Vermont, was a famous statesman and abolitionist who practiced law at Gettysburg. The furnace began operating in 1837, and the watercourse along Route 233 was once the millrace that operated the furnace waterwheel. In June 1863 Confederate cavalry under the command of General Early destroyed the furnace, and the pastures you see now were used as field hospitals for the wounded of the Battle of Gettysburg. After Stevens' death, the iron furnace changed hands many times, and in 1902 the land was sold to the Commonwealth of Pennsylvania. In 1927 the Pennsylvania Alpine Club rebuilt the stack of the old furnace as a reduced-scale monument, and this stack and a blacksmith shop that serves as a historical center are the only visible reminders of the early iron works.

Caledonia has 10 miles of hiking trails, and the Appalachian Trail crosses the central portion of the park. A brochure on the hiking trails is available at the park office. Anglers can enjoy fishing at the East Branch Conococheague and Rocky Mountain Creeks and at Carbaugh Run, which flow through the park and the surrounding Michaux State Forest. Brown trout, rainbow trout, native brook trout, and some warm-water game fish are found in these waters. About 740 acres of the park are open to hunting, trapping, and the training of hunting dogs during established seasons. Deer, rabbit, squirrel, and turkey are common game hunted, but the hunting of woodchucks, also known as groundhogs, is prohibited. The park has a swimming pool that can be enjoyed from Memorial Day weekend to Labor Day for an additional fee, and more than 450 picnic tables are located throughout the park. During the summer, campfire programs, guided hikes, and environmental education programs are offered by a naturalist. An arts and crafts fair is held in the park annually on the second Saturday of July. Admission is free, and about 200 artisans display their handcrafted items, including wood carvings, folk art, pottery, stained glass, and more. The first fair was held in 1981, and today around 10,000 people usually attend this fun event.

If you decide to spend the night, there are two campgrounds within the park, with a total of 184 tent and trailer sites available from the second Friday in April until after the end of deer season in December. Amenities include hot showers, flush toilets, and a sanitary dump station, and electricity is available at some sites. Two modern cabins are also available for rent year-round. One is a 1½-story frame house, and the other is a two-story frame house, and both houses come with a modern kitchen, bathroom, dining room, living room, central heat, and three bedrooms that can sleep 10 people.

To get to the park from Gettysburg, take U.S. Route 30 west to the intersection with Route 233.

Just outside the park is **Bobby A's Grill and Bar** (6880 Chambersburg Road, Chambersburg; 717-352-2252). About 12 miles west of Gettysburg on US 30, this is a popular restaurant. Open seven days a week for lunch and dinner, Bobby A's offers prime rib, steaks, seafood, pasta, broasted chicken, and a wide variety of appetizers. Owner Bob Arahovas knows the restaurant business—his family has owned the Lincoln Diner in Gettysburg since the 1980s. (See the Restaurants chapter for more on the Lincoln Diner.)

Codorus State Park
1066 Blooming Grove Road, Hanover
(717) 637-2816
www.dcnr.state.pa.us
The 3,329 acres of Codorus State Park sit

Caledonia State Park hosts a Sunday church service during the summer in its Cathedral of the Pines, an open area surrounded by pine trees just inside the entrance to the park. The nondenominational service is held at 10:30 A.M., and all are welcome to attend.

20 miles southeast of Gettysburg in York County, about 3 miles southeast of Hanover. The park's main claim to fame is Lake Marburg, which totals 1,275 acres and has 26 miles of shoreline. But there's more than just boating and fishing on the lake to enjoy: You can also mountain bike, hike, camp, hunt, picnic, swim, ride horses, and play disc golf. In winter you can snowmobile, cross-country ski, sled, and ice skate.

Parkland here was bought by the commonwealth between 1965 and 1966 under Project 70, a land-acquisition program that resulted in the purchase of many state parks. The design and construction of the park facilities were funded by Project 500, which raised money to improve the lands purchased by Project 70. The main boat-launching area, off Sinsheim Road, was the first project in Pennsylvania completed for public use under the Project 500 Program. The impoundment of Codorus Creek is the result of a cooperative project between the commonwealth and the P. H. Glatfelter Paper Company, a private company located in Spring Grove, Pennsylvania. The project is the first of its kind in the state, and it's designed not only to provide a public recreation area but also to satisfy the water supply needs of the company as well as the town of Spring Grove.

Lake Marburg has seven boat-launch ramps around the lake, and all but the campground launch are open to the public; the campground launch is for the use of registered campers only. Motorboats up to 20 hp are allowed, and they must display a current boat registration. Nonpowered boats must have either a launching or mooring permit from Pennsylvania State Parks (available at most park offices) or a boat registration or launching permit from the Pennsylvania Fish and Boat Commission. Mooring spaces for canoes, sailboats, and boats up to 24 feet long are available for rent if you want to bring your own boat, or you can rent pontoon boats, rowboats, canoes, paddleboats, and motorboats at the marina.

The lake is also a warm-water fishery, and popular species are yellow perch,

bluegill, northern pike, crappie, largemouth bass, catfish, and muskellunge. Bow fishing is permitted in the lake's shallow cove areas. Codorus Creek is in the Selective Harvest Program, and East Branch Codorus Creek is an approved trout stream.

For visitors who prefer to recreate on ground rather than water, there are also lots of activities. Two hiking trails are within the park. Mary Ann Furnace Trail is three interconnected loops totaling 3.5 miles that wind through hardwood forests, pine plantations, and wetlands. The 1.5-mile LaHo Trail follows the lakeshore through hardwoods and wetlands. A 7-mile network of bridle trails winds through the west side of the park, and the northern shore is the site of the 195-acre Cross-country Skiing and Snowmobile Area. This northern area also contains 6.5 miles of trails for mountain biking. Hunting, trapping, and the training of hunting dogs takes place on about 2,900 acres during established seasons. Hunting is limited to the use of shotguns, muzzleloaders, and bows during the appropriate seasons. Deer, pheasant, rabbit, squirrel, and waterfowl are available, but the hunting of woodchucks, also known as groundhogs, is prohibited. Waterfowl hunting is especially popular, and the park's 25 duck blinds are awarded by lottery each year. The park has a swimming pool that can be enjoyed from Memorial Day weekend to Labor Day for an additional fee, and picnic tables are scattered throughout the park. There's also a 36-hole disc golf course along Marina Road that is open year-round. Scorecards are at the first hole, which is by the first parking lot on the right side of Marina Road. The park also provides programs on environmental education from May to October, and birders will enjoy the park's bird-viewing station.

Winter activities also abound in this park. Registered snowmobiles are allowed on 6.5 miles of the designated Cross-country Skiing and Snowmobile Area after the end of deer season in late December. Cross-country skiing is also allowed on these trails; skiers should wear fluorescent orange during hunting season. Sledding takes place on a 2.5-acre slope near the Cross-country Skiing and Snowmobile Area, at the west end of Chapel Cove. There's another sledding area with gentle slopes in the marina area. When Lake Marburg freezes over sufficiently, you can ice skate on a 25-acre section of the lake in Chapel Cove, and ice fishing and iceboating are permitted on the rest of the lake. (A state park launch permit is required for iceboats.)

Codorus State Park has a 198-site campground that's suitable for tents or RVs up to 50 feet long. Sites are available from the second Friday in April to the third Sunday in October. Hot showers, flush toilets, and a sanitary dump station are available, and many sites have electric hookups. From Memorial Day to Labor Day, you cannot stay longer than 14 consecutive nights. Pets are allowed in some designated campsites.

To reach the park from Gettysburg, take Route 116 east through Hanover, turn right onto Route 216 East, and travel 3 miles to the park.

Kings Gap Environmental Education and Training Center
500 Kings Gap Road, Carlisle
(717) 486-5031
www.dcnr.state.pa.us
Sitting about 30 miles north of Gettysburg in Cumberland County, Kings Gap is not a traditional state park. It's operated by the Pennsylvania Department of Conservation and National Resources of the Bureau of State Parks, and its 1,454 acres of forest function as an education and

It's not uncommon to see copperheads and rattlesnakes hunting rodents around the mansion in the Mansion Day Use Area of Kings Gap. These snakes are venomous and should be left alone, although they usually will retreat if approached in their natural habitat.

training center on the environment. Sixteen miles of hiking trails interconnect three main day-use areas and wind through different habitats the hiker can explore. The grounds are open to the public year-round from 8:00 A.M. to sunset. Kings Gap is on South Mountain, and its vistas offer a panoramic view of the Cumberland Valley. A 32-room mansion on the mountaintop at the Mansion Day Use Area offers the best views, as well as functioning as the center's office and a training center for state government agencies. The center also offers interpretive environmental programs to teachers, students, and the general public. A complete schedule of the programs offered is available from the center office or at the three day-use areas. The Bureau of State Parks' Youth Environmental Learning Series for ages 4 to 17 is held here during the summer; the four programs of the series allow kids to explore and learn about the environment with other kids the same age.

Hunting, orienteering, hiking, and learning about the environment are the principle activities at Kings Gap. Several hundred acres are open to hunting, trapping, and the training of dogs during established seasons, and the entire property is open to hunting during antlerless deer season. Hunters will find deer, turkey, and squirrel to hunt, but the hunting of woodchucks, also known as groundhogs, is prohibited. The sport of orienteering involves negotiating a designated course through the use of only a map and compass. A permanent orienteering course is located here, and copies of the course map are available at the center office. Thirteen hiking trails traverse 16 miles, and each has trailheads at the three day-use areas. (See the box on hiking within this chapter for a description of the trails.)

Each of the day-use areas of the center represents a different habitat. The Pine Plantation Day Use Area is located near the entrance of Kings Gap, and here you experience a coniferous forest of white pine, Douglas fir, and larch trees. Several vernal ponds are found here in the spring.

Hiking at Kings Gap Environmental Education and Training Center

Kings Gap has 13 trails that offer 16 miles of hiking, with trailheads located at the center's three day-use areas. Here's a brief rundown of the trails, their lengths, and the difficulty rating state park authorities have assigned to them.

Boundary Trail: 1.5 miles, easy to moderate
Forest Heritage Trail: 1.6 miles, easy to moderate
Kings Gap Hollow Trail: 1.7 miles, easy
Locust Point Trail: 1 mile, easy to moderate

Maple Hollow Trail: 1.3 miles, easy to moderate
Pine Plantation Trail: 0.6 mile, easy
Ridge Overlook: 0.8 mile, moderate to difficult
Rock Scree Trail: 1.9 miles, easy to moderate
Scenic Vista Trail: 2.5 miles, easy to moderate
Watershed Trail: 1.8 miles, easy to moderate
Whispering Pines Trail: 0.3 mile, paved
White Oaks Trail: 0.3 mile, paved
Woodland Ecology Trail: 0.6 mile, easy

Vernal ponds are temporary ponds that retain water as a result of snowmelt, spring rains, and/or elevated groundwater tables. Many amphibians, including spotted salamanders, spring peepers, and wood frogs, use the ponds as breeding areas. A reconstructed log house from the 1850s sits in a small clearing within the area, and this is where a lot of the center's educational programming takes place.

The Pond Day Use Area is about 2 miles from Kings Gap's entrance, and it features a scenic pond and the mountain stream Kings Gap Hollow Run. The pond gives you a chance to observe aquatic animals adapted to slower water, such as frogs, salamanders, turtles, and water snakes. Kings Gap Hollow Run periodically dries up and reveals a stony bottom, which is home to many aquatic species when the water flow is at its peak. A deciduous forest surrounds the stream, resulting in wetland areas where you can observe sphagnum moss, cinnamon ferns, skunk cabbage, and tulip trees.

On the mountaintop 4 miles from Kings Gap's entrance is the Mansion Day Use Area. Here you can enjoy a stunning view of the Cumberland Valley from the mansion's patio. This area contains an oak forest habitat, which supports a variety of reptiles, including the box turtle, the northern copperhead, the timber rattlesnake, and the five-lined skink, one of the few lizards found in Pennsylvania. There's also a garden that is divided into three educational areas—an herb garden, a wildlife-habitat garden, and a compost-demonstration garden.

To reach the park from Gettysburg, drive north on Carlisle Street (Route 34) through Biglerville and make a left onto West Pine Street. Travel on West Pine Street for almost 1.5 miles, and then turn right onto Mountainview Road. At about half a mile, bear left onto Pine Road and follow it for almost 4 miles, and then turn left onto Kings Gap Road. The park is about 4 miles down the road. By the way, you won't find any trash containers at

CLOSE-UP

Visit Where Cannonballs Were Made for the Revolutionary War

Much of the South Mountain land in the area is dotted with iron furnaces, which were used in Pennsylvania from the 1700s through the late 1800s. Before the discovery of coal, charcoal was used to fuel the nearby iron furnaces that processed iron ore into "pig iron," which was then forged into iron tools, stoves, kettles, and other implements. The largest iron furnaces in the area were located at Caledonia, Mont Alto, and Pine Grove Furnace, and cannonballs made at these furnaces were used during the Revolutionary War.

Huge amounts of charcoal were needed to fire the furnaces; in 1786 an acre of forest would be consumed by an average furnace in one day of operation. The forests of South Mountain were clear-cut on a 20- to 25-year cycle to feed the demand, and today a relatively young forest grows on the mountain. The making of charcoal was an involved process. Wood was cut and stored during the winter, and the collier would select a site for the hearth once milder weather arrived. Here the wood would be stacked into a conical shape by standing the wood on end around a central chimney. Firing and tending the hearth was done by the collier and one or two helpers, and the men usually managed eight or nine hearths at a time. Sleeping quarters were huts near the group of hearths, and fires burned 24 hours a day for 10 to 14 days, the time needed to produce the charred wood, or charcoal. After the wood was ready, the collier would put the fire out, rake the charcoal into piles, load the charcoal onto wagons, and deliver the charcoal to the furnaces.

The demand for charcoal died once hotter-burning coal was discovered, and

Kings Gap. A carry-in, carry-out policy directs visitors to take their trash home.

Michaux State Forest
10099 Lincoln Way East, Fayetteville
(717) 352-2211
www.dcnr.state.pa.us
Michaux State Forest spans three counties, Adams, Cumberland, and Franklin, and contains three state parks within its boundaries, Caledonia, Mont Alto, and Pine Grove Furnace. It stretches from just southwest of Harrisburg, the state capital, to the Maryland border. This forest of 85,000-plus acres is in the South Mountain range, which is 6 to 7 miles wide and bordered on both sides by agricultural valleys. Within the forest are 130 miles of state forest roads and 39 miles of the Appalachian Trail. Hunting, fishing, camping, hiking, horseback riding, rock climbing, bicycling, and snowmobiling are

The rebuilt stack of the iron furnace at Caledonia State Park. The iron furnace at Caledonia was one of many in the area that forged cannonballs for use in the Revolutionary War. KATE HERTZOG

the charcoal industry was gone by the end of the 19th century. But remnants of the industry still dot the area. Caledonia State Park is named for the furnace that operated there, and the stack of the old furnace was rebuilt as a reduced-scale monument in 1927. Remains of hearth sites can be seen throughout Kings Gap—look for flat, dry spots about 30 to 50 feet in diameter that are fairly free of vegetation. The furnace in Pine Grove Furnace State Park, which is listed on the National Register of Historic Places, is still visible, as are remnants of charcoal hearths. Pieces of charcoal are still sometimes found by hikers.

among the many outdoor pursuits available on the grounds. Picnics and day-use activities go on at the Old Forge State Forest Picnic Area.

The state bought its first parcel of land here in 1901, and most of what is today Michaux State Forest was purchased by the early 1930s. The area was originally two separate forests, the Michaux and the Mont Alto, but the forests were consolidated in 1942. The first forest tree nursery in any Pennsylvania state forest was created in 1902 at Mont Alto, and a year later the Pennsylvania State Forest Academy was opened near the nursery. When it opened, the academy was one of only two schools in the country that was dedicated to training professional foresters. Mont Alto also erected the first wooden fire tower in the state parks in 1905, and in 1914 it erected the state park system's first steel structure.

Today state-forest timber is harvested to create many wood products, but potable water is Michaux's most valuable resource. The municipal water supplies of many local communities depend on the pure water found in the forest.

Mont Alto State Park
c/o Caledonia State Park
(717) 352-2161
www.dcnr.state.pa.us
With 24 acres, Mont Alto is the smallest of the state parks in the area. Located within the Michaux Forest in Franklin County, it sits about 20 miles west of Gettysburg. The Mont Alto Iron Furnace, which was built in 1807, used to operate at a site adjacent to the park. At its peak, it produced two to three tons of iron per day. In 1875 the area was turned into a summer resort by private enterprise. The commonwealth bought the area in 1902, and Mont Alto became Pennsylvania's first "state-forest park."

Excellent trout fishing can be found at the West Branch of Antietam Creek, which flows through the park. Hiking, picnicking, and riding snowmobiles can also be enjoyed, but no hunting is allowed within the park. Trash containers are not available at the park. Visitors are asked to carry only what they need into the park and to take their trash home with them. The Mont Alto Campus of Pennsylvania State University (see the Education and Child Care chapter) is adjacent to the west boundary of the park.

To reach the park from Gettysburg, take US 30 west to the intersection with Route 233, where you'll arrive at Caledonia State Park. Then travel 7 miles south on Route 233 to the entrance for Mont Alto State Park.

Pine Grove Furnace State Park
1100 Pine Grove Road, Gardners
(717) 486-7174
www.dcnr.state.pa.us
About 25 miles north of Gettysburg in Cumberland County, Pine Grove Furnace State Park occupies 696 acres within the Michaux State Forest. The park is known for its historic sites and buildings, which transport the visitor to the days when cast-iron products were made here. (See this chapter's Close-up for more on how iron furnaces in the area operated.) The first iron furnace was built at Pine Grove in 1764, and the park's visitor center operated as the furnace's gristmill. Today's park office was once an inn, and the A.Y.H. Hostel was originally a mansion built by one of the ironmasters. The final blast from a furnace here occurred in 1895, 131 years after it all began. In 1913 the company that owned the ironworks sold 17,000 acres to the commonwealth. Much of the land became Michaux State Forest, but a portion became Pine Grove Furnace State Park.

The park hosts a range of activities on its lands. There are two lakes within the park, 25-acre Laurel Lake and 1.7-acre Fuller Lake, and they offer many recreational opportunities. (Fuller Lake was created by filling the major ore quarry on the site with groundwater when mining ceased.) Swimming is allowed at both lakes, and lifeguards are on duty during the summer. Laurel Lake also has boating, with a boat launch, 85 mooring spaces, and a boat rental found at its shore. Fishing for pickerel, perch, and stocked trout goes on at both lakes, and anglers try to hook brown, brook, and rainbow trout along Mountain Creek, which flows through the park. Ice fishing is allowed at Laurel Lake, and a small area by the lake's boat launch is reserved for ice skating.

Biking is allowed on all park roads, and 3 miles of trails and access to the Appalachian Trail are available to hikers. The Buck Ridge Trail travels through Michaux State Forest and connects Kings Gap Environmental Education and Training Center with the park. The trail is marked with orange paint blazes, and a trailhead is located across from the park office. Picnic sites are available throughout the park. Hunting, trapping, and the training of dogs are allowed on 75-plus acres during established seasons. Hunters usually find deer, turkey, rabbit, pheasant, and squirrel to hunt, but the hunting of woodchucks, also known as groundhogs, is prohibited. During the winter, cross-country skiing and snowmobiling are allowed in the park and surrounding forest lands. Spring and fall in the park are excellent times for bird-watching, since the park is a rest stop for many migrating forest birds. The park is home to at least six species of woodpeckers, and waterfowl abound at Laurel Lake and its shoreline.

Overnight accommodations are available, with options ranging from camping at primitive tent sites to staying in a room in the youth hostel to staying in a modern cabin. Seventy-four tent and trailer sites are available year-round, but accessibility cannot be guaranteed during severe winter weather. Drinking water, nonflush toilets, and a sanitary dump station are available at the campground, and some sites have electricity. The hostel offers dormitory-style lodging, and cooking and dining facilities are available. (Call the hostel manager at 717–486–7575 for more information on the hostel.) A two-story frame house with

A through-hiker (someone hiking the Appalachian Trail in one trip) will reach the trail's halfway point at Pine Grove Furnace State Park. Many hikers celebrate the milestone with the "half-gallon challenge" at the Pine Grove General Store—eating half a gallon of ice cream.

a modern kitchen, bathroom, dining room, living room, central heat, and three bedrooms that can sleep eight people is also available for rent.

To reach the park, drive north from Gettysburg on Carlisle Street (Route 34) through Biglerville. After leaving Biglerville, bear left onto Main Street. The name of the road will change to Bendersville-Wenksville Road. Turn right onto Pine Grove Furnace Road in about 2.5 miles. This road will change its name to Bendersville Road and end at the junction of Route 233 (Pine Grove Road). Turn right onto Route 233, and the park entrance will be a short distance up the road.

GOLF

Golf courses abound within a short drive of Gettysburg, and many of them emphasize the rural beauty of the area. If you prefer to walk the course rather than drive a cart, all area golf clubs allow you to walk during some part of the day. All costs quoted are for the weekend rate, which is the highest rate you can expect to pay. Besides the golf courses, the Gettysburg Golf Driving Range (717–334–4308) is located east of town at Smith Road along U.S. Route 30 (York Road).

The Bridges Golf Club
6729 York Road, Abbottstown
(717) 624–9551
www.bridgesgc.com

Getting its name from the 10 bridges that are along many of the paved cart paths that meander over this 6,283-yard, par 72, 18-hole course, The Bridges is located less than 15 miles east of Gettysburg. The golf club is a member of the Audubon Cooperative Sanctuary, and the course is designed to allow woodlands and wetlands to remain undisturbed, so you have an excellent chance of seeing plenty of wildlife as you golf here. The clubhouse, which is actually a refurbished furniture factory from the 1800s, has 12 rooms for overnight stays, and golf packages are available. Meals are served at the charming Bridges Grill and Deck, which overlooks the course. A pro shop is located within the clubhouse, and a driving range, a putting green, lessons, and club rentals are available.

The course has received a four-star rating in *Golf Digest* and a top-100 rating in *Golf for Women* magazine. The lengthy 558-yard par 5 No. 8 hole is probably the trickiest, and the 534-yard par 5 No. 15 hole is probably the most scenic, with a hill that overlooks the entire back nine holes. Tee times are required, and you're not allowed to wear metal-spike shoes on the course. The Bridges requires proper golf attire, specifically a collared shirt and mid-length hemmed shorts. The cost to ride the course is $57 from 7:00 to 11:00 A.M., $50 before 7:00 A.M. and from 11:00 A.M. to 1:00 P.M., and $42 from 1:00 to 4:00 P.M. The fee is $27 to walk the course, which may be done after 1:00 P.M. A greens fee of $19 is charged after 6:00 P.M. every day.

Caledonia Golf Club
9515 Golf Course Road, Fayetteville
(717) 352–7271

The first nine holes of this golf course were built in 1922 and the second nine were added in 1926, and this oldie is still a goody. It's designed and constructed to put a premium on accuracy instead of distance, with plenty of trees and streams and narrow fairways to navigate over the par 68, 5,154-yard course. Located 12 miles west of Gettysburg behind the Totem Pole Playhouse in Caledonia State Park, club amenities include a clubhouse with a pro shop and snack bar, a putting green, and club rentals. (See the State Parks and Public Lands chapter for more activities offered in Caledonia State Park and The Arts chapter for more information on the Totem Pole Playhouse.) Although the Caledonia Golf Club is open to the public, memberships are also available.

Caledonia is usually one of the last courses in the area to open in the spring because it has small streams that crisscross the fairways, and it takes a while for the course to dry out from the winter snows. Many golfers consider the No. 9 hole to be the prettiest on the course, especially in the fall. It has about a 60-foot drop from the tee to the green and a stand of trees to the right and left of the green. The hole is a par 3 with a yardage of 169 yards. The club requests (but doesn't require) that you make tee times daily up to 3:00 P.M., and they can be made up to six months in advance if you wish. Fees run $19 to walk and $34 to ride the course.

Carroll Valley Golf Resort
Carroll Valley Resort
121 Sanders Road, Fairfield
(717) 642–8211, (800) 548-8504
www.carrollvalley.com

Carroll Valley Resort offers two golf courses, this one located at the site of the resort and the Mountain View Golf Course, located 3 miles away on Bullfrog Road (see listing later in this chapter). Carroll Valley Resort sits at the foothills of the Catoctin Mountains, and skiing is available during the winter. There are two restaurants at the resort, which is often used for conferences, meetings, and wedding receptions; its ballroom can accommodate 350 people. (For complete information on all that's offered at Carroll Valley Resort, see the Hotels, Motels, and Resorts chapter.)

The Carroll Valley Golf Resort is located about 10 miles west of Gettysburg off Route 116 (Middle Street). The hotel at Carroll Valley overlooks the course, and golf packages combining golfing, accommodations, and meals are available, as well as a clubhouse with a pro shop, a driving range, and a putting green. Golfers are not allowed to wear metal-spike shoes, and proper golf attire is required, specifically a collared shirt and no jeans or cut-offs. The newest innovation at Carroll Valley Resort is its development of a kid-friendly golfing environment. Family golf packages and new Kids on Course programs have been added, and the course has kid-friendly tees.

This 18-hole, 6,345-yard and par 71 championship course designed by Ault & Clark has received a four-and-a-half-star rating by *Golf Digest*. The course winds through the valley floor, and hills surround you as you golf. A mountain stream also cuts through the layout, making water a major factor on seven holes. One of the more challenging holes is No. 9, a 477-yard dogleg right par 4 that has water running along the right side for about 300 yards,

creating a split fairway. Cost is $42 to walk and $56 to ride the Carroll Valley course, and after 1:00 P.M. the price drops to $36 to walk and $46 to ride. Carts are mandatory before 2:00 P.M. on weekends and holidays. Tee times are required, and they may be scheduled up to one month in advance.

Cedar Ridge Golf Course
1225 Barlow-Two Taverns Road
(717) 359-4480

This 18-hole course opened in the late 1980s, and it was designed by Roger Weaver, who also later designed the Meadowbrook Golf course (see listing in this chapter). Amenities include a clubhouse with a pro shop, a restaurant, a lounge, and a putting green. No metal-spike shoes are allowed, and proper golf attire is required. Cedar Ridge Golf Course is located less than 10 miles from Gettysburg. To reach the course, travel south on Baltimore Pike for about 5 miles and turn right onto Two Taverns Road. The course is on the right in about 2 miles.

At 5,938 yards and a par 72, the course's first nine holes are relatively straightforward while the back nine are more challenging. A good round here requires accuracy—large cedar trees line many of the fairways, and about a third of the holes feature water hazards. The No. 11 hole is deceivingly difficult—although only 93 yards, this par 3 combines water and cedar trees. Tee times are recommended but not required, and it costs $21 to walk and $34 to ride the course. Seniors can ride the course for $13 on weekdays, and that price drops to $10 after 3:00 P.M. On weekends the senior rate of $16 applies after 3:00 P.M.

Flatbush Golf Course
940 Littlestown Road, Littlestown
(717) 359-7125, (877) 359-7125
www.flatbushgolfcourse.com

Don't let the windmill and gazebos that decorate the course deceive you; this is a challenging course that features open fairways, many in a dogleg configuration, water hazards, and well-placed trees. (Course rules allow the windmill and gazebos to be taken out of the line of flight without penalty.) The 6,205-yard, par 71 layout was designed by Ault, Clark and Assoc. and opened in July 1989. One of the more interesting holes is the 510-yard, par 5 No. 15, which has a double dogleg. Tee times are recommended and may be scheduled up to 10 days in advance on the Web site or 6 days in advance by phone. The fee is $25 to walk and $37 to ride the course, which is located about 10 miles southeast of Gettysburg. The best way to get there is to take Hanover Street (Route 116) east for 7 miles, turn right onto Littlestown Road, and travel for about 2 more miles. You'll also find a log cabin–style clubhouse with a pro shop and locker rooms with showers; a driving range, putting green, and practice bunker; and a lounge and snack bar. Lessons are available, and proper golf attire is required.

The Links at Gettysburg
601 Mason Dixon Road
(717) 359-8000
www.thelinksatgettysburg.com
This course was built in 1999, but it's more than just a golf course. The first homes of the Links Community Development were built in 2004, and the Links at Gettysburg course is part of the community. Its clubhouse can accommodate 260 people for weddings, receptions, and other special occasions, and a brunch buffet is offered on Sunday from 11:00 A.M. to 2:00 P.M. George T. Keeney, the chef of the place, even has a food column in the local newspaper. If you're interested in joining the

community, memberships and home sites are available, but you don't have to be a member to enjoy the golf here. Among the many amenities offered are a clubhouse with a pro shop, locker rooms with showers, a driving range and putting green, a restaurant, and a lounge and snack bar. Golf lessons are offered, and proper golf attire is required; specifically, jeans are not allowed. Golfers must also wear shoes without metal spikes. Civil War cannons serve as tee markers at The Links, which specializes in golf outings, corporate retreats, and fund-raising tournaments.

The 18-hole, 6,184-yard, par 72 layout features red-rock cliffs that come into play on 6 holes, dense forests, and 10 lakes. Precise play is necessitated by every hole being lined with one or two lakes and thick forest. The course has rated four stars in *Golf Digest,* and it's been rated the No. 6 public course in Pennsylvania by *Golfweek.* The Links is also a member course of the exclusive The National Golf Club. Its driving range and practice facility were redesigned in 2004, and tee times are required and may be made seven days in advance. This is the most expensive course in the area, with a weekend rate of $83.50 that drops to $52.25 after 2:00 P.M. To reach The Links, take Taneytown Road (Route 134) south about 4.5 miles almost to the Maryland border. Turn right onto Mason-Dixon Road, and the course is a mile farther on the right.

Meadowbrook Golf Club
835 Goulden Road
(717) 334-0569
This course began in 2000, and the final holes of this 18-hole course were completed in 2003. During the Battle of Gettysburg, Union troops occupied the land where the course sits. To reach Meadowbrook, travel Baltimore Pike south and at 0.5 mile past the intersection with U.S. Route 15, turn right onto White Church Road. Travel another 0.5 mile and turn right onto Goulden Road to the course. The clubhouse here has a pro shop and snack bar, and a putting green is available.

i

The Gettysburg Adams Chamber of Commerce began offering a PGA Golf Passport in 2005. For $39 you get special offers on more than 350 rounds of golf in central and eastern Pennsylvania, New Jersey, and Delaware. For information or to order a passport, contact the chamber at (717) 334-8151.

Meadowbrook was designed by Roger Weaver, who also designed the Cedar Ridge Golf Course (see previous listing). At 6,029 yards, it's a par 72 course, and the No. 7 hole is the most visually appealing. It has a view of the small valley that faces Big Round Top Mountain. The No. 6 hole is one of the most demanding of the course, requiring accuracy to place the ball in the sloping fairway from the tees. Tee-time reservations are preferred but not required, and it's only $10 to walk and $21 to ride the course. There are also senior specials during the week, such as those age 55 and older being able to ride the course for $15.

Mountain View Golf Course
Bullfrog Road and Route 116, Fairfield
(717) 642–5848, (800) 548-8504
www.carrollvalley.com

The Mountain View Golf Course is part of the Carroll Valley Resort, which offers this course and a sister course located at the main resort area. Golf packages that include golfing and accommodations and meals at the main lodge are available. (See the Hotels, Motels, and Resorts chapter for more on the Carroll Valley Resort; for more on the Carroll Valley Golf Resort, see the previous listing in this chapter.) Both of the resort courses are dedicated to creating a kid-friendly golfing environment, and besides kid-friendly tees, family golf packages and new Kids on Course programs have been added. Golfers are not allowed to wear metal-spike shoes on either course, and proper golf attire is required, specifically a collared shirt and no jeans or cut-offs.

The Mountain View Golf Course sits about 3 miles from the main resort area, and it's considered by many to be the easier of the two courses. Golfers here enjoy a natural grass driving range and a bit of history. The pro shop is within a pre–Civil War clubhouse that was built around 1800, and the brick farmhouse was used by the Confederates during their retreat from Gettysburg in July 1863. Slightly shorter than its sister course at 6,036 yards, this is also an 18-hole par 71 championship course

designed by Ault & Clark that's received a four-and-a-half-star rating by *Golf Digest.* Mountain View gets its name from the mountains that you can admire as you golf, and one of the best views of the mountains and the valley can be had on the No. 15 hole, a 415-yard downhill par 4. It costs nonresidents $33 to walk and $47 to ride the course, while residents pay $32 to walk and $43 to ride. Tee times are not required, but they are preferred one to two days in advance, and seniors (age 50 and older) get a reduced rate on riding the course on weekdays.

Penn National Golf Club & Inn
3720 Clubhouse Drive, Fayetteville
(717) 352–3000, (800) 221-7366
www.penngolf.com

Penn National is considered by many area golfers to be the top golf facility in the area, but it is a bit of a drive (20 miles) from Gettysburg. It features two championship courses that are drastically different, each of which has earned a four-and-a-half-star rating by *Golf Digest. Golfweek* rated it the 10th best public course in Pennsylvania. This is also a golf-course community, with residential housing blending with the golf courses. The Penn National Inn, with 52 hotel rooms, is on the grounds, and it offers stay-and-play packages that include golf, lodging, and meals on-site. Amenities include a pro shop in the clubhouse, locker rooms with showers, a restaurant and snack bar, a lighted driving range, and a putting green. Clubs may be rented here, and lessons are available at Bumble Bee Hollow Golf Academy, which offers one-, two-, and three-day programs for new as well as advanced players. To get to Penn National take Chambersburg Street west for about 18 miles to Route 997 South. Turn left onto Route 997 and follow it for 3.5 miles to the golf club, which is about 1 mile north of Mont Alto. Both courses require proper golf attire and are non-metal-spike facilities. Tee times are required and may be made up to 30 days in advance. The cost at either course is $52 to walk ($32 after 2:00 P.M.) and $69 to ride ($42 after 2:00 P.M.), and senior specials are offered.

The **Founders Course** is a traditional 18-hole course with a classic blend of tree-lined bluegrass fairways, a seven-acre lake, and large, sculpted greens. Many of the fairways are lined with mature trees, so accuracy off the tee is a must, and the lake comes into play on four of the holes. This 6,492-yard, par 72 course was built in 1968 and designed by Edmund Ault. It has a $1.3 million double-row irrigation system that was completed in 2003, and the renovation of all of the course's greenside bunkers will be complete by the 2006 season opening.

The **Iron Forge Course** is a modern course with an open-style layout with bent-grass fairways, fast bent-grass greens, and rolling elevation changes. Since it is so open, wind can dramatically factor into your game here. The par 72, 6,300-yard 18-hole course was built in 1996 and designed by Bill Love. The signature hole is No. 15, a par 4 with yardage of 347. It's a tough hole that involves steep hills, bunkers, and water, and it plays shorter than its yardage because the tee shot is downhill. A 40-foot drop from the tee to the green makes the vista from the tees just beautiful.

Construction of an additional nine holes is slated to begin in 2006 and is scheduled to be completed for play in June 2007. The new golf area and additional housing will be south of Iron Forge, between The Penn National Golf Center driving range and the campus of Penn State Mont Alto. Bill Love will design the course, and the plan is to follow the same style as Iron Forge. The club's current driving range will be moved north and modernized, and a new clubhouse is planned in the vicinity of Iron Forge's No. 8 green.

Piney Apple Golf Course
165 Slatersville Road, Biglerville
(717) 677-9264

This course's location a little more than 15 miles north of Gettysburg puts it in the middle of what's known as apple country

around here. Many points along the 18-hole, 5,287-yard, par 71 course are scenic overlooks of orchards in the valley below and mountains ringing the skyline. Amenities include a clubhouse with a limited pro shop, a driving range and a putting green, and a practice chipping area with sand traps and a green. Lessons and club rentals are available. Tee times are recommended for weekends and accepted up to two days in advance. The cost of a round is $18 to walk ($15 after 2:00 P.M.) and $32 to ride ($23 after 2:00 P.M.), and senior specials are offered during the week. To find the course, head north on Carlisle Street and continue on Route 34 (Biglerville Road) through the town of Biglerville. After you pass Rampike Hill Road, you'll want to bear left, and the name of the road will change to Bendersville-Wilkesville Road. The name of the road changes once again, this time to Wenksville Road, and you turn right onto Slatersville Road to the course.

Quail Valley Golf Course
901 Teeter Road, Littlestown
(717) 359-8453

This course in Littlestown was purchased in March 2004 by Scott and Colyn Keller, and the brothers have made many changes. They didn't alter the course's great layout, but they have improved the conditions of the tees, greens, and fairways. The clubhouse pro shop and the restaurant have also been remodeled, and amenities include a lounge and snack bar, a driving range, and a putting green. Lessons are also available. This 18-hole, 6,518-yard, par 72 course is about 10 miles southeast of Gettysburg; take Baltimore Pike southeast for about 7 miles and turn right onto Gettysburg Road. Travel 2 more miles and turn right onto Teeter Road, and the course is just another 0.75 mile down the road. Tee times are required and may be made up to eight days in advance at this non-metal-spike facility, where proper golf attire is also required. Cost is $35 to walk and $45 to ride the course.

RECREATION

Recreational choices abound in the Gettysburg area. Active folks will find plenty of ways to release their pent-up energy, with options ranging from the tame pastime of bowling to the thrill of skiing. People who prefer to watch rather than participate can enjoy cheering at a car race or at one of the horse shows hosted by the Gettysburg Riding Club. To make finding your choice easy, entries within this chapter are listed alphabetically by type of activity.

Golf is a popular leisure pursuit, and an entire chapter of this book has been dedicated to the sport. The numerous state parks in the area offer many forms of recreation, and they are also covered in their own chapter. Many carnivals and bingo nights are sponsored by area fire companies, and they are usually advertised in the *Gettysburg Times* newspaper. Also be sure to check out the Annual Events and Festivals chapter to find other fun ways to spend your time in Gettysburg.

BOATING

Codorus State Park
1066 Blooming Grove Road, Hanover
(717) 637-2816
www.dcnr.state.pa.us
Most area boaters travel the 20 miles to Codorus State Park to run their boats on Lake Marburg, which covers 1,275 acres and has 26 miles of shoreline. Motorboats up to 20 hp and nonpowered boats are both welcome, and there are six public boat-launch ramps around the lake and one ramp at the campground reserved for registered campers. If you don't have your own boat, there's a boat rental at the marina run by Appalachian Outdoor School and Adventure Sports (717-632-7484; www.appalachianoutdoorschool.com). You can rent pontoon boats,

canoes, kayaks, double kayaks, paddle-boats, and V-bottom motorboats. The cost is by the hour, with prices decreasing the longer you rent the equipment. Prices range from $12 an hour for a pedal boat for two to $49 for the first hour's rental of a pontoon boat that can accommodate 9 to 10 people. The boating season at the lake runs daily from Memorial Day to Labor Day and weekends only during April, May, September, and October. Reservations are recommended, and taxes and gas are extra.

Granite Hill Campground
3340 Fairfield Road
(717) 642-8749, (800) 642-TENT
www.granitehillcampground.com
The 150 acres that comprise Granite Hill Campground are an outdoor enthusiast's dream come true. (To get a full rundown of all this campground has to offer, see the Campgrounds and RV Parks chapter.) Even if you're not staying at Granite Hill, you can enter the property and enjoy its lake. (The campground's minigolf course and snack bar are also open to the public; see the Kidstuff chapter for information on the minigolf.) Kayaks and paddleboats are available for rent at Bass Lake, which is just inside and to the left of the campground entrance.

Pine Grove Furnace State Park
1100 Pine Grove Road, Gardners
(717) 486-7174
www.dcnr.state.pa.us
Laurel Lake, one of the two lakes found within this park, offers boating, but it doesn't allow any gas-powered motors, only small electric boats. You'll find a boat launch, 85 mooring spaces, and a boat rental at the shore of this 25-acre lake. Rowboats, electric-powered rowboats, canoes, and paddleboats can be rented,

If you enjoy dancing, check out the ball-room dance held at Gettysburg High School the second Thursday of each month. Admission is $5.00, and refreshments are available. Group dance lessons are offered about an hour before the event at a cost of $5.00. Call the Gettysburg Area Recreation Department at (717) 334-2028 for more information.

with all but the electric rowboats costing $9.00 for the first hour (the price decreases if you take the boat for more hours). The electric motorboats cost $18 for the first hour. The Laurel Boat Rental can be reached at (717) 486-3448, and rentals are available daily from Memorial Day to Labor Day and usually on weekends only during April, May, September, and October.

BOWLING

Edgewood Lanes
1880 Emmitsburg Road
(717) 337-1818

This is one of the few businesses in town that has shorter hours during the tourist season than during the rest of the year. Open daily in the off-season, during the season Edgewood Lanes is open from 6:00 to 10:00 P.M. on Monday, Wednesday, Thursday, Friday, and Saturday nights and from 10:00 A.M. to 2:00 P.M. on Monday. The bowling alley sits at the edge of town, and it offers 16 bowling lanes and a video room with a pool table and video games. Leagues bowl every evening, and there's a kids' league on Saturday. Bumper guards are also available for those learning the sport. Edgewood Lanes has been a place to relax, bowl a few games, and have fun since 1978. It will cost you $3.75 to bowl a game, and shoe rental is $2.25.

CAR RACING

Lincoln Speedway
800 Racetrack Road, Abbottstown
(717) 624-2755
www.lincolnspeedway.com

Abbottstown hosts summer dirt-track racing at the Lincoln Speedway on Saturday nights. Races are held for 410 Sprints, Thunder Cars, and 358 Sprints, and drivers compete for points, money, and bragging rights. All this racing excitement is less than 15 miles east of Gettysburg. To get to the track, take U.S. Route 30 (York Street) east for about 13 miles and turn right onto Kinneman Road. Follow Kinneman Road for almost a mile to Racetrack Road. Admission is $13.00 for adults, $8.00 for students age 12 to 17, and $2.00 for children age 6 to 11. Admission for the pit area (adults only) is $20. The speedway also offers season passes and bulk ticket rates. Gates open around 5:30 P.M., and the races usually begin at 7:30 P.M.

Trail-way Speedway
100 Speedway Lane, Hanover
(717) 359-4310
www.trail-wayspeedway.com

Friday and Saturday nights during summer in Hanover are for dirt-track racing. At Trail-way Speedway, you can see 358 Super Sprints, Thunder Cars, Street Stocks, 270cc and 600cc Micro Sprints, Scramble Cars, and Figure 8s in action. Drivers compete for points, money, and fame within local racing circles. Friday-night races feature the 358 Super Sprints, Thunder Cars, and Street Stocks, while the Micro Sprints, Scramble Cars, and Figure 8s race on Saturday nights.

To reach the track from Gettysburg, take Route 116 (Hanover Road) east about 10 miles, turn right onto Littlestown Road and then left onto Hostetter Road, and follow the arrow signs to the speedway. Admission is $10.00 on Friday night and $8.00 on Saturday night. Children younger than age 12 are admitted for free. Admission to the pit area is $18 on either night, and anyone younger than age 18 must have a parent or guardian sign a release to enter the pits. If there's a special show going on, $2.00 is added to the general and pit admission prices. On Friday nights, gates open at 5:30 P.M. and race time is 7:30. Saturdays start earlier—gates open at 4:00 P.M. and race time is 6:30.

FISHING

Adams County doesn't have the limestone substrate that makes the creeks in adjoining Cumberland and Franklin Counties so good for fly fishing, but there are still some nice fishing creeks around Gettysburg. The best-known destination in Adams County is the Conewago Creek, which has a section where only fly fishing is allowed. The stream is stocked with several hundred trout in mid-March and in October, so success comes easily here. To get to the fly-fishing section of Conewago Creek, head north from Gettysburg on Route 34 for about 5 miles and park where the bridge crosses the creek. Fly fishing is allowed upstream from the bridge; bait fishing and fly fishing are allowed downstream.

Many anglers also venture to the state parks for fishing. Codorus State Park, Mont Alto State Park, and Pine Grove Furnace State Park all offer fishing. See the State Parks and Public Lands chapter for full details.

A fishing license is required for anyone age 16 or older to fish Pennsylvania waterways. Applications are available at the Treasurer's Office, which is in the Adams County Court House (111 Baltimore Street; 717-337-9833). Tourist licenses may be purchased for three or seven days of fishing if you don't need a license for the entire year. Senior citizens who are residents of Adams County can purchase a lifetime license. An additional fee is charged if you wish to fish for trout or salmon.

GYMS

Curves for Women
705 Old Harrisburg Road
(717) 337-9886
www.curves.com
If you don't have a Curves near you, it's pretty likely you will have one soon. Curves for Women is the largest chain of franchised fitness centers in the world, with more than 9,000 locations and four million members as of July 2005. As with all Curves, this facility is equipped with hydraulic resistance machines that are arrayed in a circuit where you move from machine to machine on a time interval. The pieces of equipment in the circuit target specific body parts, and you exercise aerobically at stations between the machines to keep your heart rate up. The circuit moves you from station to station and is directed by music and taped instruction. Curves is located within the North Gettysburg Shopping Mall, and it's open Monday through Saturday. If you belong to a different Curves franchise, your membership there allows you to use these facilities while you're visiting Gettysburg.

There's probably a game of bingo going on somewhere in town during your stay. Check the numerous ads for bingo in the Gettysburg Times *newspaper. The American Legion, at 123 Baltimore Street (717-334-4513), is one of many places that host bingo, with games on Wednesday evenings.*

Gettysburg Health & Fitness
1080B Chambersburg Road
(717) 334-4777
www.gettysburgfitness.com
This coed gym is 1.5 miles west of Lincoln Square, and members range from 13 through 95 years old. When you join the club, you receive free orientations to cardiovascular training, strength training, and flexibility. You'll be shown how to use the

club's wide variety of cardiovascular equipment available in the Fitness Center, which includes StarTrac and Life Fitness treadmills, Precor Elliptical machines, StarTrac exercise bikes and steppers, and Schwinn Airdynes and Concept II rowing machines. For strength training, there's a full set of Paramount and Cybex machines and a large free-weight area. Exercise classes are held in the aerobics room, which has a state-of-the-art floating floor. Traditional fitness classes include step, hi-lo, toning/conditioning, senior fitness, low-impact, weight lifting, and kickboxing. Mind-Body-Spirit classes such as yoga, tai chi, and Pilates are also offered. Certified personal trainers are available, as are certified massage therapists, and the club also has tanning beds. Gettysburg Health & Fitness has a staffed KinderCare room that's open Monday through Friday mornings. Children age seven and younger are permitted, but only one child younger than one year old will be taken at any one time. Advance reservations are required, and you should let the staff know 24 hours in advance that you want their services. Some evening hours are available with 24-hour notice. Memberships may be for lengths of 1, 3, 6, or 12 months, and visitors to Gettysburg may purchase day passes.

YWCA
909 Fairfield Road
(717) 334-9171
www.ywcagettysburg.org
This member association offers fitness opportunities and is home to dozens of community programs. Guest passes are available for a daily fee, and membership is open to all. A basic membership gives you access to support programs and services held at the Y, while a Recreation Pass allows you the use of the fitness facilities, which include a 25-meter indoor pool, a whirlpool, two racquetball courts, and fitness and training equipment. Members must be 16 years old to use the fitness center. A variety of groups meet at the facilities, including a book group, a parent and child playgroup, and a bridge

group. CPR courses and horseback-riding lessons are also offered, and on-site babysitting services are available to members or holders of a recreation pass. The YWCA currently resides in the East and West buildings, but a decision to consolidate resources was made in 2005. An approximately 10,000-square-foot addition will be added to the East building, and certain areas of the East building will be rehabilitated as well.

HORSEBACK RIDING

Gettysburg Riding Club
102 Hounds Run
(717) 334-4396
www.geocities.com/gettysburgridingclub
Located on 10 acres east of Gettysburg off York Street and Hunterstown Road, the Gettysburg Riding Club first organized in 1952 to have trail rides and hold horse shows, and both traditions carry on today. The club grounds hold a vinyl-covered fenced riding ring, a storage shed, a secretary stand attached to a judges' stand, and a parking area. Well water and electricity are available, and a second area is graded off for use by the trail classes. Club members have trail rides about once a month, and they also have a monthly meeting at an area restaurant. A Christmas party and end-of-show-season dinner is held annually. The club is a member of two show circuits, the Maryland Pennsylvania Horse Show Circuit (MPHSC) and the Blue and Gray Hunter Circuit, and it also holds a show that benefits the Pennsylvania Sudden Infant Death Syndrome Alliance. Club grounds are rented to other horse organizations for shows and to the local 4-H club. Membership is open to anyone with an interest in horses, and you don't have to be a rider to enjoy being part of the club.

Hickory Hollow Farms
219 Crooked Creek Road
(717) 334-0349
www.hickoryhollowfarm.com
You can board your horse at Hickory Hol-

low Farms, which offers private stalls, feeding, and turning out of the horses daily. Boarders can exercise their mounts in the 100-foot by 200-foot lighted outdoor ring with all-weather footing or the 70-foot by 120-foot indoor arena. There's also an outdoor 60-foot round training ring, and the horse trails on the farm are waiting to be explored. Hickory Hollow Farms, which encompasses 70 acres of fields and woodlands, served as a Confederate field hospital during the Battle of Gettysburg. Horseback tours of the battlefield are available through the farm, with both scenic rides and historic rides offered (see the Gettysburg National Military Park chapter).

National Riding Stables
Artillery Ridge Campground
610 Taneytown Road
(717) 334-1288
(877) 335-5596 (toll-free)
www.artilleryridge.com

The National Riding Stables, located at Artillery Ridge Campground, is best known for its two-hour battlefield ride where riders listen on headsets to a CD prepared by a Licensed Battlefield Guide (see the Gettysburg National Military Park chapter). The stable also boards horses, and box stalls and corrals are available. Artillery Ridge sits about a mile south of town on Route 134 (Taneytown Road), and it's also where you can find the Gettysburg Miniature Battlefield Diorama (see the Attractions chapter). If you have little ones, the campground offers pony rides on Sunday as one of its scheduled activities. (See the Campgrounds and RV Parks to find out about all the activities available at Artillery Ridge Campground.)

MARTIAL ARTS

Dubbs Karate Academy
165 York Street
(717) 337-0315, (800) 788-5623

Dubbs Karate Academy has been teaching area residents the martial arts since

1989, and you can sometimes see people practicing their moves through the floor-to-ceiling windows that front York Street. Children and adults can earn their black belt here, and children as young as age three and four can start off with kinderkarate. Classes are held for beginners, and children and adults are taught in separate classes. Self-defense and self-confidence training are also offered, and the academy sells martial-arts supplies and has a pro shop. Dubbs is open every day but Sunday.

MOVIES

Haar's Drive-In
U.S. Route 15, Dillsburg
(717) 432-3011
www.haars.com

If you love drive-in movies and don't mind driving a half an hour or so, you might want to check what's playing at Haar's. This is an authentic 1950s drive-in, and it's been family owned since 1953. It's open only on Friday, Saturday, and Sunday nights from April through September, and two current movies are shown each night. The box office opens at 6:30 P.M., and the first show begins at dusk. To hear the movie, you tune your radio to station 101.1 FM. (The first five rows have speakers if your car doesn't have a radio.) Vans, trucks, or other high-profile vehicles are to park in the first two and last six rows, and the theater has room for about 500 cars total. Nostalgia abounds at Haar's, from

Movie buffs may want to drive about 15 miles southeast to the Hanover Movies at 380 Eisenhower Drive in Hanover (717-646-1111; www.rctheatres.com). The movie theater is one of only 100 movie screens nationwide that feature a Digital Light Processor projection system. The movie comes off a computer hard drive instead of film, which improves clarity significantly.

the layout to the traditional snack bar, but the days of pricing by the carload are long gone. Moviegoers age 12 and older are charged $7.00 each, and children age 3 through 11 are charged $2.00. Pets are not allowed, and the theater accepts cash only at the ticket office. Be aware that the bathroom situations are not the best here—the ladies' room has only two stalls, and keeping them clean does not always appear to be a high priority. To reach Haar's, drive north on U.S. Route 15, and the theater will be on your right after the third traffic light in the town of Dillsburg.

Village Cinemas
Gettysburg Village Factory Stores
Junction of U.S. Route 15 and Route 97
(Baltimore Street)
(717) 337-9705, (800) 868-7553
www.gettysburgvillage.com
These state-of-the-art theaters opened in early 2006, and they're located at the Gettysburg Village, which consists of an outlet mall, a TGI Fridays restaurant, and lodging at the Country Inn & Suites. Gettysburg Village is located just off the Baltimore Street exit of US 15, and from town you follow Baltimore Street for a few miles to reach it. Village Cinemas has nine screens that feature full stadium seating, wall-to-wall wide screens in every room, Dolby digital sound, high-back rockers, and flip-up cup holders. Armrests flip up so two theatergoers can turn their seats into a loveseat. The cinemas also have party rooms and offer VIP ticketing.

Famed pitcher Eddie Plank, who's in the Baseball Hall of Fame, was a Gettysburg native. Nicknamed Gettysburg Eddie, he joined the Philadelphia Athletics after graduating from Gettysburg College in 1901, and he pitched in the majors for 17 seasons. But Eddie was a hometown boy—he spent his off-seasons working at Gettysburg National Military Park as a battlefield tour guide.

OUTDOOR ACTIVITIES

Gettysburg Recreation Park
545 Long Lane
(717) 334-2028
The Gettysburg Recreation Park consists of 52 acres situated within the borough, and many community events take place on its grounds. Lots of exercise also gets done here; the park has a 20-station outdoor fitness trail, 7 baseball diamonds, 2 basketball courts, tennis courts, and a football field. There are also three playgrounds within the park, with one specifically designed for children age four and younger. The Gettysburg Alternative Skate Park (see separate entry within this chapter) opened in May 2005, and the outdoor amphitheater is the site for the "Sunday in the Park" concert series (see the Insiders' Tip in the Annual Events and Festivals chapter). Other park facilities include three pavilions, a seasonal snack bar, and restrooms. The park entrance is across from Gettysburg Hospital, and it can be reached from Baltimore Street by turning westward onto Breckenridge Street and then turning onto Long Lane.

Strawberry Hill Nature Center & Preserve
1537 Mount Hope Road, Fairfield
(717) 642-5840
www.strawberryhill.org
Exploring the habitats of wet and dry woodlands, three ponds, two pristine mountain streams, and more is possible within the 609 acres of Strawberry Hill Nature Center & Preserve. This private nonprofit education and conservation institution opens its land to the public for free. More than 10 miles of blazed trails meander through the property, with trails to please both the strolling family and the more serious hiker. White-tailed deer, bobcats, coyotes, and many other animals live here, and birders will be thrilled by all the species of birds to be discovered.

The Nature Center hosts a variety of programs that explore nature. In 2005 one of the programs was a 1.5-mile walk along Swamp Creek where hikers learned about vernal pools, local history, and wetland forests. Another was a full-moon spring walk to uncover nocturnal animals going about their active lives. A junior naturalist camp is also held here during the summer; see the Kidstuff chapter for full details on the camp. Strawberry Hill holds an annual pancake breakfast and maple-sugaring event, where participants actually see a maple tree being tapped and the syrup being cooked down over an open fire. Most programs are free to members of Strawberry Hill, and nonmembers pay a nominal fee, usually $2.00 to $3.00.

To reach Strawberry Hill, take Route 116 (Middle Street) west for 8.5 miles and turn right onto Carroll's Tract Road. Head north toward Cashtown to the first intersection and turn left onto Mt. Hope Road. Proceed another 3.5 miles to a parking area; the nature center is on the left. Hiking trails in the preserve are open daily dawn to dusk, and the nature center is open Monday through Friday from 9:00 A.M. to 4:00 P.M. yearlong and also open the same hours on Saturday from March to November.

SKATING AND SKATEBOARDING

Gettysburg Alternative Skate Park
Gettysburg Recreation Park
545 Long Lane
(717) 334-2028
After nearly three years of planning and construction, the grand opening of this park finally occurred in May 2005. BMX-ers, in-line skaters, and skateboarders finally have a home in Gettysburg. The fenced-in park is operated by community volunteers, and it has metal ramps and obstacles to challenge riders with varying levels of ability. All participants are required to wear helmets, and children younger than age 10 must also wear wrist guards. Children younger than age 12 must be accompanied by an active supervisor who is at least 16 years old. Everyone who uses the facilities is required to sign a liability release and a code of conduct

release. The park is generally open from afternoon to dusk, and spectators are always welcome. Cost per usage is $5.00 for Pennsylvania residents and $10.00 for out-of-state visitors; day passes are available for $10.00 for Pennsylvania residents and $20.00 for out-of-state visitors. Yearly membership is available to Adams County residents for $50 per individual or $100 per family, and residents of Gettysburg borough enjoy the park for free.

SKIING

Ski Liberty
78 Country Club Trail, Carroll Valley
(717) 642-8282
www.skiliberty.com
When you're approaching Gettysburg by heading west on US 30, Ski Liberty is visible in the distance, and swishing down the mountainside can be done after only a short drive from town. You'll find 16 slopes here, with 35 percent of the slopes geared toward beginner skiers, 40 percent toward intermediate skiers, and 25 percent toward expert skiers. The elevation of the front base is 570 feet, and elevation of the back base is 650 feet; the vertical drop on the front side is 620 feet, and on the back side it's 550 feet. You reach the mountain summit at 1,190 feet, and the longest run on the mountain is 5,200 feet. During the season, which usually runs from Thanksgiving to March, the mountain is open seven days a week for day and night skiing. Long lines are not usually a problem here—ski lifts can carry 10,920 skiers per hour. Ski Liberty has snowmaking capabilities, and you can rent all the equipment for a day on the slopes at the lodge. The Liberty Mountain Sports Shop is located on the deck level in the main lodge and is open any time the mountain is open. As at most ski slopes, snowboarding and snow tubing have become quite popular, and the ski resort offers a half-pipe and a snow-tubing area that has 10 lanes and 3 tow lifts. Ten acres are set aside for three terrain parks that are broken into beginner, intermediate, and

RECREATION

Ski Liberty offers advantage cards, which are a combination between a discount and a frequent-skier card. With an advantage card, you get 40 percent off your lift ticket each time you visit, and after you ski five times, your sixth lift ticket is free.

---

advanced areas. Skiing and snowboarding lessons are available for all ages, and many programs specifically designed for children are available.

Ski Liberty can be experienced as a day at the slopes, or you can stay overnight and make a vacation out of your adventure. The Liberty Mountain Hotel is slopeside, and the hotel at the Carroll Valley Resort is just steps away. (See the Hotels, Motels, and Resorts chapter for details on both resorts.) The ski lodge sits at the base of the mountain, and this is where you'll find McKee's Tavern, a great place to relax after skiing and enjoy a meal or snack, drinks, and often live entertainment. The resort also operates a full-service day care for nonskiing children age 6 months to 10 years, where your child can enjoy story time, movie time, games, songs, crafts, walks, free play, and snacks while you enjoy the slopes. Reservations are requested, and the fee is based on an hourly rate.

NIGHTLIFE ⓨ

Gettysburg certainly is not known for its nightlife, and most of the entertainment you'll find around town is pretty low-key. Many visitors and residents spend their evenings on the battlefield, which is open to 10:00 P.M. April through October and to 7:00 P.M. November through March. Watching the sun set while on the soil where so many gave their lives for their cause is akin to a religious experience for many, and there was quite an outcry when the park service considered shortening the park's evening hours. (Don't worry—the plans have been dropped, at least for now.) Ghost walks also fill up many visitors' evenings, and you'll see troupes of ghost hunters wandering through town on candlelight tours. (See the Attractions chapter for a complete review of all the ghost tours available.)

For those who are looking to relax with some music and/or a few drinks, there are places in town that fit the bill, and dancing happens at Mamma Ventura's, The Pike, and the Flying Bull Saloon. If you want to keep your Gettysburg trip as Civil War–oriented as possible, try the Farnsworth's Killer Angel Tavern, which has waitstaff dressed in period clothing and Civil War–era music performed live on Friday and Saturday nights. Or stop by O'Rorke's, where you'll probably run into some reenactors. And although it's not technically a nightspot, many night owls spend time at the Lincoln Diner, on Carlisle Street beside the Flying Bull. The diner is open 24 hours daily, and many residents, college students, and visitors congregate here to enjoy good yet inexpensive fare in an environment that invites you to linger. If you decide to hit the Lincoln, bring cash—that's all that's accepted as payment.

Arrow Horse
49 Chambersburg Street
(717) 337-2899

The Arrow Horse is a shop that sells banjos and bluegrass music, and bluegrass jam sessions are held here from 7:00 to 10:00 P.M. every Friday night. There's no formal schedule of performers; whoever shows up jams together. This laissez-faire attitude keeps each session fresh, and every Friday-night experience at Arrow Horse is a new adventure to look forward to.

Blue Parrot Bistro
35 Chambersburg Street
(717) 337-3739

Outside tables along the side of the Blue Parrot allow patrons to have a quiet drink or dinner while watching the people strolling by on Chambersburg Street, contributing to the "bistro" feel of the place. The lounge inside has a few small, intimate tables as well as seats at the large bar. Although the Blue Parrot doesn't offer regularly scheduled entertainment, many patrons play pool on the table that separates the lounge and dining areas. Dinner is served until 9:30 P.M., and last call is usually around 1:00 A.M. (See the Restaurants chapter for more on the delicious offerings at Blue Parrot.)

Eastside Lounge and Restaurant
1063 York Road
(717) 337-0118

You won't find musical entertainment at the Eastside, but there are three pool tables and a game room in addition to the long bar that's the main seating area. The lounge has a separate entrance, or you can enter through the restaurant area. Be sure to check out the Eastside's large and varied menu while you're enjoying a libation. (See the Restaurants chapter for a full rundown of their offerings.) The Eastside is open seven days a week from 10:00 A.M. to 2:00 A.M., and there's also a carryout six-pack store in front of the restaurant.

Flying Bull Saloon
28 Carlisle Street
(717) 334-6202

It might look small and dark from the sidewalk, but the Flying Bull is anything but. As you enter, the first thing you see is the long, long bar, which occupies the entire right side of the area, with just enough room behind the bar stools to move through the crowd that usually gathers here. About halfway down this aisle on the left is another room with plenty of space for people to dance to the music that fills the place most nights. While you're dancing, take time to read the messages written in chalk on the wall that runs along this area. The wall is reserved for military personnel, who are invited to sign it. At the end of the bar, there's another room that has some pool tables for those who prefer to cue up rather than dance. The Flying Bull usually hosts live bands on Tuesday, Wednesday is open-mike night, and DJs provide the entertainment Thursday through Saturday nights. Many local residents frequent the Flying Bull, and students from Gettysburg College also make up a good portion of the crowd while school is in session. The place is always closed on Sunday, and it's also closed on Monday when the college kids are on break.

Gettysburg Village Factory Stores
Junction of U.S. Route 15 and Route 97
(Baltimore Street)
(717) 337-9705, (800) 868-7553
www.gettysburgvillage.com

The food court at this outlet shopping center offers family karaoke every Friday night from 6:00 to 8:30 P.M. The outlet is set up to replicate an 1860s main street, with stores lining each side of a wide boulevard and parking available in front as well as behind the stores. The food court is located at the far end of the outlet, near the gazebo and the movie theaters, which opened in 2006 with stadium seating and state-of-the-art sound. While you're enjoying the karaoke, you can also munch on sandwiches, pizza, Chinese food, and more.

Hamilton's Tavern
126 Chambersburg Street
(717) 337-2719

Hamilton's Tavern is best described as "a working man's bar." When you climb the steps and open the door, it's likely all heads at the bar will swing your way. Don't be put off—everyone's just checking to see if someone they know has come in. Hamilton's is not large—one side has a long bar and a few tables along the wall and the other side has a few games and tables—but it is a friendly place where you can get drinks and food at very reasonable prices.

Killer Angel Tavern
Farnsworth House Inn
401 Baltimore Street
(717) 334-8838
www.farnsworthhouseinn.com

The Killer Angel Tavern is located on the grounds of the Farnsworth House Inn, a sprawling complex that includes a bed-and-breakfast, indoor and outdoor dining areas open to the public, a bookshop, and a sutlery. Sitting at the rear of the complex, the tavern has its own entrance, and light fare is served. South Street Pizza (717-334-4419) also operates a thriving pizza and hoagie business within the tavern. An interesting collection of uniforms and props from the movie *Gettysburg* is housed at the tavern, and the Civil War is always an avid topic of conversation, especially among the reenactors who gather here. Entertainment offered keeps with the Civil War theme of the complex, with live Civil War music every Friday and Saturday night from 9:00 to 11:00 P.M. The tavern closes after the group is done on those nights, while its regular hours are from 11:30 A.M. to 10:30 P.M.

The Livery
Herr Tavern and Publick House
900 Chambersburg Road
(717) 334-4332, (800) 362-9849
www.herrtavern.com

A casual atmosphere rules at The Livery, which sits in its own building across the parking lot from Herr Tavern and Publick House, an elegant bed-and-breakfast steeped in Civil War history. (See the Bed-and-Breakfasts and Guesthouses chapter for more on the bed-and-breakfast.) The Livery runs different food and beer specials each night, and it has a large outside deck on one side of the building. Entertainment available inside consists of blacklight pool, darts, foosball, and touchscreen video games. You'll also find big-screen TVs, and light fare is available if hunger hits. The Livery is open Monday through Friday 3:30 P.M. to 2:00 A.M., Saturday noon to 2:00 A.M., and Sunday noon to midnight.

Mamma Ventura's Lounge
13 Chambersburg Street
(717) 334-5548

Mamma Ventura's Lounge is a favorite haunt of Gettysburg College students, who gather here to dance and to sing karaoke. The lounge is actually beneath Mamma Ventura's Restaurant, and it has its own entrance. To reach the lounge, you need to walk between the buildings on Chambersburg Street to the back of the street; the entrance for the lounge is to your left as you leave the small walkway. A sign at the restaurant points you in the right direction, and you need to be careful while walking between the buildings so you don't knock into any of the stairs that are within the walkway. Once you enter the lounge, you're greeted by a large open space with tables, two bar areas on the left, and an area in the back that has pool tables. DJs spin tunes on Wednesday and Friday nights, and karaoke rules on Thursday and Saturday nights.

O'Rorke's Family Eatery and Spirits
44 Steinwehr Avenue
(717) 334-2333

Reenactors tend to congregate at O'Rorke's, which is named for Patrick O'Rorke, an Irish-born American soldier who was killed on Little Round Top during the Battle of Gettysburg. O'Rorke's has a large deck that overlooks the activity along Steinwehr Avenue, which makes it perfect for people watching. Inside you'll find good food and a nice selection of beer, wine, and specialty drinks. Six beers are on tap, including Guinness and Harp, and wine is available by the glass. Live entertainment takes place on Friday and Saturday from 8:00 to 11:00 P.M., with all types of music represented throughout the season. O'Rorke's opens daily at 11:00 A.M., and food is available until 10:00 P.M. Drinks are served until midnight except on Sunday, when the place closes an hour earlier.

If a bell rings while you're at Hamilton's Tavern, it means someone has bought a round for the entire bar. If you're not ready for another drink, just ask your waitress to enter your name in "the book." You can redeem your free drink anytime during the next 30 days.

Pike Restaurant & Lounge
985 Baltimore Pike
(717) 334-9227

Something always seems to be going on at the lounge at Pike on weekends. DJs and live bands provide dance music on Friday and Saturday nights, and on Sunday you can find a bluegrass jam and sometimes karaoke going on. Pike boasts that it has Gettysburg's largest dance floor, and although it's not really very big, you usually will find it jam-packed on weekend nights. This nightspot sits at the edge of town, and plenty of parking is available in front of and across the street from the place. A mechanical bull was a

The state of Pennsylvania allows the sale of liquor and wine through state-run stores only. Gettysburg's state store is within the Peebles Shopping Center east of town along York Road. The store is open seven days a week; call (717) 334-3814.

big draw during the 2005 season, so it's likely this will be part of the ongoing entertainment offered here. Besides the lounge, Pike also has a large deck out front and a separate bar off the deck, and live bands also play on the deck. The 6 Pack Carry Out Store (717-334-0581), which is open daily noon to 10:00 P.M., is also located here.

The Pub & Restaurant
20-22 Lincoln Square
(717) 334-7100
www.the-pub.com

The Pub doesn't have any entertainment, unless you count the people watching that goes on here. This fun place offers its patrons a bird's-eye view of all the activity that flows through Lincoln Square. There are even tables outside for those who like to be a part of the goings-on. Separate entrances for the pub and the restaurant are available, but you can reach both through either door. The pub side's rich wood lends an old-world ambience to the place, which is outfitted with a nice-size bar and a few tables. You can choose from a wide range of cocktails, wines, and beers here. In fact, there are 12 drafts on tap, one of which is always Guinness. The Pub serves until 1:00 A.M. Monday through Saturday and until 11:00 P.M. on Sunday.

Ragged Edge Coffeehouse
110 Chambersburg Street
(717) 334-4464
www.raggededgecoffeehs.com

Ragged Edge has plenty of room for you to spread out since the remodeling that took place after the place next door had a

fire in 2003. New floors, new lighting, and a new stage on the second floor make this a comfortable place to catch the live entertainment that's provided by local musicians on Saturday nights or to enjoy the unpredictability of open-mike nights on Tuesday and Friday from 8:00 to 10:00 P.M. You'll find people hanging on the front porch, in the rooms downstairs, out on the patio in back, and in the rooms upstairs. Sandwiches, salads, and baked goods are available, as well as juices, smoothies, supplement drinks, and hot and cold specialty (nonalcoholic) drinks. Ragged Edge is open daily until 10:00 P.M. except on Friday, when it's open until 11:00 P.M.

Reliance Mine Saloon
380 Steinwehr Avenue
(717) 334-9870

This unique cocktail lounge is part of the Quality Inn Gettysburg Motor Lodge, and it's within an underground coal mine. The lodge is completely nonsmoking and so is the saloon, which serves only drinks and snacks and seats about 50. Unfortunately, nonsmokers have to make it through the long hallway that leads to the lounge, where all the smokers congregate, to reach a smoke-free environment. Once you're inside the saloon, there's a small bar and lots of tables available, and the saloon's lack of windows makes you feel isolated from the outside world. The saloon is open daily from 6:00 P.M. to 1:00 A.M.

Squire Miller Tavern
The Fairfield Inn 1757
15 West Main Street, Fairfield
(717) 334-8868, (717) 642-5410
www.thefairfieldinn.com

If you like to drink in history, stop at the Squire Miller Tavern, about 8 miles west of town off Route 116. In November 2004 a colonial-era tavern license dating from 1786 was discovered by the local historical society, making the Squire Miller Tavern one of the oldest taverns in the United States still operating. The inn itself dates from 1757, and the house now serves as a bed-and-breakfast (see the Bed-and-Breakfasts and Guesthouses chapter). The tavern has its own entrance on the side of the inn, or you can reach it by turning left after entering through the front door, which has the original pulley-type lock. A key feature of the tavern is its huge fireplace, which is complete with the original kettle arm and kettle. The bar itself is magnificent. Gleaming mahogany woodwork has large archways cut into it, and this is where the liquor is displayed. The tavern serves as the smoking section of the inn's restaurant, and there are enough tables to seat about 25 people in addition to the seats at the bar.

DAY TRIPS 🚗

BALTIMORE'S INNER HARBOR

Located less than 60 miles by car from Gettysburg, Baltimore's Inner Harbor makes an easy and relaxing day trip. To reach it, travel out of town on Baltimore Street, which will become Route 97 South. At Westminster, Maryland, pick up Maryland Route 140 South and follow it to Reisterstown, where you connect with Interstate 795 South. Take I-795 South to its merger with Interstate 695. From I-695, pick up Interstate 95 East. From I-95, take exit 53 (Interstate 395 North, Downtown), and turn right at the third light onto Pratt Street. The Inner Harbor is 4 blocks up Pratt Street on your right. Once you park the car in one of the many lots near the harbor, you can walk or take a water taxi to all the area attractions, which include historic ships, shopping and dining areas, museums, and the National Aquarium.

Although Inner Harbor was created during the 1960s, it really took off as a destination spot in the 1980s when **Harborplace** opened as two glass-enclosed pavilions (Light Street Pavilion and Pratt Street Pavilion) where visitors could find small shops, lots of restaurants, and often live entertainment. In 1987 Harborplace added **The Gallery** across from Pratt Street Pavilion, with more shops and a parking garage beneath the shops. Harborplace is where most visitors begin their exploration of Inner Harbor, and for some, it's the sole reason they come to Baltimore.

---

i *One convenient place to park is The Gallery garage, which is under The Gallery and across from Harborplace. To get to the garage from Pratt Street, turn left onto Calvert Street and make an immediate right into the garage.*

Call Harborplace and The Gallery at Harborplace at (800) HARBOR-1 or visit www.harborplace.com for details on the restaurants and shops within the three locations that make up Harborplace.

Civil War buffs will not want to miss touring the **USS *Constellation*,** the only surviving Civil War–era naval vessel and all-sail warship built by the navy. Events, reenactments, and tours are always going on aboard this 1,400-ton, 179-foot sailing sloop that was built in 1854 and now serves as a museum. Once a year, the USS *Constellation* departs its berth at Pier 1 for a journey to Fort McHenry and back, with cannon firing along the way. The cost to tour the *Constellation* is $8.75 for adults, $7.50 for seniors age 60 and older and active-duty military, and $4.75 for kids age 6 through 14. Children age five and younger get to tour for free. Call (410) 539-1797 or visit www.constellation.org for more information.

No tour to Baltimore would be complete without visiting the **National Aquarium** (410-576-3800; www.aqua.org), which is located on Pier 3. This is Maryland's top tourist destination, with about 1.6 million visitors per year, and it's strongly recommended that you buy your tickets in advance of your visit. The aquarium includes an Atlantic coral reef tank that is home to more than 600 fish, a 225,000–gallon shark tank, an area filled with bottlenosed dolphins, and a replica of an Amazon River rain forest. Tickets cost $19.50 for adults, $18.50 for seniors age 60 and older, and $13.50 for children age 3 to 11; children younger than age 3 are admitted for free.

A brick-lined promenade is perfect for walking around Inner Harbor, or you can hop aboard one of the blue-and-white water shuttles that transport travelers around the harbor as well as to nearby Little Italy, Fell's Point, Canton, and Fort

McHenry. This is the oldest water-taxi service in the country, and you pay one price to ride the shuttles all day. Visit www.the watertaxi.com or call (800) 658-8947 for details. If you'd like to take a lunch, brunch, or dinner cruise, **Harbor Cruises** (800-695-BOAT; www.harborcruises.com) has been accommodating tourists since 1981. They're located at 561 Light Street, adjacent to the **Maryland Science Center** (410-685-5225; www.mdsci.org), which has three floors of hands-on exhibits, a planetarium, and a five-story IMAX theater. A sail aboard *Clipper City,* a topsail schooner that's a replica of one of the tall ships that carried coal and lumber from one East Coast port to another from 1854 to 1892, is also a possibility. Call (410) 931-6777 or visit www.clippercity.com for details.

A visitor's packet, maps, and lots of useful information on other attractions at Inner Harbor and Baltimore can be obtained by contacting the Baltimore Visitor Center at (877) BALTIMORE or by visiting www.baltimore.org. Seeing the Orioles play baseball at Camden Yards or the Ravens play football at M&T Bank Stadium, visiting Fort McHenry or the Baltimore Civil War Museum, touring the distinct neighborhoods that make up Baltimore, and a plethora of other enjoyable excursions await you.

CITY ISLAND AND DOWNTOWN HARRISBURG

Harrisburg is the capital of Pennsylvania, and locals describe the city and its environs as the East Shore and the West Shore, which are divided by the Susquehanna River. Between the two shores sits **City Island,** which has been transformed from what used to be just a large parking area into an entertainment complex with food kiosks, picnic grounds, water golf, minor-league baseball, water sports, and more. The Island is located about 35 miles north of Gettysburg, and it's a snap to reach. Just travel U.S. Route 15 north from

Gettysburg and turn right at the light at the intersection of US 15 and Market Street in Camp Hill. (This is the second light after you pass the Camp Hill Shopping Mall on your left.) Follow Market Street through Camp Hill and Lemoyne, and stay in the right lane as you go through some S curves. At the next light, take a right to head toward Harrisburg by crossing the Market Street Bridge; the entrance for City Island is about halfway across the bridge. At the stop sign at the end of the off-ramp, make a left to park closest to the activities. (Handicap parking is also to the left; follow the signs.)

Once you park the car, you can either climb the steps or walk along the ramp to the right of the steps under the overpass to begin your day of fun. Horse-drawn carriage rides are available at the stables straight ahead. Batting cages are available, and a train takes the little ones on a ride around the island. An oval paved walking track circles the Island, and you'll discover all the different activities available by following the path. The Harrisburg Senators play minor-league baseball at the Commerce Park field, and soccer and football games are held in the stadium behind the ballpark. An area to the right fronts the Susquehanna River, and you can enjoy a picnic along the banks of the river with food you bring or food you buy at the many kiosks that dot the area. This area also often features live entertainment, and there are a few shops to browse. The *Pride of the Susquehanna* paddle wheeler is located along the bank, and public cruises

The East Shore consists of the city of Harrisburg and communities to the east as far as Hershey, while the West Shore includes the communities west of the river to Carlisle. Although separated by only a river, some residents feel the shores are two different worlds, and many longtime residents never venture across the river to the other shore.

that last about 45 minutes depart through-out the day. The fare is $4.95 for adults and $3.00 for children age 3 through 12, while children age 2 and younger ride for free. Dinner and special cruises are also available, and rates on Wednesday are slightly reduced. Call (717) 234-6500 or visit www.harrisburgriverboat.com for more information.

Farther up the Island is an area espe-cially for kids, with tot-size playground equipment, and you can rent Jet Skis at the marina that's also along this stretch of the island (there is another marina off the parking lots that are to the right when you enter City Island). Swimming and sun-bathing are allowed at the far end of the island, and a water golf course is along the oval path as it starts to turn back toward your starting point. The minigolf course incorporates water on almost every hole, and this challenging course is a great way to see the river. Beyond the minigolf some hiking paths are available if you'd like to travel off the oval track into nature.

Once you fully explore the Island, you may want to stroll across the walking bridge and discover some of the fun things to do in the city. Riverfront Park is along the Susquehanna on the city side, and there's a walking path and steps that you can take down to the riverfront. If you walk straight when you leave the walking bridge and turn left when you reach Second Street, you can discover a renovated area that is called **Restaurant Row** because of all the eating establishments and night-clubs that run north for blocks. If you con-tinue on Walnut Street to Third Street and

turn left, you will reach the **Capitol Complex,** where the Pennsylvania State Legislature resides. After admiring the architecture of the capitol and the sur-rounding buildings and maybe observing a session of the legislature, you can continue up Third Street to the **State Museum of Pennsylvania** (717-787-4978; www.state-museumpa.org). This always-interesting museum covers all aspects of Pennsylvania history, and it's visited by 315,000 school-children and adults annually. Among its many significant collections is the perma-nent exhibit "The Keystone of the Union," which interprets Gettysburg's role in the Civil War. Admission to the museum is free.

After you explore downtown, you can head back to your car by either going back the way you came or heading over to the river and walking the paved path that parallels the river all the way to the walk-ing bridge.

For more information on City Island and other activities available in the capital city, call (717) 255-3040 or visit www .harrisburgpa.gov.

HERSHEYPARK

Milton S. Hershey, founder of the town of Hershey and Hershey Chocolate, opened Hersheypark in 1907, and this amusement park is still a major attraction of the area today. The park opens at 10:00 A.M., is open most nights during the summer till 10:00 or 11:00 P.M., and is located a little more than 50 miles north of Gettysburg. From Gettysburg, travel north on US 15 to Route 581 East (the sign will say to 83 North). Route 581 becomes Interstate 83 as you cross the Susquehanna River, and the road eventually splits into I-83, U.S. Route 322, and Route 283. Follow the signs for US 322, which will take you to Hershey, where you pick up Route 39, also called Hersheypark Drive. The park is a few miles up Route 39, and there are plenty of signs to guide you.

The park has 60 rides, including 10 roller coasters, 6 water rides, and more

i *You can pay a lot less for your fun day at Hersheypark by buying your tickets at a Giant Food Store, where tickets are deeply discounted. For instance, an adult ticket is only $29.95—$11.00 cheaper than at the gate. The nearest Giant is east of Lincoln Square off York Street. Call (717) 337-0017.*

than 20 kiddie rides. Games, live entertainment, paddleboats, a zoo, food, and shops round out the experience. Hersheypark is divided into the major theme areas of Comet Hollow, Founder's Circle, Midway America, Minetown, Music Box Way, and Pioneer Frontier, and the park usually adds a new ride every few years. Its latest, Storm Runner, was added in 2004, and this coaster goes from 0 to 72 mph in two seconds and intertwines with the park's monorail at two spots. Many of the coasters weave in and out of other rides. The Great Bear coaster intertwines with the Sooperdooperlooper roller coaster and the Coal Cracker water ride. Although you may love the wild rides, take time to ride the monorail and to visit the Kissing Tower, both of which give you a great view of the entire park. (The Kissing Tower is shaped like a giant Hershey's Kiss!) And check as you enter the park to see when the dolphin shows are—you definitely don't want to miss these entertaining creatures showing off their tricks.

A one-day admission in 2005 was $40.95 for those age 9 to 54, $23.95 for those age 3 to 8 and seniors age 55 to 69, and $15.95 for seniors age 70 or older; children age 2 and younger are admitted for free. Prices are reduced when buying tickets for multiple days or when entering the park later in the day. Admission includes a visit to **Zoo America,** an 11-acre walk-through zoo with more than 200 animals representing five regions of North America. Visitors to Hersheypark almost always take a tour through **Chocolate World,** which is separate from Hersheypark but located right beside it. Entrance to Chocolate World is free, and you take a ride that explains how chocolate is made. Everyone receives a free sample of a Hershey's Chocolate product at the end of the tour,

If you're leaving the park and plan to reenter later, be sure to have your hand stamped at the exit gate. Ticket stubs are not valid for reentry. Your parking ticket will allow you to reenter the parking lot upon your return.

which lets you off at a huge shopping and dining area dedicated to all things chocolate.

A daily parking fee of $8.00 per vehicle or $10.00 per camper is charged at Hersheypark. A tram service runs from the parking area to the park entrance approximately every 15 minutes during park hours. Before you get on the tram in the parking lot, look on a nearby lightpost to see which section of the lot you're parked in so you know where to get off the tram when leaving the park. If you have limited mobility but want to enjoy the park, the park rents wheelchairs and Electric Convenience Vehicles on a first-come, first-served basis. (We rented the electric scooters for my parents so they could enjoy the park with their grandkids, and it was the most enjoyable day the entire family ever had at the park—well worth the extra money.) The rental area is located behind the Tram Circle Group Sales Building. Families with children may bring in their own stroller or rent one inside the main entrance on a first-come, first-served basis.

For more information, call (800) HERSHEY or visit www.hersheypa.com. The Web site is extremely comprehensive, with details on rides, entertainment, shopping, and more within the park. You can even take some virtual rides! The site also covers area lodging, restaurants, entertainment, and other attractions.

RELOCATION

People move to Gettysburg for all kinds of reasons, and two popular ones have perpetually been to enjoy the beauty of the area and to study the battlefield and the Civil War at leisure. Today there's a third reason that's becoming more and more prevalent—to get more house for the money while commuting to Baltimore or Washington for work. Gettysburg has become a bedroom community for those two metropolitan areas, and because of this real estate is usually more expensive in the southern part of Adams County.

This bedroom-community effect has contributed to Adams County being the third-fastest growing county in the commonwealth. The 1990 census put the population at 78,274, and the 2000 census has the number at 91,292—a 16.6 percent increase. The county planning department estimates the 2004 population of the county at 99,256, an almost 9 percent increase from 2000. Housing developments seem to be springing up all over the county; in August 2005 the county planning department reported knowing of more than a dozen development plans in the works.

Nowhere is the fact that Gettysburg is a town of the "haves" and the "have-nots" more discernible than when you look at the area real-estate market. As in most towns in the United States, the cost of housing is skyrocketing. The median cost of a single-family home in the Gettysburg Area School District increased from $119,000 in 2001 to $189,000 in 2004. But wages have not increased proportionately and, according to the 2000 census, Adams County is one of the lowest ranking Pennsylvania counties in terms of average wages. Many Gettysburg residents earn $7.00 per hour, and many jobs are seasonal. Affordable housing has become a major concern, causing county officials to

form a task group on the issue. On the bright side, the 2000 census also reported that Adams County has one of the lowest unemployment rates in the state, and 80 percent of residents are homeowners. Still, the food pantry in Gettysburg serves about 750 people per month.

Where you live has a profound effect on your day-to-day existence, and this chapter will cover neighborhoods in the surrounding area. Some basic community information is included, as are places to contact early in your relocation process. Information is also provided on the humdrum but necessary chores that accompany a move, including getting a new driver's license, registering your car, and registering to vote.

REAL ESTATE

When relocating to a new area, your best bet is to contact a real-estate agent, and this is especially true in Gettysburg. Many developments have no identifying signage, so finding a particular neighborhood can be confusing for newcomers. Many of the homes are in rural settings and not part of any development, so you'll need an agent to coordinate your house hunting. (See the listings of real-estate companies later in this chapter.) Renting before you buy so you get to know your new hometown is usually advised, but Gettysburg doesn't have an abundance of apartment complexes. Two complexes are the Devonshire Village Apartments south of town off Emmitsburg Road and the Gettysburg West Apartments west of town off Chambersburg Road, both of which are managed by Michael Investments (717–334–8181). Many people also rent downtown in houses that have been converted into apartments and on the floors above stores.

Handy Numbers and Addresses

Gettysburg Hospital—147 Gettys Street; (717) 334-2121
Borough Police—59 East High Street; (717) 334-1168
Adams County Courthouse—111 Baltimore Street; (717) 334-6781
Borough Office—59 East High Street; (717) 334-1160
Post Office—115 Buford Avenue; (717) 337-3781
Adams County Public Library—140 Baltimore Street; (717) 334-5716
Adams County SPCA—11 Goldenville Road; (717) 334-8876

The neighborhoods around Gettysburg run the gamut from streets filled with mansions to mobile parks filled with trailers. New developments meld with older communities, with most new housing starting around $300,000. Housing developments in the area have homes in the $200,000 to $300,000 range on average, but exceptions do exist. You'll pay considerably more if you look in two of the most desirable locations in town—the 3 blocks along Seminary Ridge across from the seminary and West and East Broadway Avenue by Gettysburg College, where prices reach into the millions. Also very desirable for those who can afford it is the development of Ridgewood, located north of town off Mummasburg Road, which is filled with an eclectic assortment of homes surrounded by acres of woods. At the other end of the spectrum are homes within the mobile home parks, which may sell for as low as $6,000 to $20,000. Prices for homes in rural settings vary widely, with location and the amount of acreage included impacting the asking price. Expect any home with a connection to the Civil War to automatically demand a higher price. Homes close to the Maryland line are currently in demand by commuters and are therefore also higher priced.

Within the borough of Gettysburg, you'll find a lot of attached homes, and in many parts of town the downstairs are

storefronts and the upstairs are apartments for rent. There's not an abundance of crime in the area, but like most places today, crime is increasing. One area that's considered a bit questionable is South Washington Street below Breckenridge Avenue, where drug activity and crime seem to go hand in hand.

But also at the southern end of town is the beautiful neighborhood of Colt Park, where there's a nice mix of old and new homes. Residents like that they can walk to the battlefield and many restaurants and attractions, and that Recreation Park and Gettysburg Hospital are nearby. Off Emmitsburg Road beside the Eisenhower Inn & Conference Center is Devonshire Village, with condos for rent and for sale. Farther away from town to the south is the gated community of Lake Heritage, which was established in the 1960s as a vacation-home community. Today it's a thriving residential area that has a nice range of homes usually priced according to how close they are to Lake Heritage, where residents can enjoy boating and other water activities.

To the east of town there's a mobile home park behind the Giant Food Store on York Street, and the residential community of Hunter's Crossing is just outside of town off Hunterstown Road, where you'll discover newer homes that are nicely spaced out within the development. Off Hanover

Street just east of its interchange with U.S. Route 15 is the neighborhood of Hazelbrook Hills, which has a good selection of homes in different price ranges.

Many developments are to the west of town. Along Chambersburg Road are the mobile home park of Lincoln Estates and the upscale townhome community of Foxridge. Housing developments off Herr's Ridge Road include the older community of Ridgeview, the currently being built homes of Canon Ridge, and the zero-lot homes within the community of Camelot Square. A zero-lot home is one where you own only the footprint of land your house occupies. Although these are single-family detached homes, the community works much as a condo or townhome development, with an association collecting fees for maintenance and upkeep of the common grounds. Also to the west of town but along Route 116 (Fairfield Road) are the developments of Woodcrest and Twin Lakes, both older communities with a good mix of homes. Woodcrest is across from the YWCA, and Twin Lakes is just a bit farther west. Twin Lakes has expanded over the years, and today there is Twin Lakes II and Twin Lakes West in addition to the original development.

At the northern end of town along Route 34, zero-lot homes can be found within the community of Roselawn, and the Meadows community is still building condominiums and adding to its development that began in the 1990s. The Patriot's Choice development is just breaking ground on new homes, while the older community of Longview is filled with

---

Dave Ruff, one of the agents at Century 21, created and developed the Internet site www.gettysburgmarketplace.com, which lists Gettysburg-based businesses for free. The site holds a gold mine of information for visitors and residents alike, with links to many of the listed businesses.

---

sprawling homes that command a great view. Off U.S. Business Route 15 just outside of town is the Twin Oaks development, which was started in the 1960s and completed in the 1980s. Here you'll find a sprawling community with homes in an assortment of price ranges.

Real Estate Offices

Century 21 Neighborhood Realty, Inc.
705 Old Harrisburg Road
(717) 334-9131, (800) 347-6734
www.century21neighborhood.com
This Century 21 office, like all Century 21 offices, is locally owned and operated. In September 2002 Roger Sprague purchased the firm and renewed a 10-year franchise agreement. Roger brought nine years of real-estate experience to the franchise, including managing two other Gettysburg real-estate offices, and he certainly knows the area—he was a dairy farmer in Adams County for 20 years. This Century 21 office has 16 agents in addition to Roger, and they deal in residential, commercial, and investment properties. One agent is dedicated full time to finding tenants for investment properties and apartments and homes for renters. Century 21 Neighborhood Realty is a member of the Multiple Listing Services computer network and the National Association of Realtors.

Coldwell Banker Bigham, REALTORS®
121 Buford Avenue
(717) 334-7666
www.cbbigham.com
www.coldwellbanker.com
In business since 1955, this locally owned and independently operated company is the oldest continuously operating real-estate firm in the area. The president and broker/owner of the company is Adams County native Barbara M. Hartman, who is the daughter of the company's deceased founder, William A. Bigham. In 1982 the company became a member of Coldwell Banker Residential Affiliates and changed

its trade name to Coldwell Banker Bigham, REALTORS®. The company is licensed in both Pennsylvania and Maryland, and it provides a full range of real-estate services, including residential and commercial/investment brokerage services, property management, and real-estate consulting services.

Bigham's employs eight agents besides the owner, and its philosophy is "Expect the Best." The company goal is not to necessarily be the largest company in the area but to provide the highest possible level of service to clients and customers.

Coldwell Banker Bob Yost–Sites
1270 Fairfield Road
(717) 334–7636, (800) 274–7636
www.cbhomesale.com
Coldwell Banker has operated in central Pennsylvania since 1949, and it opened this local office in 2000. The company takes full advantage of our high-tech world, advertising access to agents 24/7 via e-mail, voice mail, pagers, cell phones, and fax. But their high-tech approach doesn't diminish their personal touch. Every year since the 1980s, the company has planted flags at random throughout local communities in York and Adams Counties—in 2005 they placed 24,000 flags. Coldwell Banker Bob Yost–Sites handles residential, commercial, and rental properties, and this one-stop Realtor also offers mortgage and title insurance services.

Jack Gaughen Realtor ERA
224 Baltimore Street
(717) 334–6283, (800) 289–6283
www.jgr.com
Jack Gaughen Realtor ERA was established in 1963 in Camp Hill, a suburb of Harrisburg. Today the company has grown to include 15 offices in 7 counties covering central and southcentral Pennsylvania. Much of its growth has been through acquisitions, and it expanded into Adams County in 2000 by buying ERA Miller. The Gettysburg office has 27 agents who handle residential, commercial, and rental

properties. Jack Gaughen Realtor ERA has a relocation division, and you can request a free relocation guide to the area by visiting their Web site or calling the number above.

Long & Foster Real Estate, Inc.
430 Baltimore Street
(717) 338–3406, (800) 667–2027
www.longandfoster.com
Sixteen agents are ready to assist you at this office of Long & Foster Real Estate, Inc., whose parent company, the Long & Foster® Companies, is the largest privately owned residential real-estate and related financial services company in America. The states of Pennsylvania, Virginia, West Virginia, New Jersey, Maryland, Delaware, and North Carolina as well as the District of Columbia are serviced by Long & Foster offices, and the Gettysburg office handles the counties of York and Adams in Pennsylvania. The company works with residential, commercial, and rental properties, and relocation services and mortgage services are available.

If you have a computer, ask your agent to implement the system that sends you daily e-mails that show houses for sale. The information comes from the Multiples Listings book, and this is an easy way to become familiar with the local real-estate market.

Re/Max of Gettysburg
18 Carlisle Street, Suite 300
(717) 338–0881, (800) 765–3280
www.gettysburgrealestate.com
Re/Max is a global real-estate system of franchisee-owned and -operated offices, and throughout the network more than 100,000 agents do business in more than 50 countries in more than 50 languages. This Gettysburg franchise was established in 1995, and it's currently experiencing lots of growth. In fact, it claims that no other real-estate office in Adams County has

Homes & Land *is a free publication that is chock-full of local real-estate companies showing you properties they have for sale. Pick up your copy at shops around town, on the Internet at www.homesandland.com, or by calling (800) 277-7800.*

grown at the pace it has in the last six years. The office offers residential, commercial, and rental services, and there are currently about 20 agents available to help you find your new home. If possible, check out the main Re/Max Web site of www .remax.com. It offers lots of great information, including the basics of buying or selling property, a glossary of real-estate jargon, and mortgage tools that help you calculate how much house you can afford.

SOCIAL SERVICES

South Central Community Action Programs, Inc. (SCCAP)
153 North Stratton Street
(717) 334-7634, (800) 232-6562
www.sccap.org
Acting as an umbrella agency, SCCAP coordinates charitable programs in Adams County (and neighboring Franklin County) that help low-income individuals help themselves. At one place, those in need can find access to a variety of programs that want to lend a hand. SCCAP is a private, nonprofit corporation that was established in April 1965, and its funding comes from federal, state, and local government, foundations, businesses, and individual donations. Programs that help you find day-care services and help you pay for them, that help you get a job, that help you keep your house up to code, and that help you with emergency assistance are just a few of the many programs SCCAP offers. The federal program Women, Infant, and Children (WIC), which helps families feed their children, is also

run by SCCAP, as are the local food pantry and homeless shelter. The food pantry is open seven days a week at the same address as SCCAP, and the homeless shelter is located at 102 North Stratton Street.

United Way of Adams County
123 Buford Avenue
(717) 334-5809
http://national.unitedway.org
This nonprofit organization delivers services to those in need and also provides links to local volunteers and businesses. Across America, there are approximately 1,400 community-based United Way organizations, and each is independent, separately incorporated, and governed by local volunteers.

Veterans Affairs of Adams County
Union Square Building
23 Baltimore Street
(717) 337-9835, (888) 337-9835
www.va.gov
This local office of the Veterans Affairs can give you contact information and help you apply for veterans' benefits. It's staffed by one person and open on weekdays (closed for lunch from noon to 1:00 P.M.). Although its address is on Baltimore Street, its entrance is easily accessible from Middle Street.

COMMUNITY INFORMATION

Gettysburg Convention & Visitors Bureau (CVB)
102 Carlisle Street
(717) 334-6274, (800) 337-5015
www.gettysburgcvb.org
The Gettysburg CVB provides Gettysburg visitors and residents comprehensive information about area events. The official visitors guide distributed here is a compact booklet chock-full of information. You'll find listings for accommodations, restaurants, tours, attractions, shops, golf courses, and more along with a concise discussion of the Battle of Gettysburg and

Grocery Stores

Giant Food Stores—44 Natural Springs Road; (717) 337-0017
Kennie's Market—217 West Middle Street; (717) 334-2179
Weis Markets—735 Old Harrisburg Road; (717) 337-1753

a calendar of special events planned for the area. Brochures from area businesses are displayed on two walls of the office, and a very knowledgeable and pleasant staff is available to help with any questions you might have. The Gettysburg CVB also distributes an annual calendar of events at their office or by mail, as well as a quarterly newsletter titled "Destination Gettysburg," which features events, packages, and activities in the area. Located just a little more than a block off the square, the Gettysburg CVB should definitely be one of your first stops in town. The office is open daily.

Gettysburg Adams
Chamber of Commerce
18 Carlisle Street
(717) 334-8151
www.gettysburg-chamber.org
The Gettysburg Adams Chamber of Commerce began way back in 1919, and this is where new residents head to get vital information about the area. A relocation packet distributed by the chamber gives new or potential residents a good overview of Gettysburg and Adams County, and it's bursting with information on everything from top area employers to the median cost of a house in the area. Maps of Adams County, including an excellent map of Gettysburg, are available from the chamber, and telephone books are given to anyone who stops by the office for them. You can also pick up a community calendar of events open to the public in the upcoming year (the calendar is really comprehensive); school, church, and real-estate information; lists of mem-

ber clubs, organizations, banks, contractors, attorneys, and major employers; census information; and much, much more. The chamber is open Monday through Friday, and it's located within the first block off the square.

LICENSES AND REGISTRATIONS

Drivers' Licenses

IF THIS IS YOUR FIRST LICENSE

The state of Pennsylvania issues a learner's permit to residents at least 16 years old who have returned a completed physical form and paid the permit fee. The fee must be paid by check; no cash is accepted. You can pick up your permit and a booklet that gives you all the information you'll need to pass the license test at 59 North Fifth Street. This is also where you will take the tests for your license. The written exam is given from 8:30 A.M. to 4:15 P.M. on Wednesday and Friday, and the driving exam is given by appointment only on Wednesday and Friday.

IF YOU MOVED HERE FROM ANOTHER STATE

You are required to replace your out-of-state license with a Pennsylvania license within 60 days of moving to the state. To do so, head to 59 North Fifth Street on either a Wednesday or Friday with your current driver's license; your social security card, birth certificate, passport, or military ID; and a check for the fee (no cash is accepted). You must also present two forms of ID that provide your current Pennsylvania address (an electric bill, a telephone bill, etc.). If your out-of-state license has expired, you'll be required to take both the written and driving test.

IF YOU NEED TO GET YOUR LICENSE RENEWED

Every four years, you'll receive a camera card for a new photo license in the mail. For renewal of the license, you take the card to the License Photo Area at 59 North Fifth Street (717-334-0308). Hours are Tuesday, Wednesday, Friday, and Saturday from 8:30 A.M. to 4:15 P.M. and Thursday from 8:30 A.M. to 8:00 P.M.

Car Registration

Technically, you're required to register your car with the state within 30 days of moving to Pennsylvania, but most people begin this process once they acquire their Pennsylvania driver's license. To register your car, you'll need to fill out a Pennsylvania Auto Registration Form, which can be picked up at any notary public or at the AAA office at 1275 York Road (717-334-1155). You will need the car's out-of-state title, the vehicle mileage, proof of Pennsylvania insurance, and a legible pencil tracing of the Vehicle Identification Number (VIN). If you don't want to do a tracing, pick up an MV-1 form from the notary or AAA and take it to a state inspection mechanic to verify the VIN. The title fee is $22.50 for all vehicles, and the registration fee for passenger cars is $36.00. A new license plate is $10.

Voter Registration

You can vote in Pennsylvania public elections at age 18 if you have been a citizen of the United States for at least a month, you have resided in the state for at least

30 days before the election, and you are registered to vote.

Voter registration forms are available at all public libraries, municipal offices, and post offices throughout the state. The forms are also available at the Voter Registration Office at the Adams County Courthouse, 111 Baltimore Street; (717) 337-9832. The completed form can be mailed to or dropped off at the registration office. To vote in the state's primary elections, you must declare a party affiliation when registering. Registration closes 30 days before a primary or general election and opens 1 day after the election.

The League of Women Voters of Pennsylvania is a nonpartisan organization that disseminates information on voter registration, elections, national and state legislators, government agencies and services, and many more topics. Call (800) 692-7281 or visit their Web site at www.pa.lwv.org. The league has a branch in Adams County, which can be reached at (717) 334-7607.

WORSHIP

More than 100 houses of worship of all different Christian denominations can be found within Adams County. The Gettysburg area chamber of commerce's countywide roster of churches lists more than 35 churches with a Gettysburg address. Jewish synagogues, Muslim mosques, and Buddhist temples are not located within the county, but they can be found in Cumberland and Dauphin Counties to the north.

The area was settled by pioneers of German, Scotch, and Irish descent in the mid-1700s, and religion has always been an important part of the community. Reverend Alexander Dobbin, a leading early settler, headed a Presbyterian congregation, and the Gettysburg Lutheran Theological Seminary was established in 1826 by Samuel Simon Schmucker, a prominent American Lutheran. Schmucker also founded Pennsylvania College, now called

Gettysburg College, in 1832. Christ Evangelical Lutheran Church (30 Chambersburg Street) was deeded in 1835, and its congregation formed in November 1836. Although it wasn't the first Lutheran congregation in Gettysburg, it was the first to use English rather than German as its exclusive language, and it is the oldest church in Gettysburg used continuously for worship. St. Paul AME Zion Church, at 269 South Washington Street, dates from 1835, and it's the oldest African-American congregation in the area.

When the Battle of Gettysburg began, churches in the area opened their doors to the wounded and became makeshift hospitals. The Historic Church Walking Tours feature eight town churches used in this way, and performances portray the events of those days through narratives, plays, and music. (For details on the Historic Church Walking Tours, see the Attractions chapter.) If you see a wayside marker outside a church, it's likely to describe the church's use during the battle. When President Lincoln visited Gettysburg to say a few words at the dedication of the National Cemetery, he attended services at the Presbyterian Church of Gettysburg, located at 208 Baltimore Street, and you can see the pew where he sat.

Religion is interwoven into many aspects of the local community. Many retirement and continuing-care centers are religiously affiliated, and there are many religiously affiliated schools throughout the area. Every Saturday about two pages of the *Gettysburg Times* newspaper are devoted to listing area churches and their services.

If you'd like to attend services on the battlefield, the Gettysburg Battlefield Summer Amphitheater services are held on Sunday at 8:00 A.M. rain or shine from the beginning of July to the end of the summer. The services are both interdenominational and ecumenical, and they're provided by the Gettysburg Ministerium. Offerings given during the service go to the Ministerium Transient Fund to help those in need. Outside services are also held at Caledonia State Park (see the State Parks and Public Lands chapter) and the National Shrine Grotto of Lourdes at Emmitsburg, Maryland (see the Attractions chapter).

EDUCATION AND CHILD CARE

Almost from its very existence, Gettysburg has been a place of higher learning. Less than 45 years after the first settlers came to the area in 1734, the first classical school west of the Susquehanna River opened at the home of Alexander Dobbin, an Irish minister and community leader who had come to the area in 1773. He built his home in 1776, and today the Dobbin House serves up delicious food in an authentically restored building brimming with 18th-century atmosphere. (See the Close-up in the Restaurants chapter for more on the history of the Dobbin House.) Within 100 years from its beginnings, Gettysburg was also home to the Gettysburg Lutheran Theological Seminary (1826) and the Pennsylvania College, which is now known as Gettysburg College (1832).

Both the seminary and the college still exist today, and Gettysburg itself is a place where the history of the Civil War is studied in depth by tourists, scholars, lovers of history, and students of all ages. This history is an integral part of the area, and most public schools teach an entire course during sixth grade on the Civil War battle fought here and its aftermath. Students are required to learn the entire Gettysburg Address, not just the first few lines that most people are familiar with. This knowledge of Gettysburg and its historical significance is inspiring, and it infuses the area with a sense of pride.

The educational opportunities here are as varied as the area. A rural public school system shines with state-of-the-art technology, and arts and music are an integral part of a student's academic experience. An extension of the Harrisburg Area Community College has joined Gettysburg College and the Lutheran Theological Seminary as institutions of higher education located within Gettysburg. About 20 miles west of Gettysburg is the university of Mont Alto, an undergraduate extension campus of Penn State University. And less than 15 miles to the south is Mount St. Mary's College, located in Emmitsburg, Maryland. Back in Gettysburg, the YWCA runs an Elderhostel for older adults that centers on the Battle of Gettysburg and the Civil War.

Families will also find many child-care options in the area. Some are franchises of national chains, others are private day cares, and still others are affiliated with church organizations. Both Gettysburg College and Gettysburg High School have centers at their facilities, and other centers are located throughout Gettysburg and the outlying areas.

PUBLIC SCHOOLS

In Pennsylvania, geographic areas are divided into boroughs and townships, and school districts draw their students from these areas. Adams County has a total of six public school districts, with an aggregate student population of almost 15,000 students in the 2003–2004 school year.

The Gettysburg School District encompasses 185 square miles and includes students in the borough of Gettysburg and six surrounding townships. Total enrollment is around 3,400 students, and pupils are divided among four elementary schools, one middle school, and one high school. Each school has a library, and all classrooms are equipped with computers. Three of the elementary schools enroll students from kindergarten through third grade, while the fourth elementary school

Adams County School Districts

Bermudian Springs School District
7335 Carlisle Pike, York Springs
(717) 528-4113
www.bermudian.org

Conewago Valley School District
130 Berlin Road, New Oxford
(717) 624-2157
www.conewago.k12.pa.us

Fairfield Area School District
4840 Fairfield Road, Fairfield
(717) 642-8228
www.fairfieldpaschools.org

Gettysburg School District
900 Biglerville Road
(717) 334-6254
www.gettysburg.k12.pa.us

Littlestown Area School District
75 Maple Avenue, Littlestown
(717) 359-4146
www.lasd.k12.pa.us

Upper Adams School District
161 North Main Street, Biglerville
(717) 677-7191
www.uasd.k12.pa.us

enrolls students in fourth and fifth grades. Student/teacher ratios average 20:1 in kindergarten through third grade and 24:1 in grades four and five. Among the many programs offered is the America Reads program, in which students from nearby Gettysburg College tutor students who need extra help. Extracurricular activities include music, art, and numerous clubs and organizations.

Students in the sixth through eighth grades attend Gettysburg Area Middle School. Activities available include Band-front, Intramurals, Knowledge Matters, and Mathcounts programs, and there are clubs involving agriculture, art, mountain biking, skiing, writing, and other areas of interest. Sports include basketball, field hockey, football, track, wrestling, volleyball, and cheerleading. The middle school implemented a Bully Prevention Plan during the 2001–2002 school year, and the class of 2008 was the first to complete all three years of the program. In this class, the number of reported incidents of bullying dropped from 68 during the 2001–2002 school year to 13 during the 2003–2004 school year. A "peace party" is held for

students who have no bullying infractions.

Gettysburg High School provides vocational/technological education as well as traditional academic education. Since 1995 the school has focused on creating teams of teachers and students, develop-ing alternative education, integrating the curriculum, and restructuring the use of time. As of the 2003–2004 school year, Gettysburg High School is a Project 720 Implementation high school. Project 720 is a statewide initiative named for the num-ber of days in a high-school student's career, and it is designed to increase academic rigor for all students, provide educational opportunities, and create con-nections with post-secondary educational venues. During the 2003–2004 school year, the high school enjoyed a 98 percent graduation rate, with SAT test scores aver-aging 514 in the verbal part of the test and 517 in the mathematics part. More than 70 percent of graduates advance to higher educational opportunities.

See above for a listing of contact infor-mation for the Gettysburg School District and the other public school districts in Adams County.

PRIVATE SCHOOLS

About 2,100 students in Adams County attended private and nonpublic schools during the 2003–2004 school year. Many of the schools are quite small and religiously based. The Gettysburg-area private schools included here enroll more than 100 pupils.

Adams County Christian Academy
1865 Biglerville Road
(717) 334-9177
The Adams County Christian Academy has about 150 students enrolled in prekindergarten through 12th grade. The school is coed and affiliated with the Baptist religion. There is one teacher for each grade, and the teacher-to-student ratio is 1:12.

Delone Catholic High School
140 South Oxford Street
McSherrystown
(717) 637-5969
www.delonecatholic.org
This is the only Catholic high school within Adams County, and its student population comes from numerous local Catholic elementary schools. It enrolls more than 500 students and has a teacher-to-student ratio of 1:14.

St. Francis Xavier School
45 West High Street
(717) 334-4221
www.sfxs.org
This Catholic elementary school was established in 1877, and about 280 stu-

---

Since 2002 Go-Sport Physical Therapy (705 Old Gettysburg Road; 717–337–3300) has held a speed and agility camp annually. The camp is for middle-school and high-school athletes who want to increase their speed and quickness. Students meet twice a week during the monthlong camp, which is usually held during July and August.

---

dents attend kindergarten through eighth grade here. Its staff consists of the Sisters of Mercy and Christian lay teachers, and enrollment is not limited to those of the Catholic faith. The teacher-to-student ratio is 1:20.

HIGHER EDUCATION

Gettysburg College
300 North Washington Street
(717) 337-6000
www.gettysburg.edu
Samuel Simon Schmucker, a prominent American Lutheran who had founded the Lutheran Theological Seminary at Gettysburg in 1826, also founded Gettysburg College in 1832; today it covers 200 acres in the north end of town. Its beautiful campus is filled with stately buildings that fit perfectly with the town's Civil War history, even though the college predates the Civil War by about 30 years. It is situated less than a mile from the battlefield, and Pennsylvania Hall, the college's first building, served as a hospital for the wounded during the battle. More than 700 Union and Confederate soldiers were treated at Pennsylvania Hall, and in November 1863, Gettysburg College students were among the crowd that attended President Lincoln's short speech that would forever after be known as the Gettysburg Address. Another president, Dwight D. Eisenhower, spent a good deal of time at the college. He retired to Gettysburg after his presidency and wrote his memoirs in what is today the college's admissions office, now known as Eisenhower House. Gettysburg College is still a place where presidents like to visit; in 2000 President George W. Bush delivered a speech to the Republican National Convention from Eisenhower House.

Today nearly 2,500 students attend this four-year liberal arts and science college, and the student population is pretty evenly split between men and women. About 96 percent of students live on campus, in more than 40 residence halls. The students come from 40 states and 35 countries, with the majority of students hailing from Pennsylvania, New Jersey, Maryland, Connecticut, and New York. More than half the student body receives · some type of financial assistance, and need-based and merit-based aid is available. Students may choose from 36 majors, pursue interdisciplinary and self-designed majors, or complete one of several cooperative and dual-degree programs. Majors include those in the social sciences, the natural sciences, and the humanities, and study-abroad programs are also available. Faculty is composed of more than 180 full-time members, 95 percent of whom have a doctorate or the highest earned degree in their fields. Individualized teaching reigns at this small private school, with the student-to-faculty ratio at 11:1 and the average class size at 18 students. Gettysburg College is home to one of only 19 Phi Beta Kappa chapters in Pennsylvania, as well as honorary or professional societies in 16 academic areas. About a quarter of the students participates in 24 intercollegiate sports programs, and there are varied intramural and club activities available. There are also fraternities and sororities to join.

The college is an integral part of the town, and free community events are often held here, such as art exhibitions and artist receptions, musical performances, lectures, film showings, and planetarium shows. In addition, nearly 1,300 students participate annually in community-service programs at the national, international, and regional level. Local and regional community-partnership projects include Big Brothers Big Sisters, community gardening, after-school tutoring and mentoring of grade-school students, swim clinics for migrant farmworker children, volunteering at the community soup kitchen, working with the homeless, and working with children in inner-city Baltimore schools.

Programs that bond the students as a community are also available. First-year students can select a seminar that appeals to their interests, and students who choose the same seminar are housed together in theme residence halls, where they share living space and classroom experiences with others who have similar interests. There's the Artistic Mind House, the Civil War House, the Environmental Awareness House, the Skiiing/Snowboarding House, the Writing House, and many more theme houses. Every other Thursday, students, professors, and administrators set aside an hour of the day to come together on campus to discuss world issues, trends, and events. And the Gettysburg Recreational Adventure Board (GRAB) is a popular program in which students enjoy weekend climbing, caving, kayaking, or backpacking excursions.

The academic achievements that can be attained here as well as the emphasis placed on developing each person as an individual have earned Gettysburg a reputation as a fine institution of higher learning. For four years running (2001–2005), the college was ranked among the top 50 liberal arts colleges in *U.S. News & World Report,* ranking 45th in the 2005 report. It also was ranked 40th in the 2005 list of "Great schools, great prices" published by *U.S. News & World Report.* Gettysburg was one of only five liberal arts colleges in Pennsylvania that were named a "good deal."

Harrisburg Area Community College–Gettysburg Campus
731 Old Harrisburg Road
(717) 337-3855
www.hacc.edu/gettysburg

This branch campus of the Harrisburg Area Community College (HACC) was opened in September 1999. The school is located within the North Gettysburg Shopping Center, and 100 parking spaces in a designated area are reserved for students. The facility features a library, classrooms, three state-of-the-art computer laboratories, a hardware repair lab to facilitate hands-on training in PC repair and testing, an Allied Health–equipped training classroom, a student multipurpose room, and offices for faculty and staff. In addi-

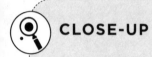

Famous Gettysburg College Alumni

Carson Kressley, one of the hosts of the Emmy award-winning fashion makeover show *Queer Eye for the Straight Guy,* received his bachelor's degree from Gettysburg College in 1991. He majored in management, was elected to Phi Beta Kappa, and was a member of the management club, the equestrian team, and Alpha Phi Omega. An accomplished horseman, Carson was a member of the U.S. team for the 1999 World Cup Equestrian Games in Capetown, South Africa, and the team took home a silver medal. Before *Queer Eye,* Carson worked as division director of the U.S. Equestrian Federation. He then went on to work as associate director of retail advertising and then director of creative development for Polo Ralph Lauren. In addition to his TV show, Carson has written a book titled *Off the Cuff: The Essential Style Guide for Men and the Women Who Love Them,* and he made his movie debut in 2005 in *The Perfect Man.*

Other Gettysburg alumni who have made a name for themselves are:

Fred Fielding, who served on the 9/11 Commission and who, at one time, was thought to be "Deep Throat." He served as deputy to former White House counsel John Dean during the Nixon administration.

Ron Paul, a Republican congressman from Texas who was the 1988 Libertarian Party presidential nominee.

Eddie Plank, a native of Gettysburg who was inducted into the Baseball Hall of Fame for his pitching record.

Bruce S. Gordon, former business executive and current head of the NAACP.

Carol Bellamy, executive director of Unicef since 1995.

Although not an alumnus, Dwight D. Eisenhower is closely associated with Gettysburg College. He used an office on campus to write his memoirs, and this statue of him is outside Eisenhower Hall, which currently serves as the admissions office. KATE HERTZOG

tion, the Gettysburg Campus utilizes existing public school facilities in the Gettysburg High School (Gettysburg School District) and in New Oxford High School (Conewago Valley School District).

HACC employs an open-door admission policy, which allows high-school graduates, GED recipients, and individuals 18 years or older to attend regardless of their educational background. The Gettysburg branch offers 23 associate degree, certificate, and diploma programs; credit and noncredit courses; and customized employee training programs for business, industry, and other organizations. Some of the associate degree programs are defined as transfer programs, geared toward students who plan to complete their education at a four-year college. Other associate degree programs are designated as career programs, and these are for students wishing to complete school with a two-year associate degree. About a third of the programs require taking some classes at the main campus in Harrisburg. A full range of student services are available at the Gettysburg campus, including placement testing, advising and counseling, financial aid, career planning, and student activities.

HACC–Gettysburg Campus has formed a partnership with the Adams County Tech Prep Consortium to develop industry-driven curriculums to guarantee local high-school students a seamless secondary and post-secondary and technical education that can be completed in Gettysburg. Current programs include Allied Health technology, computer repair technology, and the culinary arts.

Lutheran Theological Seminary at Gettysburg
61 Seminary Ridge
(717) 334–6286
www.ltsg.edu
Founded in 1826 by Samuel Simon Schmucker, a leading churchman in American Lutheran circles (and founder of Gettysburg College in 1832), the Lutheran Theological Seminary at Gettysburg is the oldest continuing Lutheran seminary in

the Americas. It was created to fill the specific need at the time for American-trained clergy. In 1832 the seminary moved from modest quarters in the center of town to its current 52-acre location on a ridge overlooking the borough of Gettysburg from the west. On July 1, 1863, the first day of the Battle of Gettysburg, the campus became a battleground and then the center of the Confederate line for two days. The cupola of the Old Dorm served as an observation tower first for Union and then for the Confederate officers. From that day and for two additional months, the rest of the building served as a hospital for the wounded from both sides. Three original buildings still stand at the seminary: Krauth House, Schmucker House, and Schmucker Hall. A fire on November 8, 2004, damaged Krauth House, but reconstruction and restoration of the house are under way.

The primary mission of the Lutheran Theological Seminary at Gettysburg (LTSG) is to prepare leaders for service in the Evangelical Lutheran Church in America as pastors, deaconesses, associates in ministry, and diaconal ministers. Two degree programs, the Master of Divinity and the Master of Arts in Ministerial Studies, serve as the academic foundation for that preparation. The seminary's Master of Arts in Religion program offers an opportunity for broad study in theological disciplines, while at the same time permitting specialization in one particular area of interest. The Master of Sacred Theology (STM) degree provides an opportunity for concentrated study in a given area of theological inquiry for persons who have completed a first theological degree or its equivalent. The Doctor of Ministry degree is received through the Eastern Cluster of Lutheran Seminaries, of which Gettysburg is a part. The seminary also offers a long list of one-day events and public lectures intended for broad audiences of both clergy and laypersons, and the Lay School of Theology has been held on campus each summer since 1963.

The student body numbers around 270

full- and part-time students, and there's a faculty of 18, plus another 10 part-time, adjunct, and distinguished visiting teachers. Students travel from 30 states and another half dozen countries to study theology here. Even though most students are members of the Evangelical Lutheran Church in America (ELCA), a growing number of students have religious backgrounds from other Christian traditions.

The Seminary Ridge Historic Preservation Foundation is in the process of creating an interpretive walking tour on Seminary Ridge. The 1.5-mile path will be for pedestrians and bicyclists, and there will be three primary entry points to the path and more than 20 wayside stops along the way. The walkway will focus on the importance of the battle on Seminary Ridge on the first day of the Battle of Gettysburg and the religious history of the seminary. The foundation raises money for the pathway by selling engraved bricks, and it recently completed the construction of a plaza of 1,200 bricks, 300 of which are engraved with the names of alumni, friends, and notable former residents of the ridge. Archaeological studies of the proposed pathway area have been completed, and engraved bricks are again being sold to raise more money for the construction of the pathway. Engraved bricks cost $100 each; to order a brick, call the seminary at (717) 334-6286.

Penn State Mont Alto
1 Campus Drive, Mont Alto
(717) 749-6000, (800) 392-6173
www.ma.psu.edu

Both the Civil War and the area's iron furnaces played a role in the creation of a school at Mont Alto. Col. George Wiestling came to Mont Alto in 1864 after his medical discharge from the Union army. As a shareholder in the Mont Alto Iron Company and its last ironmaster, Wiestling lived here during the waning years of the iron furnaces, which converted local iron ore into pig iron. During peak production, the fires of an iron furnace would use up to an acre of forest in a day, and the

forests of South Mountain were clear-cut on a 20- to 25-year cycle to feed the demand. (For more on the many iron furnaces that were in the area, see the Close-up in the State Parks and Public Lands chapter.) All the clear-cutting eventually took its toll on the forest around the Mont Alto Furnace, as it did on the forests throughout Pennsylvania. After Wiestling's death, the state purchased his estate as part of public use lands for reforestation.

Wiestling's abode became the site of the Pennsylvania State Forest Academy, a school devoted to the study of forestry and the reforestation of the state of Pennsylvania. The school opened in 1903 with an enrollment of 13 at the site of the present-day Mont Alto campus, becoming the only state-established and -operated forestry school in the nation. The Pennsylvania State Forest Academy merged with Penn State (then the Pennsylvania State College) in 1929; academy students protested, feeling Penn State's forestry curriculum was inferior to theirs. Mont Alto served as Penn State's forestry campus, and students completed the first year of their four-year degree here until 1942. The campus was closed due to World War II and reopened in 1946. Penn State Mont Alto became a Commonwealth Campus in 1963, offering the first one or two years of many Penn State degrees, as well as some associate degrees (including forest technology). In 1997 Mont Alto joined Penn State's Commonwealth College and began offering bachelor's degrees.

Today Penn State Mont Alto offers the first two years of study for more than 160 Penn State bachelor-degree programs, and 4 bachelor's degrees or 7 associate degrees may be attained while taking all classes at the Mont Alto campus. Bachelor's degree programs are in business, nursing, human development and family studies, and English. Two-year associate degree programs are in forest technology, business administration, nursing, physical therapy, occupational therapy, human development and family studies, and letters, arts, and sciences. Enrollment numbers around 1,100 students, with a student-to-faculty ratio of 17:1 and an average class size of 24 students. Mont Alto is one of only 10 Penn State campuses to offer on-campus housing, with 3 residence halls that can accommodate 440 students on the campus's 91 wooded acres. Varsity sports include basketball, tennis, golf, soccer, volleyball, softball, cheerleading, and cross-country. Club sports and intramural sports are also offered.

Mount St. Mary's University
16300 Old Emmitsburg Road
Emmitsburg, MD
(301) 447-6122
www.msmary.edu

Mount St. Mary's University was founded in 1808 by Fr. John Dubois, and its 1,400-acre campus is located less than 15 miles south of Gettysburg off U.S. Route 15. This Catholic liberal arts university shares its space with Mount St. Mary's Seminary, the second-largest seminary in the country, and the National Shrine Grotto of Lourdes, America's oldest replica of the Lourdes shrine in France. (For more on the National Shrine Grotto of Lourdes, see the Attractions chapter.) The Mount is home to about 1,600 undergraduate and 500 graduate students and about 150 seminarians. The student body men-to-women ratio is approximately 60:40, and about 60 percent of undergraduate students come from the state of Maryland. The rest of the student population hails from 28 states and approximately 10 foreign countries. The undergraduate student-to-faculty ratio is 14:1, and the average class size is 20. More than 90 percent of students receive financial aid.

The university offers 40 undergraduate majors, 5 post-graduate degrees, and the chance to study abroad in England, Italy, France, Costa Rica, Ireland, and Spain. In 2005 it made *U.S. News & World Report*'s top college list for the ninth consecutive year. Mount St. Mary's is one of the few universities where undergraduate students are guaranteed four entire years of on-campus housing. Eighty-two percent of

undergraduates take advantage of this and live on campus in traditional or apartment-style residence halls or theme homes. Theme homes include Wellness Housing, the Women in Science floor, and Special Interest Housing. Wellness Housing is for students who wish to live in a substance-free (alcohol, drugs, tobacco) residence, and the Women in Science floor is for female residents majoring in or considering a major in science, math, or computer science. Special Interest Housing is for students who share a common interest. All undergraduate students may apply to live in Wellness Housing or the Women in Science floor, and sophomores, juniors, and seniors who maintain a minimum grade point average of 2.5 may apply to live in a "Make Your Own" house or floor.

Students at the Mount have lots of activities to pick from, and 80 percent of students stay on campus on the weekends. There are 18 varsity sports to participate in as well as club sports, a full intramural program, and more than 70 clubs. The campus schedule is also full with dances, concerts, and guest lecturers.

CONTINUING EDUCATION

Elderhostel
YWCA of Gettysburg & Adams County
909 Fairfield Road
(717) 334-9171
www.ywcagettysburg.org

The first elderhostels in the United States began in 1975 on a few college and university campuses in New England. Then, as now, they were dedicated to providing high-quality and affordable educational opportunities to older adults. At Gettysburg the elderhostel program is put on with the association of the YWCA of Gettysburg, and the Gettysburg battlefield serves as the campus. Rather than staying at a college dormitory, accommodations are at the Historic Gettysburg Hotel, a premier hotel located on Lincoln Square (see the Hotels, Motels, and Resorts chapter).

Elderhostel offers a wide array of programs throughout the United States. Some are held entirely at Gettysburg while others include Gettysburg as part of a longer itinerary. The Gettysburg elderhostel programs focus on the battlefield, the surrounding area, and Civil War–related subjects. Stays usually are for three or five days. Grandparents may want to check out the program that allows them to bring grandchildren along on their learning experience. There's also a service program where participants work on the preservation of the Eisenhower National Historic Site.

CHILD CARE

Child Care Information Services (CCIS)
153 North Stratton Street
(717) 334-7634, (800) 232-6562
www.sccap.org
This service will supply you with listings of available child-care providers in the area. It also provides subsidies for day-care services for lower-income caretakers. The listing of day-care providers is available to anyone, regardless of income level, and it contains a wealth of useful information, including names, addresses, hours, curriculums, fees, and more. Child Care Information Services (CCIS) is one of the programs of the South Central Community Action Programs, Inc. (SCCAP), which coordinates charitable programs in Adams County that help low-income individuals help themselves. (For more on SCCAP, see the Relocation chapter.)

Day Cares and Preschools

Following are just a few of the many day cares and preschools that operate in the area. The list you receive from CCIS will also include names of caregivers who operate within their homes, but those included here are centers that operate at a place of business. Many of the centers participate in subsidy programs, so be sure to ask about available financial assistance.

Babes in Arms
150 Hunterstown-Hampton Road
(717) 337-2619
This day-care center is open Monday through Friday 6:00 A.M. to 6:00 P.M., and it offers after-school, before-school, early-dismissal school-day, school-holiday, snow-day, and full-year day care. Babes in Arms enrolls newborns to children age 15, and it gives a multichild discount.

Christ Lutheran Nursery School
44 Chambersburg Street
(717) 334-6532
Preschool education is offered here for children age three through five from September through May. The preschool program for children age three or four meets on Tuesday and Thursday mornings from 9:00 to 11:30 A.M. Children age four and five may choose a morning or afternoon prekindergarten program held on Monday, Wednesday, and Friday. The morning session meets from 9:00 to 11:30 A.M. while the afternoon session runs from noon to 2:00 P.M. The program is sponsored by the Christ Evangelical Lutheran Church, and scholarships are available.

Gettysburg High School Preschool
1130 Old Harrisburg Road
(717) 334-6254, ext. 6149
This preschool is part of the school district's vocational child-care education program, and it has its own private entrance at the high school. It operates two sessions, a fall session that runs 9:00 to 10:10 A.M. from mid-October to early January and a spring session that runs 8:00 to 10:10 A.M. from late January to mid-May. Monday and Wednesday are reserved for children age three and four, while children age four and five are welcomed on Tuesday and Thursday.

Gettysburg's Growing Place
Gettysburg College—West Building
first floor
(717) 337-1255
www.gettysburg.edu
Gettysburg's Growing Place is managed
by Hildebrandt Learning Centers (HLC),
which operates 18 child-care centers in
Pennsylvania. The day care is open Monday through Friday 6:30 A.M. to 6:00 P.M.,
and after-school, early-dismissal school-
day, and full-year day care are available.
The program enrolls newborns to children
age 15, and it offers a multichild discount.

Head Start
705 Old Harrisburg Road
(717) 337-1337
Head Start is a preschool program that
offers a wide range of services to both
children and their families, including educational, health, nutritional, and social
services. The program is open to three-,
four-, and five-year-olds who come from
income-eligible families or who have a dis-
ability or special need. Services are
offered during the regular school year on
a part-day or full-day basis, with part-day
classes running from 9:00 A.M. to 1:00 P.M.
and full-day classes operating from 8:30
A.M. to 3:00 P.M.

Learning Tree Child Care
Gettysburg Lutheran Home
1075 Old Harrisburg Road
(717) 334-6204
www.lutheranscp.org
This day care is affiliated with Lutheran
Social Services, and it's located in the nursing-center building of Gettysburg Lutheran
Retirement Village. Activities often include
visits with the residents who live at the

retirement village. Learning Tree is open
Monday through Friday 6:00 A.M. to 5:30
P.M. and offers full-year day care. Newborns
to children in kindergarten are eligible for
the program.

St. James Lutheran Church
109 York Street
(717) 334-7171
Open Monday through Friday 6:30 A.M. to
5:30 P.M., the program at St. James offers
after-school, before-school, early-dismissal
school-day, school-holiday, snow-day, and
full-year day care. Applications are
accepted for newborns to children age 15,
and a multichild discount is available.

Wee Care Learning Center
75 Springs Avenue
(717) 334-5347
Wee Care is open Monday through Friday
6:30 A.M. to 6:00 P.M. and offers after-
school, before-school, early-dismissal
school-day, school-holiday, snow-day, and
full-year day care. Enrollment is open to
infants 2 months old to children age 15,
and employee and early-payment discounts are available.

YWCA of Gettysburg & Adams County
909 Fairfield Road
(717) 334-9171
www.ywcagettysburg.org
The day-care center is one of many programs held at the YWCA. (See the Recreation chapter for more on the YWCA.) It's
open Monday through Friday 6:30 A.M. to
6:00 P.M. and offers after-school, before-
school, early-dismissal school-day, school-
holiday, snow-day, and full-year day care.
The program accepts infants from 2
months old to children age 15.

HEALTH CARE Ⓗ AND WELLNESS

Although it's a rural community, Gettysburg has a complete system of health-care services. It has one of the two hospitals located within Adams County (the other is Hanover Hospital) within its borough, and WellSpan, the hospital's parent company, offers integrated health services throughout southcentral Pennsylvania and northern Maryland. Home-care services are available to give people a bit of help so they can stay in their homes, and health-care centers offer medical and rehabilitation services.

HOSPITALS AND HEALTH CENTERS

Gettysburg Holistic Health Center
2311 Fairfield Road
www.GettysburgHolisticHealthCenter.net
Located about 3 miles west of town, practitioners at this health center provide services related to natural health care and natural healing. The mantra here is that the client's emotional, physical, and spiritual health is always of the utmost importance. The center offers yoga, naturopathic medicine, acupuncture, therapeutic massage, and counseling services in a serene, rural setting. Although they share a building and a common outlook on holistic healing, each practitioner runs an independent operation. The Sacred Lotus Yoga Studio located within the center is run by Lynn Roby, who follows the Kripalu methodology of yoga. Lynn is director and owner of the center as well as one of the center's two counselors. The other counselor is Betsy Tresselt, and together Lynn and Betsy have more than 30 years of experience helping others.

You can call Lynn or Betsy at (717) 338-9777. Therapeutic massages are given at the center by Marti Thomas and Nancy Lyon. Nancy specializes in deep-tissue massage, Swedish massage, stone therapy, and craniosacral therapy, while Marti's areas of expertise are deep-tissue massage, Swedish massage, cranial-sacral therapy, Samyama healing, and Reiki I and II. Both may be contacted at (717) 334-5140. Ted O'Brien is a Pennsylvania-licensed acupuncturist, and he also writes the "Holistic Living" column for the *Gettysburg Times* newspaper. Ted has worked with hundreds of patients using acupuncture and Chinese herbs and treating mostly pain-related disorders, and he can be reached at (717) 586-7044. Dr. Len Maza, a chiropractic doctor, joined the staff in January 2006.

Gettysburg Hospital
147 Gettys Street
(717) 334-2121
www.wellspan.org
Gettysburg Hospital has been serving the community for more than 80 years. Today it is a 99-bed acute- and emergency-care facility run by WellSpan Health, a community-based, not-for-profit organization that has more than 50 locations providing health and wellness services in southcentral Pennsylvania and northern Maryland. The hospital is located southwest of the square, surrounded by neighborhoods and the Recreational Park on Long Lane. The grounds include a medical building and the Gettysburg Hospital Heart Center, which offers patients leading-edge diagnostics, access to state-of-the-art treatment, and comprehensive cardiac rehabilitation. The heart center also has a program that's especially

Gettysburg Pharmacies

CVS Drug Store—1275 York Road; (717) 337-2812; open Monday through Friday 8:00 A.M. to 9:00 P.M., Saturday 8:00 A.M. to 6:00 P.M., and Sunday 9:00 A.M. to 5:00 P.M.

The Medicine Shop—6 Springs Avenue; (717) 337-0881; open Monday through Friday 9:00 A.M. to 6:00 P.M. and Saturday 9:00 A.M. to noon (closed on Sunday)

Giant Food Stores Pharmacy—44 Natural Springs Road; (717) 337-0585; open Monday through Friday 9:00 A.M. to 9:00 P.M.,

Saturday 9:00 A.M. to 6:00 P.M., and Sunday 10:00 A.M. to 4:00 P.M.

Rite Aid Discount Pharmacies—236 West Street; (717) 334-6447; open Monday through Saturday 8:30 A.M. to 9:00 P.M. and Sunday 10:00 A.M. to 6:00 P.M.

Wal-Mart Pharmacy—1270 York Road; (717) 334-1313; open Monday through Friday 9:00 A.M. to 9:00 P.M., Saturday 9:00 A.M. to 6:00 P.M., and Sunday 11:00 A.M. to 5:00 P.M.

designed to address the unique needs of women with heart-related health issues. Besides acute care and heart care, Gettysburg Hospital also provides the area's only Transitional Care Center, a Medicare-certified skilled nursing facility for patients who have been discharged from the hospital but are not quite well enough to go home on their own. Residents in the 19-bed center receive a number of medical and rehabilitative services to help them return to an independent lifestyle as quickly as possible. The Transitional Care Center also provides adult respite care on a short-term (3 to 13 days) basis.

Gettysburg Hospital Rehab offers comprehensive inpatient and outpatient rehabilitation services that provide treatment, exercise, and education for injuries and functional impairment. Physical, occupational, and speech therapy are offered. Inpatient and outpatient care is given within the hospital, while the WellSpan Health Center on Chambersburg Road offers only outpatient care. This center at Herr's Ridge features a warm-water aquatic therapy pool and certified aquatic therapist.

A sleep disorders lab is also housed at Gettysburg Hospital. It consists of two

patient-friendly sleep rooms with bathroom and shower and a dedicated control room. More information on the sleep lab is available at (717) 337-2412. The hospital is justly proud of its maternity center, where you can choose to have a physician or a midwife deliver your baby. Childbirth classes and sibling-preparation programs are also offered, and family members can view a picture of your new baby at the hospital Web site's online nursery.

The hospital is well equipped for visitors also, with a cafeteria on the ground floor that's open till 6:15 P.M. and a snack bar and gift shop located just off the main lobby that's open till 7:00 P.M. With the exception of Pediatrics and Maternity, children younger than 12 years of age are not permitted to visit unless special permission is given from the patient's physician.

State Health Center
424 East Middle Street
(717) 334-2112

This is one of 57 health centers throughout the state run by the Pennsylvania Department of Health. The department implements its public health programs through the center, with the goal of protecting and improving the health of Penn-

HEALTH CARE AND WELLNESS

sylvanians and visitors to the state. The clinic part of the center conducts childhood and adult immunizations, HIV testing and counseling, and tuberculosis treatment and management. Programs on health education and the prevention of injuries and disease are also available, and the center also handles communicable disease reporting and investigation. The center is open weekdays, and you should call for an appointment if you need the services of the clinic.

WellSpan Health Centers
820 Chambersburg Street

450 South Washington Street
www.wellspan.org

The center on Washington Street is across from the hospital, and many women-related health services are available here. A variety of doctor's groups dedicated to women's issues have their offices in the building, as does Gettysburg Hospital Women's Imaging Services. Women in need of a mammogram, a breast biopsy, or a bone density test can have their tests done here. The other center houses a family medicine practice (717-337-4103) and the Gettysburg Hospital Rehab/Aquatic Center (717-337-4206), which offers massages as well as outpatient rehabilitation services.

REFERRAL SERVICES

Gettysburg Hospital
Health Information Line
(717) 334-4646

This is a physician-referral service that will match you with a physician affiliated with Gettysburg Hospital. It also supplies information on community health programs.

WellSpan Health Source
(717) 851-3500, (800) 840-5905

This service imparts information on the services provided by all of Well-Span Health's various organizations. WellSpan Health can register you for a

variety of health and wellness classes and provide referrals to physicians on staff at Gettysburg Hospital who are accepting new patients.

HOME CARE

Comfort Keepers
2819 York Road
(717) 337-1409, (800) 207-4693
www.comfortkeepers.com

Comfort Keepers is a national network that has franchises in 47 states. The Gettysburg location is a satellite office of the franchise that's located in Fayetteville, about 20 miles west of Gettysburg. More than 80 caregivers are employed by the franchise, which has been in business since 2000. Nonmedical in-home care is provided, and services include companionship, light housekeeping, transportation, meal preparation, grocery shopping and errand running, personal-care assistance, bathing assistance, walking assistance, medication reminders, and escorting clients to appointments. Most clients are fairly mobile, and Comfort Keepers rarely assists individuals who are bed bound. Caregivers are employed by the company, not independent contractors, so clients do not have to deal with paying one fee to the agency and one fee to the actual caregiver. Comfort Keepers also screens all caregivers, and the franchise and the caregivers are fully insured. All care is provided either at the client's home or assisted-living facility at times requested by the client, and the client determines how much care he or she needs. A minimum of 3 hours up to the day's entire 24 hours may be scheduled, and schedules are made up weekly to allow flexibility. If they desire, clients can change their schedules weekly.

Lutheran Home Care Services Inc.
1075 Old Harrisburg Road
(717) 334-6208
www.lutheranscp.org

Lutheran Home Care Services provides a

wide range of medical and nonmedical services delivered in the comfort of your home, whether "home" is a private home residence or an assisted-living-facility residence. Home-support services range from a few hours of help to 24-hour care, on a short- or long-term basis. Help is given with dressing and bathing, preparing meals, housekeeping and laundry, grocery shopping and errands, transportation, companionship, lab services, medication box fills, and a variety of other services, including respite care. For complete peace of mind, a home telemonitoring service is also available. By teaming with HomMed, the nation's leading provider of home tele-monitoring equipment, Lutheran Home Care Services can collect vital signs and monitor clients every day—from the comfort of the client's home. The tele-monitoring system is about the size of a clock radio, and each day a gentle, friendly voice guides the client through the simple procedure to collect the vital signs (weight, temperature, and blood sugar). The client is then asked up to 10 questions about his or her condition that can be answered by pressing a yes or no button on the monitor. The monitor auto-matically transmits the data via telephone connection to the offices of Lutheran Home Care Services, where it is reviewed daily by a nurse. For clients with other monitoring needs, medical devices and attachments such as a spirometer, glu-cose meter, an ECG device, and more are available.

Visiting Angels
18 Carlisle Street, Suite 105
(717) 337-0620
www.visitingangels.com
Visiting Angels is a national network of franchised nonmedical senior home-care agencies whose goal is to help elderly and older adults continue to live in their

homes rather than having to move to nursing homes or assisted-living facilities. They will also tend to your nonmedical needs if you're in an assisted-living facility and realize you need some help with daily-living activities. This local Visiting Angels franchise is owned by John Palone, who also runs an office in Carlisle, and it's one of 250 franchises of Visiting Angels oper-ating across America. Living-assistance services provided include hygiene assis-tance, meal preparation, light housework, companionship, errand running and shop-ping, and respite care. Caregivers are employed by the franchise, and they are licensed and bonded. A unique feature of Visiting Angels is that the client gets to select his or her caregiver. The agency matches your needs to the best possible caregiver, and the caregiver is not assigned until you meet and approve the person. Caregivers are assigned tempo-rary or long-term assignments, and they're available on weekends and holidays. You can schedule care in your home for just a few hours up to 24 hours per day, and the schedule is flexible to allow for client's changing needs.

Visiting Nurses Association (VNA)
Home Health
49 North Fifth Street
(717) 334-1490
www.wellspan.org
VNA Home Health is part of the WellSpan Health system, and it offers medical ser-vices in the comfort and privacy of a patient's home. Services are available for patients of all ages and postpartum moth-ers and children and include skilled nurs-ing care, home health aides, physical therapy, speech therapy, respiratory ther-apy, IV therapy, patient education, and more. Medicare, Medicaid, and most pri-vate insurances are accepted as payment.

RETIREMENT 🌴

Seniors have a wealth of programs and activities available to them in the Gettysburg area. Most area attractions offer special admission pricing, and many local restaurants also discount meals for seniors. In this area, age is something to be respected, and elderly wisdom is passed along and cherished. A good number of resident seniors were not born in the area. They decided to relocate here for sundry reasons, with the area's beauty, relaxed pace, and wealth of history being three main incentives. Many seniors spend the majority of their time studying the battlefield and the Civil War at their leisure. Recreational opportunities are plentiful around Gettysburg, and active seniors can spend their days golfing, horseback riding, and fishing (see the Recreation chapter). Activity for the mind can be found at the area colleges and the elderhostel program held here that studies the Battle of Gettysburg (see the Education and Child Care chapter).

If you're in the area long enough, you're bound to see the buses of the Adams County Transit Authority on the roads, dropping off and picking up seniors as they go about their daily lives. This is just one of the many low- or no-cost programs available to seniors, and the Adams County Office for Aging runs a dynamic agency that can give you all kinds of information on senior programs and senior-related issues. This agency also runs the area senior centers, where seniors can always find companionship and activities.

The local Gettysburg chapter of AARP meets the third Wednesday of every month except July and August at the Recreational Park Building at Gettysburg Recreation Park (Long Lane; 717-334-2028).

The Gettysburg area also boasts numerous retirement communities and nursing homes, and many have a range of options to suit each person's independence level. In short, there's plenty here to occupy your time and keep you engaged in the community, and support systems are in place to help you deal with the health issues that come along with age.

SENIOR AGENCIES AND SERVICES

Adams County Office for Aging (ACOFA)
318 West Middle Street
(717) 334-9296, (800) 548-3240
ACOFA, one of 52 agencies on aging located throughout Pennsylvania, is a private, not-for-profit operation dedicated to providing assistance to and advocacy for older people. They offer a wide range of services to seniors age 60 and older. Some of the services are free while others are billed on a sliding-fee scale, where seniors pay a portion of the fee for the services based on monthly income. And donations are always welcome!

Services available range from helping seniors fill out health insurance and government forms to providing help with everyday activities, such as meal preparation, bathing, dressing, and light housekeeping. ACOFA also runs the senior centers, delivers hot meals to homebound seniors through the Meals on Wheels program, and provides domiciliary care for adults who can't live independently. Seniors can also borrow limited medical equipment for a short time, such as canes, walkers, and shower benches, from the agency. In short, if you're a senior and you have a question about a service or a problem you need help with, ACOFA is the place to call. The staff is extremely knowl-

Adams County Senior Centers

ACOFA runs seven senior centers in Adams County. Open to anyone age 60 or older, each operates on a part-time basis, either four or five days per week. Each center serves a hot meal, and games, conversation, exercise programs, health screenings and programs, educational and volunteer opportunities, trips, and much more are available. Senior-center staff will work with the Adams County Transit Authority (ACTA) to get seniors to and from the center. There's no charge to participate in center activities, but donations are gladly accepted.

East Berlin Senior Center
East Berlin Community Center
Fourth Street and North Avenue, East Berlin
(717) 259-9630
Open Monday through Thursday 9:00 A.M. to 1:00 P.M.

Fairfield Area Senior Center
St. Mary's Catholic Church
350 Tract Road, Fairfield
(717) 642-8465
Open Monday through Friday 10:00 A.M. to 2:00 P.M.

Gettysburg Senior Center
Harold Court
142 North Stratton Street
(717) 334-5012
Open Monday through Friday 9:00 A.M. to 1:00 P.M.

Littlestown Senior Center
10 Locust Street, Littlestown
(717) 359-7743
Open Monday through Friday 8:30 A.M. to 2:00 P.M.

McSherrystown Senior Center
201 South Third Street, McSherrystown
(717) 632-7998
Open Monday through Friday 9:00 A.M. to 1:00 P.M.

Upper Adams Senior Center
2950 Table Rock Road, Biglerville
(717) 677-6370
Open Monday through Friday 9:00 A.M. to 2:00 P.M.

York Springs Senior Center
Lion's Club Building
Main Street, York Springs
(717) 528-8921
Open Monday through Thursday 9:30 A.M. to 1:30 P.M.

edgeable about senior issues and who provides what services to seniors throughout the county.

Adams County Transit Authority (ACTA)
Rear 257 North Fourth Street
(717) 337-1345, (800) 830-6473
The ACTA provides transportation throughout the county for seniors, and the fare depends on the age of the rider,

the rider's income level, and the purpose and distance of the trip. Trips to medical appointments, senior centers, grocery stores, and banks are usually free for seniors age 60 or older. All subsidized transportation requires you to verify your qualifications for a particular program, so you need to call ACTA or the Adams County Office for Aging (see the listing within this chapter) for information before you begin to use the transportation. Reservations for your trip must be made by noon the day before transportation is needed. Service for ambulatory seniors is available 24 hours a day, 7 days a week in the Gettysburg area. Residents who live in the Gettysburg area who require the use of a wheelchair can have transportation provided at various times Monday through Friday. Rides in other parts of the county are usually available from 6:00 A.M. to 6:00 P.M. on weekdays only, but times are limited in some outlying areas. If you use a wheelchair or live outside the Gettysburg area, ACTA suggests you call them to check on transportation availability before you schedule an appointment. The ACTA is closed and does not provide transportation on New Year's Day, Good Friday, Memorial Day, Independence Day, Labor Day, Thanksgiving and the day after Thanksgiving, and Christmas.

NURSING HOMES AND RETIREMENT COMMUNITIES

Beverly Healthcare Gettysburg
741 Chambersburg Road
(717) 334-6764
www.beverlycares.com
This skilled nursing home located at the western outskirts of town is one of 354 nursing homes run by Beverly Healthcare across the United States. Although area residents have received health-care services at the site since the 1960s, it became a part of the Beverly system in

---

The Web site for Comfort Keepers, a nonmedical in-home care company, has a section called Senior Resources that has links to more than 50 senior-related Internet sites. Visit www.comfortkeepers .com to check it out. More information on services offered by Comfort Keepers can be found in the Health Care and Wellness chapter.

1981. The goal of this 102-bed facility is to provide personalized quality health care in a homelike environment. To that end, residents are encouraged to personalize their rooms with furniture, pictures, and mementos from home. Short- or long-term care is available, and patients may be admitted on weekends. Beverly considers rehabilitation to be an essential element of life in all their nursing homes, and rehabilitative services include physical therapy, occupational therapy, and speech therapy. Though most residents require only general nursing services, complex medical services such as wound care and IV therapy are available. Beverly Healthcare Gettysburg also has an entire wing designed especially to address the needs of Alzheimer's patients. The nursing staff working on this unit must undergo continuing education specifically for Alzheimer's disease care. Hospice care is also available, and a nurse is available 24 hours a day to work with the hospice team. Recreational activities are available to residents, and respite care can be arranged. Beverly Healthcare Gettysburg is a for-profit center that accepts payment for its services from Medicare, Medicaid, private insurance, and private pay.

Brethren Home Community
2990 Carlisle Pike, New Oxford
(717) 624-2161, (888) 624-8242
www.brethrenhome.org
This nonprofit, faith-based continuing-care retirement community that sprawls across a 251-acre campus situated less than 15 miles east of Gettysburg has more than 900 residents who call the place home. The Brethren Home Community began in 1908, and today it includes apartments, cottages, and single homes in addition to its assisted-living center and health-care center. Individual retirement homes come in three different floor plans ranging from 1,782 to 2,041 square feet with 9-foot ceilings, two bedrooms, two baths, a two-car garage, and walk-in closets. Cross Keys Village features more than 320 cottages in 21 different models, from a roomy one-

bedroom to large two-bedroom models with a garage. One- and two-bedroom apartments are found at Harmony Ridge, and most feature a private patio or balcony in addition to modern conveniences. If you prefer not to cook your own meals, you can dine at The Campus Inn Restaurant, which is open seven days a week. The campus also boasts a fitness center, a church, a community center, banking services, a gift shop, scheduled campus transportation, and walkways that let you take in the rural setting at a leisurely pace.

The assisted-living center of the Brethren Home Community is a licensed personal-care facility that allows you to continue your independent lifestyle while knowing personal assistance is available from the staff 24 hours a day. Meals are served restaurant style in the dining room three times a day, and a kitchenette is located on each floor of the center. Each floor also has a spacious living room where you can relax, and activities that provide social interaction with other residents take place every day.

Medical care is offered at the Health Care Center, which offers long-term and short-term nursing care as well as respite care. Short-term medical treatment or rehabilitation that's needed after a hospital stay is given at the Cross Keys Subacute Center, and the Health Care Center also offers special-care nursing for clients with Alzheimer's and other dementia-related disorders. Adult day-care services are part of the Brethren Home Community, and day care is provided to those in the surrounding community as well as to campus residents. The day care is designed for adults who need some degree of daily supervision, and it's open to persons at least 18 years old who are physically challenged and/or cognitively impaired. Services at the day care include a hot meal and a wide range of activities, such as cooking, field trips, arts and crafts, music, gardening, and pet visits. Personal-care services, such as bathing and hair care, are also provided. A noon meal is served as well as morning and afternoon snacks. The cost for the

adult day care is $38 for a full day and $30 for a half day. The noon meal costs $3.00. More information on the adult day care may be obtained by calling (717) 624-5955.

Gettysburg Lutheran Retirement Village
1075 Old Harrisburg Road
(717) 334-6204
www.lutheranscp.org

Gettysburg Lutheran Retirement Village is a continuing-care retirement community (CCRC) that is part of Lutheran Social Services, an agency of the Evangelical Lutheran Church in America. Its attractive campus less than 2 miles north of Lincoln Square features residential-living townhomes and apartments, assisted-living/personal-care rooms, and a skilled-care center.

As a resident of Gettysburg Lutheran Retirement Village, your abode is a maintenance-free home and you choose your level of activity and independence. The village has 57 one-, two-, and three-bedroom units, as well as 21 one- and two-bedroom apartments. Transportation is provided for local medical needs and grocery shopping as well as for cultural and pleasure trips. If you prefer not to cook, you can take advantage of the meal service that's available. While you're enjoying your carefree lifestyle, you are also ensuring that if you need more help, you have admission, as space allows, to any other level of care you may need in the future. A call system is provided in the apartments to obtain medical assistance in an emergency situation, and townhome residents are provided with a telephone number to gain access to medical assistance for medical emergencies.

If daily assistance is needed but daily medical care is not, the Assisted Living/Personal Care facility may be the ideal solution. Here you have a private or semiprivate room in a building that also has a communal dining room, a lounge area, and an outdoor walking trail. You choose your activities and daily routine with the security of knowing that support is available when you need it. The village bus is available to take you to local medical appointments and scheduled shopping and pleasure outings. A beauty shop and laundry service are available on a fee-for-service basis.

Physical or mental limitations may necessitate your living in a skilled-care center for either a limited or an extended period of time. The 100-bed skilled-care center here provides skilled nursing care and full rehabilitation services including physical therapy, occupational therapy, and speech therapy. Programs focusing on social, creative, and intellectual interests are available, and there are plenty of group activities to participate in, including cooking, sports, crafts, parties, bus rides, and discussion groups. Beautician and barber services are provided on campus, and residents can also enjoy activities and visits with the young children from Learning Tree Child Care, the Lutheran Social Services child-care center that's located right in the nursing-center building. (See the Education and Child Care chapter for information on Learning Tree Child Care.)

Hospice services are offered by Lutheran Social Services through the Hospice of the Good Shepherd (717-334-6208), which employs a team of skilled professionals, para-professionals, and volunteers dedicated to caring for the dying patient and the patient's family. The team works with the family and caregivers to help them understand what to expect, to teach them special care-giving techniques, and to help them with emotional difficulties. Hospice

care can be provided in the home, in a skilled nursing facility, in a personal-care setting, or in a hospital. Hospice of the Good Shepherd has a bereavement program designed to help families address issues that may arise after a loved one's death, and the program provides resources and support to aid in the family's grief recovery process.

For information on the varied home health-care services provided by Lutheran Social Services, see the Health Care and Wellness chapter.

Green Acres
Adams County Nursing
& Rehabilitation Center
595 Biglerville Road
(717) 334-6249

Green Acres is a not-for-profit skilled nursing facility with 154 beds that sits amid a rural setting of peach and apple orchards less than a mile north of Lincoln Square. The center is state licensed and Medicare and Medicaid approved, and it accepts payment for its services from Medicare, Medicaid, private insurance, and private pay. Green Acres has been providing care to area residents since it was established in 1891 as an alms house. Today state-of-the-art medical treatment is offered here, including dementia treatment and physical, speech, and occupational therapy. Residents have their choice of a wide range of activities; some activities are held at the center and some involve the community. Popular programs include interacting with pet-therapy animals, baking, caroling, gardening, and trick-or-treating. The center also coordinates with hospice workers when clients need those services, respite care is available, and the Share and Care Adult Day Care (717-334-5970) is on the premises.

The goal of the Share and Care Adult Day Care is to improve or maintain an impaired adult's physical and mental functioning so he or she can remain living within the community. The day care is open Monday through Friday from 7:00 A.M. to 4:30 P.M., and adults may attend for

either a half or a full day. Full-day participants receive lunch and two snacks, while
those who attend for half a day receive
one snack. Activities include music, bingo,
painting, exercising, cooking, movies, and
more. For an additional fee, clients may
have personal bathing assistance and
podiatry services, and the services of the
beauty/barber shop at Green Acres are
available to them. Physical, occupational,
and speech therapy, all of which must be
ordered by the client's doctor, are offered
here, and these services may be billed to
the client's insurance. Applicants must
have their doctor complete a patient history and physical, a tuberculosis test must
be taken, and admission interviews are
conducted before the adult is admitted to
the program. The cost of the day care is
$50 for a full day and $25 for a half day.

Shepherd's Choice Nursing and Rehabilitation Center
867 York Road
(717) 337-3238

This center's name is an acronym for its
mission statement. It provides a Christian
community extending God's love and
compassion; Home environment for
changing needs; Overall commitment to
residents, families, employees, and the
larger community; Individualized, professional services; Complete care for the
body, mind, and spirit; and Empowerment
to achieve the highest potential and vic-
tory in all areas of daily living. This 118-bed
facility that opened in 1987 embraces the
concept of resident-centered care, where
nurses and assistants provide 24-hour
hands-on individualized care with a team
approach. Services include physical,
speech, and occupational therapy, and
hospice and respite care are available.
Shepherd's Choice is also a secured facility that uses a watch-mate system to protect residents who suffer from Alzheimer's
or dementia-related diseases. At-risk
patients wear a bracelet that triggers the
outside doors to lock or alarms to sound
if the patient begins to wander away. Residents' rooms feature floor-to-ceiling windows, providing an opportunity to watch
deer and other wild animals, and clients
are encouraged to personalize their
rooms. The center provides dental and
optometry services on-site, and it has a
beauty/barber shop. Planned group and
individualized activities are also available.
This nonprofit skilled nursing facility
accepts payment for its services from
Medicare, Medicaid, private insurance, and
private pay.

MEDIA

Local and national information can easily be obtained in Gettysburg, via print, radio, or television. Many places of business have an area by the door where you can find brochures for local attractions and events, and Lincoln Square and many street corners have coin-operated newspaper boxes. Gettysburg has its own newspaper, as well as publications that focus on what to do around the area. It also has an AM and an FM radio station, and cable TV is available throughout the area.

PRINT MEDIA

Gettysburg Companion
Times & News Publishing Company
1570 Fairfield Road
(717) 334-1131
www.gettysburgcompanion.com
The *Gettysburg Companion* is a glossy magazine that began publication in April 2004, and it's put out by the same company that publishes the *Gettysburg Times* newspaper. Issues come out five times a year on a bimonthly basis (there isn't a December/January issue). Each issue spotlights an area business in addition to having articles and pictures relating to Gettysburg people, places, and events. One article always features the Readers' Choice Award, which highlights an area overnight accommodation or restaurant that was nominated by readers of the magazine. In addition to the article, the winner also receives a wood plaque featuring the cover of the issue that their business was named in. You can pick up the *Gettysburg Companion* for free at area businesses or have it mailed to you for a fee.

Gettysburg Experience
P.O. Box 4271, Gettysburg 17325
(717) 359-0776
Community events are highlighted in this free publication that's published monthly by Leonard and Diana Loski. Its 6½-inch by 10½-inch black-and-white format is designed like a small book, and its 100 or so pages are chock-full of interesting articles on Gettysburg and the Civil War and lots and lots of ads for area businesses. There are also articles that feature area businesses. If you're wondering what to do or where to go while in town, the *Gettysburg Experience* will give you lots of choices to pick from. The center of the booklet also features a fantastic map of downtown Gettysburg, making finding where you want to go a breeze. Trivia questions are at the bottom of every other page, and the answers are contained within the articles, and there's also an answer key at the end of the booklet. The *Gettysburg Experience* is in just about every store you walk into, so finding a copy is never a problem, and most locals consider this the best reference when planning their leisure activities.

Gettysburg Times
1570 Fairfield Road
(717) 334-1131
www.gettysburgtimes.com
The *Gettysburg Times* newspaper is published daily Monday through Saturday (except Christmas and New Year's Day) by the Times and News Publishing Company. It has a circulation of about 10,000 subscribers, and it covers all the news of Gettysburg and the surrounding townships as well as national news. The *Times* isn't a thick paper, but it packs a lot of local news into its pages. The "Good Old Days" series runs once a week, and it gives locals a chance to write in and reminisce about how things used to be and

what was where back in the day. Sides of national issues are represented with editorial pieces by Molly Ivins, Cal Thomas, and other notable journalists. Local issues take up a good amount of the space, with weekly columns devoted to pet issues, tourism, senior news, and other local interests. The *Gettysburg Times* is essentially a small-town newspaper, with birthday greetings that include pictures, announcements of divorces, engagements, and marriages, and pictures of reporters who cover the local scene. The paper also has weekly listings of events going on and an in-depth religion section, which lists all the activities the local churches are sponsoring. In 2004 the *Times* received the Keystone Press Award and the Pennsylvania Associated Press Managing Editors Award. The paper's banner is ADAMS COUNTY NEWS FIRST and their slogan is MORNING'S GREAT, EVENING'S TOO LATE.

RADIO STATIONS

Gettysburg has two local radio stations, both of which have been locally owned by the Jones family for many years. Both stations are part of the Times and News Publishing Company, which also publishes the *Gettysburg Times* newspaper and the *Gettysburg Companion* magazine.

WGTY-FM (107.7 FM)
1560 Fairfield Road
(717) 334-3101
www.wgty.com
This is a country station, and its signal serves Adams and York Counties and nearby Maryland. You can hear the latest country hits as well as perennial favorites and bluegrass sounds. The station also broadcasts Nextel Cup Racing, making it York and Adams Counties' country home for NASCAR.

WGET-AM (1320 AM)
1560 Fairfield Road
(717) 334-3101
www.wget.com

WGET is a CNNRadio News affiliate, and local topics are covered each weekday morning during the popular Breakfast Nook program that begins at 8:30 A.M. The segment features on-air personality Fred Snyder, who's been at the station for 10 years, interviewing prominent local, national, and international figures on a variety of topics. Sports are also big at this station, which is an affiliate of SportingNews Radio. Local residents tune in to hear coverage of the Phillies, the Redskins, Penn State University athletics, NFL games, and NASCAR races.

TV STATIONS

Cable television is provided by two local companies, Adelphia Communications and Susquehanna Communications, commonly known as SusCom. Adelphia is the 5th-largest cable television company in the country, with customers in 31 states, while SusCom is the 16th-largest cable television company in the country, with customers in 6 states. Which provider you use will be based on your geographic location, with Adelphia servicing most of Gettysburg and SusCom servicing the outer regions of the Gettysburg area and the towns of Hanover and York. Weekly TV listings can be found in the Wednesday edition of the *Gettysburg Times,* and both providers' stations are listed.

Adelphia Communications
2720 Baltimore Pike
(717) 337-1630, (888) 683-1000
www.adelphia.com

Susquehanna Communications
221 West Philadelphia Street, York
(717) 846-4551
www.suscom.com

Adams Community Television
44 C South Franklin Street
(717) 334-3000
www.actv.org
Adams Community Television, or ACTV, as

it's known, was founded in 1988 by Raymond Gouker, a teacher of visual communications at Gettysburg High School. He created the station as a way to showcase the history, people, and culture of the local communities, as well as to provide educational programming of interest to area residents. ACTV started out with 10 hours of airtime per week telecast to 6,000 households. Today it telecasts more than 96 hours per week to more than 32,000 households. It receives support from Adelphia Communications and can be found on the company's cable lineup on channel 10.

INDEX

ABOUT THE AUTHOR

Kate Hertzog resides in Mechanicsburg, Pennsylvania, where she works as a freelance editor and proofreader. *Insiders' Guide to Gettysburg* is her first book, and her Maine coon cats, Dexter and Dillon, always had their paws in it from day one. Both deserve kudos for giving up many walks and lots of playtime to ensure the book stayed on schedule. Kate's husband, Tim, contributed greatly by being a loving and supportive husband, a role he has played to perfection for more than 25 years.

Kate began her career as an analyst who helped coordinate the systematic updating of the supplies for the Trident submarines, and she was bitten by the publishing bug when she went to work as an inventory analyst for Book-of-the-Month Club. From there, Kate moved on to become a book club manager for the McGraw-Hill professional book clubs. When she left McGraw-Hill in 1996, she decided to establish her own business and perform freelance editorial work from home.

You may reach Kate at katehert@comcast.net.